# NOT A CHOICE, NOT A JOB

## ALSO BY JANICE G. RAYMOND

*The Transsexual Empire: The Making of the She-Male*

*A Passion for Friends: Toward a Philosophy of Female Affection*

*The Sexual Liberals and the Attack on Feminism,*
ed. with Dorchen Leidholdt

*RU 486: Misconceptions, Myths and Morals,*
with Renate Klein and Lynette J. Dumble

*Women As Wombs: Reproductive Technologies
and the Battle over Women's Freedom*

# NOT A CHOICE,

# NOT A JOB

## EXPOSING
### THE MYTHS ABOUT
## PROSTITUTION
### AND THE GLOBAL
## SEX TRADE

JANICE G. RAYMOND

**Potomac Books**
*Washington, D.C.*

Potomac Books is an imprint of the University of Nebraska Press

**Library of Congress Cataloging-in-Publication Data**
Raymond, Janice G.
  Not a choice, not a job : exposing the myths about prostitution and the global sex
trade / Janice G. Raymond. — First edition.
     pages cm
  Includes bibliographical references and index.
  ISBN 978-1-61234-626-7 (hardcover : alk. paper)
  ISBN 978-1-61234-627-4 (electronic)
  1. Prostitution. 2. Human trafficking. I. Title.
  HQ118.R39  2013
  306.74—dc23

                                                          2013006152

Printed in the United States of America on acid-free paper that meets the American
National Standards Institute Z39-48 Standard.

Potomac Books
22841 Quicksilver Drive
Dulles, Virginia 20166

First Edition

10 9 8 7 6 5 4 3 2 1

In Memory of

*Raquel Edralin Tiglao*, the Philippines, 1947–2001
*Zoraida Ramirez Rodriguez*, Venezuela, 1949–2002
*Denise Pouillon Falco*, France, 1916–2013

# CONTENTS

# PREFACE

In mainstream media articles about sex trafficking and prostitution, we read "prostitution is inevitable," "prostitution is the oldest profession," "men need the sex of prostitution," "legalized prostitution regulates the industry," "prostitution is a choice." In progressive media, we are told "prostitution is sex work," "trafficking is migration for sex work," "prostitution is a job, like any other service job," "the numbers of trafficking victims are wildly exaggerated in both NGO and government estimates," "trafficking is a myth," "trafficking and prostitution are not the same."

This book challenges these claims based on many years of experience working on issues of trafficking, prostitution, and the global sex industry. From 1994 to 2007 as codirector of the Coalition Against Trafficking in Women (CATW), an international non-governmental organization (NGO), I worked with victims of prostitution and trafficking, national and international policymakers, women's rights and human rights advocates, and the United Nations to promote the fundamental human right of women and children to be free from sexual exploitation and to develop programs in almost twenty countries on prostitution and sex trafficking.

A particular strength of CATW is that it combines education, research, and policy work with direct services and prevention programs for victims of trafficking and prostitution through its many coalitions and affiliates worldwide. CATW has been at the forefront of programs not only to prevent trafficking and sexual exploitation but also to teach young men in schools and communities about their role in creating the demand for prostitution as well as their potential role in being catalysts for change. CATW has also supported legislation that makes men accountable for their abuse of buying women and children for the sex of prostitution.

As an activist I have met hundreds of women in many countries who have been in systems of prostitution and whose lives have been ravaged by it. I have met women who thought they were migrating out of their countries for work and ended up in the sex industry. I have encountered runaway girls in the United States who left home because male relatives had sexually abused them, only to find themselves smooth-talked into the sex industry by pimps. I have been in brothels where I have seen girls as young as nine servicing male buyers. And I have talked with men who are habitual prostitution users and feel entitled to purchase women's and girls' bodies to meet their alleged sexual needs.

Also as an activist I have learned that working against the sex industry is like working against nothing else that I have experienced. The industry has friends in high places and has become a major lobbyist on behalf of national and international legislation that would favor its expansion.

As a researcher I have published numerous articles on prostitution and sex trafficking, lectured internationally on these topics, and served as an expert witness in legal cases. I have testified before the U.S. Congress, the European Parliament, and legislative committees in various countries against the legalization and decriminalization of prostitution and the sex industry. A large part of my scholarly and activist life has been spent fighting the legal normalization of prostitution.

## SCHOLARSHIP AND ADVOCACY: RESPONSIBLE RESEARCH

Research provokes responsibility if experience and ideas are to have any effect in the real world. In responsible research the researcher is accountable for her ideas and conclusions and works to make them tangible in society. If research shows that smoking is bad for a person's health, the researcher might promote programs and public policy that help to persuade people not to smoke, or serve as an expert witness in a legal case against the tobacco industry.

Scholarly advocacy means that the researcher does not "float lightly above the fray." As a professor in a women's studies program in a large public university, I encountered many students who were victims of male violence against women. The content of women's studies classes often calls forth the experiences of women who have lived that "content," especially when violence and sexual exploitation are discussed in the classroom. In meeting with students in my office, I would often hear that some were caught up in the sex industry—strip dancing that quickly became prostitution, or modeling that turned into pornography. I was aware that my role was not only to provide understanding, sensitivity, and help, but also some kind of framework about the complexities and confusions that plagued their experiences.

As I listened to the students speak in and out of classes, I knew that I was a witness to not only their individual experiences but also to the history and politics of sexual crimes against women. These encounters with students, and later with women and children abused for years in systems of prostitution and trafficking, were powerful testimonies that called for an analysis of the wider context in which the sexual objectification, abuse of, and violence against women are allowed to continue. For me this investigation also meant examining the common claims and arguments that subsidize the system of prostitution and the global sex industry and that truly mystify many.

Empirical research is important and valuable in any study for the evidence it produces. Some academics writing on trafficking and prostitution have interviewed few trafficked or prostituted women. For example, Ronald Weitzer is a sociologist best known for publishing critiques of researchers who conclude that prostitution is violence against women. His tack is to malign their research as advocacy. He especially has attacked evidence-based researchers, who have interviewed hundreds of women in prostitution, for not being evidence based. When we examine Weitzer's own research, however, he proves to be a typical library-based scientist. His is the view of an armchair critic who has not published his own evidence-based interviews with prostituted women in the field.

Coincidentally those he criticizes, including myself, disagree with his conclusions countenancing state-sanctioned prostitution. Weitzer frequently claims that our research is tainted by our advocacy. However, a major difference between Weitzer and the scholars he criticizes is that we are honest about how our evidence grounds our advocacy and that we are activists who use our research to inform public policy. Weitzer's work is bound by his own biases and by the information he cherry-picks to fit his particular ideological bent. Confirmation bias plays a large role in his essays, masked by the posture of an academic critic. Certainly, confirmation bias exists on both sides of the prostitution debate, but Weitzer pretends it doesn't feature in his own work or in the work of his ideological allies.

Data are always mediated by *interpretation* of the evidence. It is not true that empirical data *directly* produce evidence-based conclusions, as if there is an unswerving line from the data to the conclusions. Interpretation intervenes between data and conclusions. Data are increasing, especially with Internet access to it, but often one sees noticeable errors in interpretation of the data. Also, competing interpretations follow from similar information. For example, researchers who interview women in prostitution may conclude that a high percentage of women have a positive attitude about their activities and voluntarily entered the sex industry. Other researchers may use broader questions to test this positive response and ask women interviewed whether they would want their daughters to enter the sex industry. Given this question, women most often respond more negatively about their own past journeys into prostitution and express their desire for a different path for their daughters.

Competing interpretations may owe to genuine ambiguities in the studies themselves, the way in which interviews are conducted and data are collected, or the interpretation of what is "voluntary." My own research shows that a high percentage of women, social service providers, and law enforcement officials respond to the question of choice by emphasizing that whether women choose to be in prostitution can only be discussed in the context of their other options. Many speak about prostitution as women's final option, or as an involuntary way of making ends meet.[1] Poverty, predatory recruiters, deception, and gross exploitation mark their alleged choices.

Other factors complicating empirical research are how subjects are selected for interviews, how questions are framed, and the environment in which subjects are interviewed. Much of what passes for evidence depends on *where* the research is conducted. Sex work advocates often gain access to interviewing women in the sex industry through pimps, brothel owners, or other self-interested parties who give permission for researchers to query women within the confines of a brothel or sex club. Leaving aside for the moment the ethical implications of these alliances, we can recognize that brothels are controlled environments not conducive to honest and open discussion.

Researchers who obtain interviews with women through agencies and organizations that provide services to prostituted and trafficked women conduct the most reliable evidence-based studies. These organizations over a period of time have built up trust with women who become clients of the organization. This is the reason why good anti-trafficking legislation gives organizations and agencies multiple months to work with victims whose trust has been violated by recruiters, pimps, traffickers, and buyers. Service providers know that what women tell them at the beginning of the contact is often quite different from what women relate after trust is obtained. Initially, many women in prostitution will deny the exploitation and violence that has happened to them for various reasons including: to tell the truth about their experiences could be dangerous; they come from backgrounds of sexual abuse where the sexual exploitation they are subjected to is accepted as sex, not as violence; they see violence as part of the "job" and as an occupational hazard; and they have survived the violence done to them in the sex industry by dissociating from it.

Advocacy is often seen as a threat to objectivity. Some researchers, public authorities, and persons in general think that scholars are or should be neutral in what they study and write about and should not be advocates, as this may compromise their job of being professional researchers. In a Canadian legal case in which I was an expert witness, the lawyer for the applicants sought to undermine the credibility of my testimony by constantly impugning my advocacy in opposing legalization and decriminalization of the sex industry.

Other experts believe that if researchers are also advocates, it should be as a consequence of what they have researched, not in advance of it. Often ignored is that the subjects researchers choose may express their existing advocacies and opinions. *What* scholars research and discover can inform or modify their advocacies. Robert Jay Lifton in his 2011 memoir makes this point about his past work on the Nazi doctors: "It is often assumed that scholars perform their work more or less neutrally . . . and take on their moral advocacies as a result of what they discover. But I have come to an almost opposite view . . . what we choose to study as scholars is a reflection of our advocacies, our passions spoken or otherwise."[2]

Combining research with advocacy gives a researcher's work external validity, rather than simply internal validity in which research is mostly discussed and understood within the academic guild. I believe that uniting research and advocacy is a scholarly strength rather than a liability, that researchers should be accountable for their data and interpretations, and that part of the job of being a researcher is to test ideas and conclusions in the real world of programs and policy.

Academics in many fields typically do not see themselves as public policy advocates. They subscribe to a conservative standard against making public policy claims. It is deemed more appropriate to discuss limitations of a particular study and to emphasize the complexity of drawing conclusions from the data.

Other researchers who do advocate for particular positions make judgments within the dominant paradigm of their peer group. Combined with a strong need to be part of the club and to be recognized as a nuanced thinker, many academics are reluctant to make judgments about their data that don't fit in with the conclusions of their colleagues. Most researchers know that entering policy debates as dissidents can be very costly in the damaging of professional credibility, especially in opposing decriminalization of the sex industry. This is a highly politicized debate where critics of legalization and decriminalization of the sex industry are often dismissed as ideological, biased, and moralistic.

---

This book begins by looking at the common arguments that promote prostitution and sex trafficking and the mythmakers who invent them. Since these arguments are widely used, not only in policy and academic circles but also in media, many people accept them or don't know how to respond. The purpose of chapter 1 is to excavate these arguments, analyze them from different angles, and examine them in ways that make sense, ultimately exposing them as fictions. I hope this method and content will inform and motivate readers, inspire action, and promote good public policy.

Although people react to the viciousness of traffickers and pimps and sympathize with victims, many are genuinely confused when they are fed truisms—for example, that legalization of prostitution will control the sex industry, protect the women, and reduce sexually transmitted diseases. Although people may be unsure whether these assumptions are true, they may sound realistic, and many don't know how to respond. These myths continue to confound people.

I remember a conversation with a university dean who, upon hearing that I opposed legally institutionalizing and regulating prostitution, was shocked and said, "But isn't that counterintuitive?" I would venture that a large segment of people, like this dean, accepts that it is more sensible to regulate prostitution than try to eliminate it. People don't understand who and what is decriminalized in legal regimes of prostitution. Also, the mindless platitude that "prostitution is the oldest profession" seems to have the weight of history on its side.

Chapter 2 looks at the prostitution users, the men who constitute the demand for prostitution. Answers to the question of *why* men buy women in prostitution depend on who is asked. This chapter lists thematic responses from the buyers themselves, prevalent in media features and research studies, as well as the words of men who trade information about prostitution and the sex industry on Internet sex sites. Each quote is a narrative in itself. The very existence of this body of information turns the question of "why do women do this?" to "why do men do this?" All of these accounts give us a picture of the buyers, a picture that is qualified by the perspectives of the women they use in prostitution.

Civil society in many countries is undecided about the legal status of prostitution users. Even fining the buyers, as in Sweden and Norway, has to be defended because opponents will argue that boys will be boys, relying on this and other myths that rationalize and excuse what men do to women in prostitution. Chapter 2 will also show how this situation is changing. Most of the Nordic countries have passed legislation criminalizing the purchasing of sexual activities.

Chapter 3 examines the Netherlands in depth because it has become the poster country for others considering legalization or decriminalization of prostitution and the sex industry. This chapter looks at the history of prostitution legislation in the Netherlands, and the role of "state feminist" NGOs in leading to the lifting of bans on pimping and brothels in the year 2000. Several years later the pillars of the legalization regime—tolerance zones, licensed brothels free of organized crime, and a regulated business of prostitution—began to crumble and are now in shambles.

By legalizing prostitution, Dutch politicians opened up their cities to international organized crime, trafficking in women and children, and drug cartels. After only several years of the legalized results, Amsterdam mayor Job Cohen stated it was impossible to set up a safe zone for women in prostitution that was not controlled by organized crime. In 2008 the Dutch National Police Report confirmed that a clean, normal prostitution business sector in the Netherlands "is an illusion." Chapter 3 will demonstrate that all the reasons given for how legalization would reduce trafficking, promote women's well-being in the sex industry, control child prostitution, and neutralize organized crime have not come true.

Although few countries admit the economic incentive to regulate prostitution, chapter 4 looks at why certain governments are dependent on institutionalizing a prostitution economy to increase a country's commercial development. It also clarifies that prostitution is an economic option for mostly *poorer* women.

Sex—or what passes for it—has become a big business as the international sex industry grosses over $US35.7 billion per year.[3] Prostitution markets ensure not only the future of a globalized sex industry but also the future of organized crime, which controls many of the prostitution venues—legal and illegal.

This chapter also examines the "human capital costs" of prostitution and spotlights another fiction that prostituted women earn lots of money, or more than they could get anyplace else. One researcher has developed a methodology for estimating the lifelong costs of young women leaving prostitution in Manitoba, Canada, showing the immense *economic diversion* of what they earn into drugs and alcohol, pimps, drivers, and sex venue owners, as well as the more indirect costs of chronic health problems and lost job opportunities.

In many developing countries, prostitution has a history of colonialist underpinning. I saw this legacy of prostitution colonialism in the Philippines in visiting the former U.S. military base cities of Olongapo and Angeles City. The integration of military colonialism and prostitution shaped the twentieth-century U.S. military–prostitution complex globally, continuing into the twenty-first century.[4]

This chapter also discusses the migration-trafficking debate. Sex work apologists argue that women who end up in prostitution from poorer countries are simply part of the larger global migration stream, not victims of trafficking. Equating trafficking with migration covers a multitude of misinformation. Although there are linkages between trafficking and migration, to equate trafficking with migration is fraught with problems, one of the worst being that trafficked persons are treated as criminals.

The overarching theme of the final chapter is the necessity to address both innovative policies and programs to combat globalized sex trafficking and prostitution so that we do not simply apply Band-Aids to problems. Not only is it necessary to prevent sexual exploitation but also we need good practices that prevent legalization and decriminalization of the sex industry.

*Not a Choice, Not a Job* is concerned with exposing the myths about prostitution and the global sex trade. This also means exposing the myths about good practices promoted by the pro-prostitution lobby, not simply criticizing but also presenting alternatives. Chapter 5 focuses mainly on alternative good practices that challenge the normalization of prostitution as work and confront the demand for prostitution that promotes trafficking for sexual exploitation. It highlights exemplary legislative and policy initiatives in addition to projects and programs that challenge the demand for prostitution.

This book has a point of view. It proceeds from years of being a scholar and an advocate (i.e., a scholar-advocate). The failure to recognize prostitution as violence against women is a failure to challenge *both* liberal and conservative ideas of sexuality. In the liberal view, prostitution is a woman's choice; in the conservative view, prostitution is her determined behavior. In the liberal view, prostitution is a woman's economic necessity; in the conservative view, prostitution is a man's natural need. In the liberal view, prostitution is female sexual liberation; in the conservative view, prostitution is female sexual perversion. In the liberal view, prostitution is a woman's basic human right; in the conservative view, prostitution is her essential moral failing. In my feminist abolitionist view, prostitution is one of the final strongholds of sexualized male dominance.

# ACKNOWLEDGMENTS

This book has taken me seventeen years to compose. During much of this time, I was privileged to be the co-director of the Coalition Against Trafficking in Women (CATW). It was a consuming job, which left me with very little time for writing. During that period, I met many courageous and inspiring individuals who were committed to the elimination of violence against women perpetuated by a global system of prostitution and trafficking. Much of what I have written is their story as well.

The three women to whom this book is dedicated are a key part of CATW's history. Raquel Edralin Tiglao was a founding member of CATW Asia-Pacific (CATW-AP). She was also a former political prisoner during the Marcos dictatorship in the Philippines, the founder and director of the Women's Crisis Centre in Manila that services all victims of violence against women, and a dear friend. Zoraida Ramirez Rodriguez was the founder of CATW Latin America and the Caribbean (CATW-LAC) and a fierce advocate for women in prostitution. Zoraida's advocacy during the drafting of the UN Protocol on trafficking was critical to gaining Latin American country support for a definition of trafficking that protected all victims. Denise Pouillon was part of the early generation of feminist abolitionists of prostitution who laid the groundwork for all of us today. She founded one of the initial anti-trafficking organizations called the Union Contre le Trafic des Femmes, and co-organized the International Abolitionist Federation. All these women devoted their lives to women's human right to be free from all forms of sexual exploitation.

In the course of visiting numerous countries and partnering with organizations that promote women's rights to be free from sexual exploitation, I have been fortunate to work with many dedicated abolitionists who believe that prostitution is not a human right but a violation of women's human rights.

From the Philippines, Aurora Javate de Dios (Oyie) is the president of CATW International, director of the Women and Gender Institute at Miriam College in Manila, and the Philippines' representative to the ASEAN Commission on the Rights of Women and Children. During the drafting of the UN Trafficking Protocol in Vienna, Oyie was one of the governmental committee heroes who fought valiantly for a definition of trafficking that protected all victims of trafficking. Also from the Philippines, Jean Enriquez, the director of CATW-AP with her team in Manila, has developed a program for boys and young men promoting a different standard of masculinity to combat male sexual exploitation of women in prostitution. Jean and all the survivors I have met from the Philippines have a very special place in my heart. I also thank Cecilia Hoffman who, for many years, shepherded the work of CATW-AP and developed it into the strong organization it is today.

From India, Ruchira Gupta is the founder and director of Apne Aap, a model program that promotes the empowerment of prostituted women in various parts of the country. Ruchira has won many prestigious prizes for her work, among them the Clinton Global Citizen Award. I had the honor of visiting the Apne Aap center in Calcutta and the many women and young girls served by Ruchira and her colleagues. Also in Calcutta, more than twenty-five years ago, Indrani Sinha established an early feminist center for survivors of prostitution. Sanlaap serves both the women and the girls who are vulnerable to second-generation prostitution.

From Indonesia, Siti Ruhaini Dzuhayatin is a co-builder of the first Women's Crisis Centre in Indonesia and a faculty member in Islamic law at the State Institute of Islamic Studies in Yogyakarta. I thank Siti for organizing a course on gender and Islam and for inviting me to join the faculty where I met many of the best "students" I have ever taught and learned from. From Bangladesh, longtime women's rights activist and lawyer Sigma Huda became the UN Special Rapporteur on Trafficking and courageously wrote one of the first UN reports that linked prostitution and trafficking. Sigma has spent much of her life defending women's legal rights. From India and Thailand, Jean d'Cunha is now the global migration advisor for UN Women who worked closely with CATW in the 1990s. From South Korea, Young-Sook Cho, Kim Na Youn, and the staff at the former Center for Women's Human Rights developed prostitution prevention and public education programs at the same time that they monitored the new Korean law on prostitution and engaged in policy planning. When in Seoul, I was inspired to meet the many Korean activists who work in the network of the numerous shelters that exist for survivors of prostitution, shelters that were established as a consequence of the Prostitution Act in 2004, which also penalizes the prostitution users.

From Latin America, Giovanna Merola worked with Zoraida Ramirez Rodriguez in Venezuela to put CATW on a firm footing in the region. Giovanna died shortly after Zoraida, having suffered through a long illness during which she worked tirelessly for CATW-LAC. From Mexico, Teresa Ulloa Ziáurriz, the second director of CATW-LAC, expanded the coalition's reach into twenty-one countries in the region. The impunity of the drug cartels in Mexico has fueled many disappearances of women and children thought to be trafficked and prostituted. Teresa has rescued and assisted hundreds of women and children who have been in internal and international trafficking situations in her region. From Argentina, Sara Torres has been a long-standing representative of CATW and a persistent advocate of justice for prostituted women in Argentina. Sara has drawn public attention to the impunity of traffickers who escape prosecution from a complacent judicial system. From Chile, Marlene Sandoval established CERSO, the early and well-known center for young girls caught in prostitution, providing them with housing, education, and job training. Maria Boniface from Ecuador, now living in Britain, was a brilliant translator who worked with CATW and translated many of our meetings and key projects. She labored over and above the call of hours and duty.

From Africa, Esohe Aghatise established Association IROKO in Italy that provides services to Nigerian women who have been trafficked there. She publicizes the plight of these women, many from the state of Edo, who through jiujiu rituals become bonded to their traffickers. Esohe has bravely challenged the pro-prostitution lobby in Italy and in Nigeria. From Mali, Fatoumata Sire Diakite, a well-known advocate against female genital mutilation, was the former director of CATW in the African region who, under a past government, became Mali's ambassador to Germany.

From Australia, well-known scholar and writer Sheila Jeffreys has directed the Coalition in the Australian and New Zealand region. Facing the impediment of working in a country that has legalized prostitution, Sheila has courageously critiqued Australia's prostitution and trafficking policies both within the country and abroad. Mary Sullivan's book *Making Sex Work: A Failed Experiment with Legalised Prostitution in Victoria, Australia* makes one of the most comprehensive contributions to our knowledge about what happens when a country institutionalizes prostitution and the sex industry. Publisher-activists Renate Klein and Susan Hawthorne have made an enduring gift to the campaign against prostitution, pornography, and all forms of violence against women in their numerous publications through Spinifex books. They have given the feminist movement against prostitution and pornography a life that will be remembered in libraries and personal collections across the globe.

From the Balkans, journalist Briseida Mema, correspondent for Agence France Presse and co-founder of the Women's Media Group in Albania, co-organized a project called "No to Sexual Tourism, Yes to Cultural Tourism." Briseida is a remarkable woman and a skilled organizer who arranged meetings in Tirana for CATW representatives with Albanian parliamentarians to discuss and critique proposed legalization initiatives there. From Zagreb Croatia, Nela Pamuković, director of the Center for Women War Victims—ROSA, Rada Borić from the Center for Women's Studies, and Nera Komarić from the Women's Room, partnered with CATW and the European Women's Lobby to organize a government/NGO hearing to challenge legalization initiatives that had surfaced in Croatia. They also organized an international conference on Preventing Trafficking in Conflict and Post-Conflict Situations. From Bulgaria, owing to the extraordinary efforts of MP and former minister of foreign affairs Nadejda Mihailova—in conjunction with her director of security Nikolay Radulov from the Institute for Democracy, Stability and Security in Southeast Europe and Genoveva Tisheva and Iliana from the Bulgarian Gender Research Foundation—organized meetings for CATW representatives with the Bulgarian prime minister as well as an international conference to present the case against legalization of prostitution. Because of these efforts, the minister of the interior reversed his earlier pro-legalization position and publically distanced himself from legalization initiatives. From Romania, Gabriela Chiriou of Caritas brought together a diverse coalition of governmental, feminist, human rights, and religious organizations including ARTEMIS, ADPARE, APoWer, AIDROM, to launch symposia, press conferences, and public awareness campaigns to present the case against legalization of prostitution.

From the Baltics, Ilvi Joe-Cannon, acting director of ENUT, the Estonian Women's Studies and Resource Centre, in conjunction with social worker Eha Reitelman from the Tallinn Women's Shelter and Julia Kovalenko from the Legal Information Center for Human Rights, focused on organizing projects related to the demand for prostitution. Ilvi authored a primer on male demand that was translated into Russian,

Latvian, and Lithuanian, and it served as a model for a general primer on male demand published by CATW. These projects were followed by a conference to raise public awareness regarding male accountability for purchasing women in prostitution, and a signature campaign signed by prominent men who pledged not to buy women for sexual activities. From Lithuania, Dovile Rukaite and Jurgita Peciurene from the Women's Issues Information Centre and Kristina Misiniene from Caritas led a brilliantly organized campaign that included life-size posters of men with partially opened trouser front zippers with the words, "It is shameful to buy a woman." Other posters informed sex tourists, "Buying sex is a crime in Lithuania." The posters were placed in public places, including bus kiosks, in the biggest cities of Lithuania. These posters were made possible by a law passed in 2005 as a result of the campaign that penalizes buyers for purchasing sexual activities. From Latvia, Inete Ielite of the Coalition for Gender Equality in Riga with representatives from the Resource Centre for Women "Marta" organized a hearing with members of the Latvian parliament and concerned NGOs to discuss the campaign against legalization and focus on demand activities. The campaign challenged the current legal system in Riga where prostitution is regulated in violation of Latvia's ratification of the 1949 Convention.

From Russia, my earliest experience of the trafficking situation there was informed by Luobov Vertinskaya, a passionate defender of women's rights who helped to organize the Women's Crisis Network in the Arctic city of Murmansk. I witnessed the flooding of Murmansk with sex tourists from several of the Scandinavian countries and learned at the same time that Russian women were being bussed through Norway's indigenous Sami lands on rolling brothels. In later years, I also traveled to Moscow to help initiate the Volga Campaign led by representatives from MiraMed and the Angel Coalition—Juliette Engel, Afonsa Kadyrova, Svetlana Yakimenko, and Marianna Solomatova. Three cities along the Volga, sites from which women are trafficked, were targeted to conduct information campaigns with governmental authorities, police, medical and court personnel, social workers, NGOs, journalists, and village people. Since its founding, the Angel Coalition has assisted fifteen thousand victims of trafficking.

From the Nordic countries, the Feminist Group Ottar, led by Asta Haland and Jane Nordlund, has worked for many years to eliminate prostitution and pornography in northern Europe. Ottar organized the Network North working across feminist borders in Russia, Norway, and Sweden, and worked to bring a law against the buyers to Norway.

The Network North—joining with Luobov and other Russian women, as well as with Marit Smuk Solbakk from the Sami organization, Sarahkka—coordinated the first international conference in Russia to address prostitution, pornography, and violence against women in the year 2000.

From Norway, Agnete Strom and Anne Rothing from Kvinnefronten (the Women's Front) have supported CATW for so many years in so many ways that have been key to its survival. From the first day I met Agnete in Beijing in 1995, she believed in our work and helped make it possible. I am also grateful for the short time I knew Anne Soyland from Kvinnefronten who, the week before she died, was writing letters in support of CATW's work. The Women's Shelter Movement in Norway is led by Tove Smaadahl who has labored on the grassroots level for many years to provide assistance to all victims of male violence against women. Tove actively participated in the efforts to pass the 2009 Norwegian law penalizing the purchasers of sexual activities. Thanks also to Harald Bøhler from the Oslo police department who has given me information on the workings of the Norwegian law penalizing the buying of sexual activities.

In Sweden from the governmental sector, I thank Margareta Winberg, former deputy prime minister of Sweden and former minister of gender equality, who is the model of a feminist politician working to eliminate prostitution and trafficking. Margareta hired Gunilla Ekberg as the anti-trafficking point person in the ministry of gender equality, where Gunilla was responsible for many of the activities and reports that were integral to generating world support for the Swedish law against demand. Marianne Eriksson from the Swedish Left Party and former member of the European Parliament (MEP) participated in many of the CATW campaigns in Europe and elsewhere. She also initiated the first hearing in the European Parliament on "The Consequences of the Sex Industry in the European Union." Inger Segelström, MEP from the Swedish Social Democratic party, was an early parliamentary advocate for the Swedish law prohibiting the purchase of sexual services. I thank Jonas Trolle from the Stockholm police department for his public presence in speaking about the positive consequences of the Swedish law in global forums and for his communications that responded to my questions about the law. Max Waltman generously shared many of his articles on the Swedish law. From the non-governmental front came the impetus for the Swedish law prohibiting the purchase of sexual services. Ebon Krom and Angela Beausang, both former directors of ROKS, the Swedish Women's Shelter Movement, assisted many victims of male violence against women including those prostituted and trafficked and were staunch defenders of the Swedish law. Wiveca Holst, Swedish representative to the European Women Lobby (EWL), has been a faithful source of information for my work.

From Iceland, Gudrún Jónsdóttir and the committed women at Stigamot have been dedicated activists working against violence against women. Gudrún has faced many threats from the sex industry in her country as Stigamot worked successfully to close down the strip clubs in Reykjavik. Due to the efforts of Stigamot in partnership with Icelandic female politicians, Iceland became the third Nordic country to pass a law penalizing the prostitution users.

From Finland, I thank researcher Marjut Jyrkinen and statistician Tuomo Niskanen for providing me with information on the numbers of buyers charged for purchasing trafficked/forced women into prostitution. Marjut was also the Finnish representative to the UN ad hoc governmental committee that drafted the Palermo Protocol on Trafficking. She fought through some very difficult sessions, advocating for a definition of trafficking that protected all victims, not just those who could prove force.

From Denmark, Hanne Helth has been an abolitionist force to be reckoned with who organized the March 8 Initiative in 2011—an international conference to educate Danes about the necessity to pass the Nordic model prohibiting purchasing persons in prostitution. At an earlier time, Hanne worked with survivors of prostitution at the Danish abolitionist organization Reden. If and when Denmark passes a law penalizing the buyers, it will be due in large measure to Hanne's efforts and the group she has organized in Copenhagen.

From the Republic of Georgia, Nugzar Sulashvili founded the Center for Foreign Citizens and Migrant Rights (FCRS) to protect the rights of Georgian citizens migrating abroad and to prevent persons from being trafficked. Nugzar had been a former border guard who, when he launched FCRS, wrote a courageous and comprehensive report on government complicity and corruption, much of it related to trafficking. Because of subsequent threats to himself and his family, Nugzar left Georgia and sought asylum in France where he remains today. Lela Shatirishvili, a cofounder of FCRS, continued the work on prevention of trafficking, setting up programs to warn potential migrants across the country of the tricks of traffickers and initiating training programs on migrant rights and responsibilities.

From Moldova, Veronica Lupu founded the Association for Women in Contemporary Society. The association has bravely worked to release and repatriate Moldovans and other victims of trafficking from the jails of the United Arab Emirates (UAE), traveling to the UAE and going into the prisons, where victims have been confined under laws punishing them for supposed immorality and adultery. The association under Veronica's direction has trained police, judges, prosecutors, and NGO representatives on the UN Trafficking Protocol and challenged legalization of prostitution proposals in Moldova.

From Hungary, Zsuzsa Forgacs as part of the Movement for a Prostitution-Free Hungary organized early campaigns against legalization of prostitution in Hungary. She worked with The Way Out With You Association, CATW's partner in Budapest, to establish a drop-in center for women in prostitution that provides an alternative to one that promotes legalization. One of Zsuzsa's most creative projects has been codesigning and developing hard-hitting posters that were placed in male urinals and other public places in Budapest featuring seven men urinating with the message: "Every Seventh Man Buys Vulnerable Women and Children for Sexual Use—They Generate Prostitution with Their Money."

From Britain, Julie Bindel as an opinion writer for the *Guardian* has consistently addressed issues of violence against women in her columns. With her "wicket wit" and incisive editorials, she has become one of the most recognized journalists writing on global women's issues. Julie worked with the Joint Project of CATW and the EWL to develop a press packet for journalists writing on issues of prostitution and trafficking.

From Glasgow, Scotland, Ann Hamilton has been the driver of the Routes Out Partnership, a municipal government program that clearly views prostitution and sexually exploitative activities as violence against women. This partnership shows what strides a city can make when it recognizes prostitution as violence against women rather than as a normal job, and Ann has been in the forefront of the city's efforts. I have seen this program in action several times and met so many of the good women and men in Glasgow who are a part of it. Thanks also go to Councilor Jim Coleman, who has led the city council in rejecting licenses to strip clubs in Glasgow and helped support the Routes Out Partnership.

From Ireland, Good Shepherd Sister Gerardine Rowley coorganized the Ruhama Project in Dublin, Ireland. Ruhama provides services for women in prostitution and has also been a powerful force behind efforts in Ireland to legislate against the male demand for prostitution. Many years ago, I went out with the Ruhama street team and witnessed firsthand their courageous work.

From Belgium, I thank Collette De Troy from the European Women's Lobby. She and I worked closely for several years on a joint project supported by the governments of Sweden and the United States to address gaps in current anti-trafficking programs and policies that avoid challenging demand for prostitution and legalization/decriminalization policies. We launched this program in twelve different countries of Europe, including the Balkans and the Baltics, Hungary, the Czech Republic, Moldova, and Russia—all countries where the trafficking situation was critical.

Ascuncion (Choni) Miura put the feminist abolitionist agenda on the map of Spain. In several key government jobs, Choni promoted abolitionism, sometimes at the risk of job security. When Spain faced legislative reform on prostitution, Choni organized international conferences and forums in Spain to convince legislators and the public of the failed consequences of legalization of prostitution in other European contexts. Marta Torres is CATW's superb UN representative in Vienna and Geneva and has been a longtime feminist abolitionist who was part of our team in Vienna during negotiations over the UN Protocol on Trafficking, working to translate many of our documents.

From France, Algerian Wassyla Tamzali who worked at UNESCO for many years was one of CATW's earliest supporters. Because of Wassyla, CATW had a strong presence at the Beijing World Conference for Women in 1995, and she continued to showcase our work during her time at the UN agency. Berenice Dubois has been a longtime advocate for women in France and in the wider European context and has never hesitated to speak clearly about the right of women to be free from sexual exploitation. No acknowledgment can adequately express my thanks to Malka Marcovich. I cannot begin to list the work that Malka has done for CATW and the passionate advocacy she brings to the work against violence against women. It has also been a great pleasure to meet with Sabine Salmon and other members of Femmes Solidaires when I attended a planning conference for the Mediterranean Network in Paris.

I thank Rachel Eapen Paul from India and Norway for bringing me into the NCA Capacity Building, Democracy and Human Rights Project for women in Iraq. Rachel's leadership at every stage of a challenging project was responsible for the success of this remarkable program. Along with her capable assistant Dima Baqain and the team at NCA in Amman, Jordan, the Iraqi women's project served as a model for women working on violence against women in a Middle Eastern context. While being a small part of this program, I had the privilege of meeting many courageous Iraqi women, as well as women from other parts of the Middle East, who were working against violence against women during the American war in Iraq. I especially was inspired by Zeinab Al Kattrani from Basra, one of the most dangerous areas in the country where women were experiencing wholesale slaughter on the streets and from which many were trafficked. Equally inspiring was the work of Khanim Latif from the organization, ASUDA Combating Violence Against Women in Kurdistan. From Lebanon and now working from France, Mariam Abdo has been a great pleasure to meet. She is one of the organizers of the Mediterranean Network Against Trafficking in Women and its coordinator in the Middle East.

From the United States, I thank my former codirector Dorchen Leidholdt who was a cofounder of CATW International. For as many years as I have known Dorchen, she has been a courageous advocate working in the most entrenched arenas of violence against women, i.e., prostitution and pornography. Also as the legal director at Sanctuary for Families in New York, Dorchen has provided aid to hundred of victims of male violence against women. Norma Ramos, the current director of CATW, has continued the work of the Coalition, especially in her campaigns to promote a prostitution-free Internet. For over a decade, Barbara Kryszko has been CATW's listserv and website manager, its participant in the joint CATW-Apne Aap project in India, and its representative who testified before the Canadian Commission on the Status of Women—all during the same time that she has maintained a full-time job as director of the Family Justice Center Legal Project in Brooklyn, New York, for Sanctuary for Families. I also thank my former assistant, Derek Kipp, who worked with me for several years doing many of the detailed jobs that supported our programs worldwide. Thanks to Dave Block who during some critical moments provided support to CATW.

Twiss and Pat Butler have been with CATW since its inception in 1988, and they continue to be our strongest supporters. They have not only helped ensure financial support but have been personally involved in many of our projects. Twiss continues to serve on our board of directors. For too short a time, I was pleased to know and work with Taina Bien-Aimé, former executive director of Equality Now before she became executive director of the Women's City Club of New York. For many years, Taina worked with CATW in New York on joint campaigns to eliminate trafficking and sexual exploitation. Lisa Thompson, the Salvation Army's Liaison for the Abolition of Sexual Trafficking, has played a vital and inspiring role in the organizing of faith-based coalitions against trafficking. Melissa Farley's work documenting the situation of women in prostitution and the men who use them has been critical to the cause of feminist abolitionism. Her work has rigorously documented what happens to women who are trafficked and prostituted.

John Miller, the former director of the U.S. Office to Monitor and Combat Trafficking, is a true compassionate conservative with a heart of human rights who, from the beginning of his tenure, understood the connections between prostitution and trafficking and what needed to be done to protect victims and to create public policy. I thank Eleanor Kennelly Gaetan, who during her time in the government and after has played a key role in supporting many of CATW's projects and is a committed abolitionist. Mark Lagon, who followed John Miller as director of the U.S. Office to Monitor and Combat Trafficking, was very supportive of CATW's work, especially of our efforts in Mexico and Bangladesh. Democratic congresswoman Carolyn Maloney from New York worked with CATW for several years when she was cochairperson of the Congressional Caucus on Human Trafficking. As a staunch opponent of legalization of prostitution, she is well aware that normalizing prostitution as work is a myth that does nothing to protect women.

None of these acknowledgments would be complete without thanking the many survivors of prostitution and trafficking that I have been privileged to meet and work with. Their experiences have informed all my work and research about the global sex trade. I especially want to recognize the survivors who participated in a joint press conference at the European Parliament in 2005 and issued a manifesto about "Who Represents Women in Prostitution?"; from the United States, Vednita Carter, who founded the organization Breaking Free in Minneapolis/ St. Paul; from Korea and the United States, Chong Kim, who founded MAISIE; from Britain, Fiona Broadfoot, part of the NIA project for women in prostitution in London; from Brussels, Yolande Grenson, who founded Pandora in Antwerp; and from Denmark, Odile Poulsen, a writer. The manifesto they issued at the conference was based on an earlier declaration written by Filipino survivors.

One of the early survivors that I met was Evelina Giobbe who founded one of the first survivors' organizations in the United States called WHISPER. Evelina gave an eloquent testimony before the UN Working Group on Contemporary Forms of Slavery in 1999 in Geneva. Norma Hotaling founded SAGE in San Francisco and became a powerful force worldwide as a public authority in representing the voice of survivors. In conjunction with the San Francisco police and district attorney's office, Norma founded what became known as the John's School, a program to educate first offenders who purchase sexual activities and which has been replicated in many U.S. states, as well as in other countries. It was a great loss when Norma died in 2008.

From the Philippines, I have known Alma Bulawen, the founder of BUKLOD in Olongapo, for many years. When I first visited BUK-LOD in 1998, I had the chance to see the inspiring work that Alma and her BUKLOD staff had accomplished. Since then, Alma has joined with CATW-AP, both in their programs to aid survivors and in their summer camps for boys where she and other survivors teach young men the truths about prostitution. In Calcutta, I met many of the women in prostitution in Sonagachi, as well as their children, who helped start the Apne Aap program and publish its newsletter called the *Red Light Despatch*.

Other survivors have inspired me like Louise Eek, now a Swedish journalist who has written not only about her experience in prostitution but about what this means for public policy and legislation. Numerous survivors remain unnamed such as the women and girls I met in the mega Tanbazar brothel and the Kandupatty brothel area in Bangladesh where the authorities do little to address the situation, as well as the women and girls in prostitution from the Sonagachi streets and brothels in India.

Finally, I would like to thank my editor at Potomac, Hilary Claggett, who backed this book and guided it during the initial part of the publication process and the other editors and production team at Potomac. I thank Charlotte Raymond, my longtime agent for her help in negotiating the labyrinthine terms of a book contract and her husband, Alan, for thinking of the title. Norma Johnson, in the course of carefully proofreading this book, read the entire work aloud with me.

My partner of thirty-eight years, Pat Hynes, has been my in-house editor for as long as she has been my constant companion. Living with another committed writer and political advocate is an exhilarating experience in which the personal and political most often merge effortlessly. For me to say anything about Pat is to say everything about all that I respect and love.

# INTRODUCTION

> It is said that slavery has disappeared from European civilization. This is a mistake. It still exists; but now it weighs only upon the woman, and it is called prostitution.
>
> —*Victor Hugo*, Les Misérables

Many people have heard of sex trafficking and understand its gravity. As much as the public has become informed about the depravities of trafficking, many persons are ill-informed or confused about the ethical, legal, and policy questions, and the political debate surrounding how sex trafficking is related to prostitution.

Articles with titles such as "Human Trafficking: Exploiting Misery and Creating It" or "21st Century Slaves" describe the plight of victims caught in the sex trade by unscrupulous traffickers who recruit them inside or outside their countries of origin, force or deceive them, prey on their vulnerabilities, and subject them to continuous abuse. These articles are often presented with little emphasis on the role of the global sex industry. When I was codirector of the Coalition Against Trafficking in Women (CATW), media would frequently phone asking if I could provide a victim willing to talk with them. Of course this is understandable because people learn through real-life experiences, but most of these accounts do not provide any analysis of the larger picture behind the sex trade, offering no context and little substance.

Numerous articles include the gratuitous and unfounded statement that prostitution is inevitable—the conservative view; others, that all aspects of "adult consensual sexual activities," including pimping and brothels, must be decriminalized—the liberal view. When people hear about decriminalization, they often assume that only women are decriminalized.

Critics of the view that prostitution should be decriminalized agree that *women* should be decriminalized, but not pimping, buying, or brothels. They argue that legal decriminalization of prostitution is a gift to pimps and traffickers to harm more women and children. This view, however, is rarely presented not only in the mainstream but also in the progressive media. A recent media event confirmed the one-sided picture given in the progressive media that the sex industry should be decriminalized, allegedly to protect women.

Amy Goodman on *Democracy Now!*, a U.S. television program that is favored by many concerned Americans and that features many thoughtful interviews, ran a one-sided show, ostensibly about the travel restrictions barring "sex workers" from the 2012 AIDS conference in Washington, D.C. Goodman interviewed Meena Seshu of SANGRAM, a group that works for "sex worker" rights in India, and Annah Pickering, former "sex worker" and manager of the New Zealand Prostitutes Collective, also an advocate of "sex work." Under the banner of "sex worker" rights, both women and their organizations promote the decriminalization of buyers, pimps, and brothels. When Goodman asked Pickering to respond to those who say that decriminalization of "sex work" could lead to the exploitation of vulnerable women and girls, Pickering claimed that decriminalization works in New Zealand because the country has "removed most of the laws against adult consensual sex, [thereby allowing people to live] off the earnings of prostitution [pimping] and soliciting [buying and selling sex]."[1]

It is unfortunate that Goodman did not ask this question of survivors of prostitution who do not identify as "sex workers" because they don't want their exploitation institutionalized as a normal job (see chapter 1). People do not hear the opposing view mainly because many good interviewers such as Goodman rarely invite them and their allies on the show to speak for themselves. Additionally, the AIDS issue has been a powerful tool used by sex work apologists to normalize prostitution as work around the world.

## SEXUAL SLAVERY AND RACE SLAVERY: ABOLITIONISM VS. REGULATIONISM

Most of us have heard of "abolitionism" not in the context of female sexual slavery but as a philosophy and practice of eliminating race slavery. As with race slavery, those who work to abolish prostitution understand it as sexual slavery—not always the slavery of those in physical chains who have been brutally forced into prostitution but a more complex form of slavery in which women are subjected to prostitution through deception, fraud, abuse of their vulnerabilities, or abuse of power. The UN Working Group set up to monitor the 1949 *Convention for the Suppression of the Traffic in Persons and of the Exploitation of the Prostitution of Others* declared prostitution to be a contemporary form of slavery. We tend to forget that recognizing racial oppression as slavery took centuries for people to acknowledge and act against.

Some of the same issues that we are now debating in the prostitution context were historically debated in the race slavery context. Most contentious was the issue of abolitionism versus regulationism. The historical debate over race slavery included proposals to administer it as a business and make it "better" for those who were enslaved. Rather than abolish the system of slavery, advocates proposed regulating slavery as a state-sanctioned "economic sector." Likewise in the prostitution debate, a controversial 1998 report published by the International Labor Organization (ILO), the official labor agency of the United Nations, called for economic recognition of the sex industry. The report recommended that four countries in Southeast Asia cash in on the booming profits of the sex industry by taxing and regulating it as a legitimate job.[2]

Initial British legislation against race slavery was regulationist based on the principle that "the Trade was in itself just but had been abused."[3] British opponents of race slavery mostly confined their attacks to the slave *trade*, not to slavery per se, as modern-day prostitution advocates limit their criticisms to sex trafficking or forced prostitution, not prostitution itself. Early anti-slavery measures proposed in Britain are comparable to harm reduction schemes advanced by prostitution advocates today who want to train women in safe-sex techniques, including self-defense to ward off dangerous buyers and requiring prostitution entrepreneurs to put panic buttons in brothel rooms allegedly to prevent violence—a backhanded acknowledgment that prostitution *is* violence against women.

Some pro-slavery countries wanted to regulate race slavery by official inspection of the slave ships, and some even promoted standards of hygiene on vessels carrying the enslaved from Africa. Others argued a variation on the forced/free distinction now prevalent in the prostitution debate, stating that only if slaves had been kidnapped, not legally bought, should they be returned to Africa. Portugal regulated conditions in the slave trade by restricting the duration of the slave ship voyages. France elected to reap the profits of slavery by opening its ports in the Caribbean to foreign slave traders, provided they paid a tax.[4]

And many argued, as did Cotton Mather, that slaves in North America "lived better [as slaves] than . . . as free men in Africa."[5]

In the United States, there were arguments that slavery was justified on the basis that not all slaves were "enslaved," such as house servants, and that others were free agents at some point along the slavery spectrum. For example, some researchers maintain that Sally Hemings, owned by Thomas Jefferson and who "was likely the mother of four of his children,"[6] was privileged. They say that although Hemings began her life as a slave, she later led the life of a free woman and chose to stay with Jefferson when he came back to the United States. They point to evidence that Hemings learned French in Paris with Jefferson when he was posted in France as the new nation's envoy, that he bought her fine clothing, that their relationship was very intimate, and that she could have stayed in Paris as a free woman when Jefferson returned to America but chose to return with him.[7]

Sex industry advocates have touted a similar deconstruction of sex trafficking as a temporary coerced situation that later somehow evolves into a freer and chosen existence within the sex industry. As a 2011 UNAIDS Advisory Group report states, "People who . . . find themselves tricked or coerced once within the sex industry, can find their way out of situations of coercion but remain in sex work operating more independently and usually with the support from their fellow sex workers, their clients, their intimate partners and their managers or agents."[8] It is doubtful, however, that most trafficked women would be snookered into believing that clients, managers, and agents—better known as johns, brothel operators, and pimps—are their future safety net.

Britain and the United States outlawed the *international slave trade* before they outlawed race slavery itself. In 1808 the U.S. Congress banned the importing of more slaves into the country. In other words, it banned international trafficking in persons for purposes of slavery but not the domestic slave trade. This legislation did little to obstruct internal slavery but instead helped to increase it. The sole domestic market for slavery made African American women into sexual and reproductive commodities for producing the next generation of slaves. Economically this domestic market expanded profits for the owners so much so that at the beginning of the Civil War, "the dollar value of slaves was greater than the dollar value of all of American's banks, railroads, and manufacturing combined."[9] Domestic slavery was not abolished in the United States until 1865 when the U.S. Congress ratified the Thirteenth Amendment, only to be followed by the Jim Crow laws.

Similarly, under the U.S. federal anti-trafficking act, domestic prostitution, which is largely domestic trafficking, is not outlawed but left to the states to decide whether to regulate it or determine the penalties for pimping, solicitation, and brothels. A Romanian woman trafficked into the country and forced into prostitution is offered protection under the federal Trafficking Victims Protection Act (TVPA), but a U.S. woman forced into prostitution is treated as a criminal and arrested. Her pimp, if caught, receives a lesser sentence than a trafficker who imports foreign women into U.S. prostitution. Also under the TVPA, all trafficked children, whether forced or not, are offered protection. However, U.S. children, many fleeing abusive homes, who end up selling their bodies on the streets of major U.S. cities can be arrested for prostitution, considered criminals, and sent to juvenile detention centers. Girls as young as eleven, having been sexually exploited at an early age, are treated as criminals.

A self-serving argument used to maintain race slavery in the nineteenth century was that if Britain gave up the slave trade, France and other countries would take it over.[10] In the same way, opponents of abolitionist legislation to criminalize demand for prostitution, passed in countries such as Sweden, Iceland, and Norway, argue that these countries are simply exporting their prostitution problem and that penalizing prostitution users drives them elsewhere.

In the nineteenth century the British West India Committee was dedicated to preserving slavery on its plantations in the Caribbean. When its slavery industry came increasingly under attack, the committee employed lobbyists to launch a propaganda campaign against those who opposed plantation slavery.[11] Today the sex industry and its apologists not only use ever more malicious tactics to discredit abolitionists of prostitution but also have curried favor with politicians in promoting legislation that favors normalizing buying, pimping, and brothels. Many captains of the sex industry have become savvy contributors and advisers to politicians, including those in the United States, Australia, Germany, and the Netherlands who vote for legalization and decriminalization of the sex industry.[12]

When British abolitionist Josephine Butler began her campaign against the system of prostitution during the last third of the nineteenth century, regulation of prostitution was the dominant trend especially in Europe. This system prevailed until the mid-twentieth century. Women were kept in brothels mandated by the state, subjected to police harassment and arrest if caught outside the brothels, and forced to undergo medical examinations at which point they were simply discarded if found with a disease. In 1949 the legal tide turned, and Josephine Butler's abolitionist campaigns took root in a UN convention that endorsed the abolition—not the regulation—of prostitution.

The 1949 *Convention for the Suppression of the Traffic in Persons and of the Exploitation of the Prostitution of Others* was a leap forward in human rights legislation. It decriminalized the victims but not the perpetrators, as happens in state-sanctioned systems of prostitution. In the aftermath of the passage of the 1949 convention, prostitution was viewed as more akin to slavery than to work, and the language of "sex work" would have been anathema to those who drafted this legislation. In the 1970s and '80s, however, there was a movement to abolish abolitionism and its key UN convention and to replace them with a public policy that distinguished between forced and free prostitution and between sex trafficking and prostitution. This movement made *consent rather than exploitation and harm* the foundation and focus of national and international law and policy. Abolitionism was attacked as outdated and moralistic.

The anti-abolitionist position is based on a labor model of prostitution and international sex trafficking, where both are redefined as *sex work*, or as *migration for sex work*. The labor model rebranded the entire system of prostitution by transforming pimps into business agents, brothel owners into sex entrepreneurs, prostitution users into consumers, and women in prostitution into sex workers. This discourse is reminiscent of a pro-slavery strategist in the West Indies who wrote, "Instead of SLAVES, let the Negroes be called ASSISTANT PLANTERS; and we shall not then hear such violent outcries against the slave-trade by pious divines, tender-hearted poetesses, and short-sighted politicians."[13]

An essential challenge of the British abolitionists was to convince the citizenry that race slavery was indeed a form of slavery, not a form of work to be accepted as such despite all the pro-slavery efforts to humanize it. It is sobering to remember that to many ordinary people in these bygone centuries, race slavery seemed as normal and natural as many consider prostitution to be today. In the century of Enlightenment, with its emerging ideals of the possibilities of reason to shape human destinies of life, liberty, and the pursuit of happiness, few saw the contradictions between freedom for white men and suppression of blacks. Those who preached progressive secular and religious ideas—John Locke, Voltaire, George Whitefield—gave their assent to slavery in various ways.[14] To the early abolitionists, the task of eliminating race slavery was as daunting as the elimination of prostitution is to abolitionists today who see the long haul ahead, not to mention the extensive campaigns against sexual slavery that have already transpired.

This does not mean that prostitution is inevitable. Like race slavery, sexual slavery is socially and politically constructed "out of men's dominance and women's subordination. An 'idea of prostitution' needs to exist in the heads of individual men to enable them to conceive of buying women for sex. This is the idea that women exist to be used, that it is a possible and appropriate way to use her."[15] The system of prostitution will not end until many men are disabused of this idea, until many more people recognize that sexual slavery, like race slavery, is the buying and selling of human beings, and until more people understand that prostitution is just as solvable as any other kind of oppression.

In many ways this book is about the lack of policy resolve to address what in fact has become a documented human rights crisis—the continuing commercial sexual exploitation of women and children in most countries of the world. Not to leave readers with this picture, it is also a testimony to the changes that feminist abolitionism has made to policies and programs that combat this crisis.

## THE FEMINIST CAMPAIGN TO ABOLISH PROSTITUTION: HISTORICAL AND CONTEMPORARY MOVEMENTS

Feminists with some supporting male allies waged the early campaigns for abolition of prostitution. They boldly named prostitution for what it was and still is—a class of women created and regulated to minister to the sexual appetites of men. Inveighing against the double standard that permitted "male lust" and male sexual "incontinence" to rule the lives of women in prostitution, abolitionists opposed a system of female "cleansing" by enforced medical examinations mandated by British law. These exams subjected women to bodily intrusions that were continual, degrading, and torturous.

Josephine Butler, the founder of the movement to abolish prostitution, challenged men's entitlement to prostitution by initiating a campaign against the Contagious Diseases Acts of mid-nineteenth-century Britain that targeted women in prostitution, as well as single women, widows, and others suspected of being "immoral." Butler regarded the acts as a system of apprehending vulnerable women, subjecting them to degrading exams, and disinfecting them for the safe enjoyment of men. And she pointed out that many women who were not in prostitution and had undergone these exams then turned to prostitution because they were stigmatized as prostitutes.

Like new generations of feminist abolitionists that she would inspire, Butler and the courageous women who followed her labored for many years to build and then globalize an international abolitionist movement that campaigned against state normalization and regulation of prostitution. Butler's influence was wide-ranging both across Europe[16] and in India where women were being subjected to prostitution to serve the British Army. Butler founded the international abolitionist movement on feminist principles that targeted the double standard of morality in prostitution. By challenging the essentialist ideology of male sexual need, she assailed the (still) reigning value system that prostitution is both necessary and inevitable. She was very clear in expressing that a social and political economy of sexuality propelled mainly poor and working-class women into selling their bodies for financial survival to mostly middle- and upper-class men, an economy for which men were ultimately responsible.[17]

Following the results of their enforced medical examinations, women could be confined in prison-like infirmaries called Lock Hospitals for nine months. Speaking for the hundreds of women in prostitution who she had personally assisted, Butler quoted the words of one woman who found herself detained in one of these hospitals:

> It is men, men, only men from the first to the last that we have to do with! To please a man I did wrong at first, then I was flung about from man to man. Men police lay hands on us. By men we are examined, handled, doctored, and messed on with. In the hospital it is a man again who makes prayers and reads the bible to us. We are had up before magistrates who are men, and we never get out of the hands of men until we die.[18]

In India, Britain also enforced the Contagious Diseases Acts. Butler wrote of her "wrath" over the brutal subjection of Indian women in the British Army's cantonment brothels, and she deplored the fact that sympathy and public awareness were more difficult to elicit for "anonymous" Indian women in prostitution than for prostituted women in Britain. A majority of Indian women in the military brothels were widows who had been sold into prostitution by their husbands' families. Many were children who the military housed in wretched conditions and who lived in fear of abusive soldiers. The British government in India actively solicited "sufficiently attractive" and younger women for British soldiers who had complained about the "quality" of women they had been supplied with.[19] For many years after the acts were outlawed in Britain, Indian women and girls were forced to undergo the hated medical examinations.

The commander in chief of the British army in India and the architect of the policy, Gen. Sleigh Roberts, issued a racist response to Butler's public campaign against military prostitution in India. "Prostitution is a trade amongst the natives which is practised all over India; shame, in a European sense, does not attach to it." Butler responded furiously, threatening the general with an Indian mutiny and telling him "nothing so surely produces a spirit of rebellion as the trampling on the womanhood of a subject race by their conquerors."[20]

Butler led the abolitionist campaign to challenge prostitution as sexual slavery. She put the spotlight on men's legal impunity for using and abusing women in prostitution at a time when the state treated them with legal exposure and imprisonment in the Lock Hospitals. As a result of Butler's work, the Contagious Diseases Acts in Britain were suspended in 1883 and finally repealed in 1886 but, in practice, did not end in India until 1895. The issue of men's responsibility for promotion of prostitution, and Butler's campaign against men's "irrepressible" need for the sex of prostitution, would be taken up again by feminist abolitionists in the twentieth and twenty-first centuries.

As in Josephine Butler's time the current debate over prostitution centers on abolition or regulation. This book is a philosophy of feminist abolitionism—not simply a matter of theory but of strategies, practices, and policies based on abolitionist principles. The principles of feminist abolitionism are basic to women's liberation and put women's freedom front and first.

- Prostitution is not inevitable, just as genocide, torture, war, or poverty is not inevitable.
- Prostitution is constructed and can be deconstructed.
- Prostitution is not the oldest profession, pimping is.
- Prostitution is sexual slavery. As with race slavery, the regulationists want to civilize slavery by making prostitution "better," not eliminate it.
- Regulating prostitution is based on the premise that some women can be segregated from others into a class that provides sexual services for a price and used as instruments of sexual gratification for men.
- Those who construct prostitution are the men who buy women and children for sexual activities and the pimps, brothel owners,

recruiters, and other perpetrators who sell them for profit and other gain.
- Prostitution has become a global industry and requires a global solution.
- Every woman has the right to be free from sexual exploitation and not to be sold as a sexual commodity or service.

In 1979 Kathleen Barry gave new life to feminist abolitionism with the publication of her book on trafficking and prostitution entitled *Female Sexual Slavery*. She began *Female Sexual Slavery* with a tribute to Josephine Butler, documenting the history of Butler's abolitionist campaign and placing it at the beginning of the modern-day feminist movement to eliminate prostitution and the global sex industry. In 1988, with Dorchen Leidholdt, Barry cofounded the international Coalition Against Trafficking in Women (CATW).

Like Butler, Barry was very clear in challenging the male demand for prostitution. She reminded us that other early feminists recognized the centrality of prostitution in the struggle for women's human rights, and they targeted male demand, male violence against women, and lack of economic opportunity for women as being responsible for prostitution. She quoted Emma Goldman in writing that "fully fifty percent of married men are patrons of brothels. . . . Yet society has not a word of condemnation for the man, while no law is too monstrous to be set in motion against the helpless victim."[21] Christabel Pankhurst's words are as incisive as Goldman's: "Intelligent women are revolted by men's commerce with white [*sic*] slaves. It makes them regard men as inferiors. . . . Men have a simple remedy for this state of things. They can alter their way of life."[22]

Josephine Butler did not live to see her work culminate in the UN *Convention for the Suppression of the Traffic in Persons and of the Exploitation of the Prostitution of Others*. Adopted in 1949, this convention was an abolitionist instrument that obliged ratifying countries to "repeal or abolish any existing law, regulation or administrative provision against women in prostitution." It put the onus on those who "procure, entice or lead" others into prostitution and included measures to prevent trafficking and prostitution and to protect and assist victims. The convention required that victims not be penalized for their own exploitation and stipulated that consent could not be used as a defense to trafficking or the exploitation of prostitution. And the convention prohibited states that ratified it from passing any legislation that regulated prostitution or recognized it as a legal, economic, or administrative sector. Most national legislation especially in Europe, now in existence against pimping, procuring, and living off the earnings of a person in prostitution, came into existence during the 1950s—a testimony to the influence of this convention. "Nevertheless, the question of the 'buyer' is not mentioned in the Convention, in spite of the fact that abolitionist feminists had historically called attention to the ways in which men created the demand for prostitution."[23]

Legally challenging male demand for prostitution would become the work of a new generation of feminist abolitionists, including members of the CATW, who would be successful in influencing another UN instrument (the *Protocol to Prevent, Suppress and Punish Trafficking in Persons, Especially Women and Children, Supplementing the United Nations Convention against Transnational Organized Crime*). The Palermo Protocol, as it is called, is the first UN mechanism to address the demand that results in women and children being trafficked, calling on countries to take or strengthen legislative or other measures to discourage this demand that fosters all forms of exploitation of women and children (article 9.5).

Critics promote the view that abolitionism is difficult to implement and lacks a pragmatic content. However, feminist abolitionists have not only exposed the failures of "pragmatic" legal regimes of prostitution (see chapter 3). They have also shown how to implement abolitionism in public policy by confronting the male demand for prostitution (see chapter 2). Penalizing male demand for the sex of prostitution is an existing successful pragmatic alternative to state-sponsored prostitution, enacted in several countries such as Sweden, Norway, Iceland, and South Korea.

## LANGUAGE

Reality hangs on the thin thread of the language. The conclusions reached concerning prostitution often reside in the words used to describe it. For example, terms such as "sex work," "sex with girls," "transactional sex," and "child prostitution" do not shed light on what happens to women and children in situations of sexual exploitation. Polite and comfortable ways of describing sexual violence, exploitation, and predation inoculate us to the harm of prostitution for women and children. Working girls, ladies of the night, and escort workers are convivial terms and mask what is essentially a grim, sordid, and dangerous

industry, obfuscating the pimps, the prostitution users, and other
perpetrators.

Sex worker and sex work are terms that I do not use because such
terms function to endorse the view that prostitution is and should be
normalized as simply another form of work. Many individuals and organizations believe that the terms "sex worker" and "sex work" dignify the
women. In my experience, I have learned that these terms serve mostly
to dignify the sex industry by giving buyers, pimps, recruiters, and other
key perpetrators of sexual exploitation more legitimacy than they could
otherwise obtain. Instead I use the terms "women or persons in prostitution," "in systems of prostitution," and those who are "prostituted"
within the sex industry.

Sex industry advocates are fond of distinguishing between legalization and decriminalization. They argue for decriminalization of prostitution, maintaining that the prostitution industry should be free-flowing
and not subject to any state regulation. However, the consequences of
legalization and decriminalization are similar. Both legalization and decriminalization make aspects of the sex industry legal, i.e., by not making them illegal.

*Legalization* of prostitution means that the state makes parts of the
prostitution system legal by regulating prostitution and the sex industry
through, for example, registration of women in sex venues, health monitoring, location of brothels, and taxation.

*Decriminalization* of prostitution means elimination of the penalties
for all or certain aspects of the prostitution system, such as solicitation,
pimping, and the keeping of brothels. It does not mean elimination
of pimps and brothels, but rather the rebranding of pimps as benign
business managers for women in prostitution and brothels as cottage industries controlled by women. Government implementation of decriminalization is impossible without some form of government regulation
of prostitution. In no country or state that I know of does decriminalization exist without some form of regulation. Unencumbered decriminalization of prostitution without regulation is a myth.

When prostitution is decriminalized, control is mostly taken out of
the hands of the police and given to the local councils. For example, in
countries and states that have decriminalized pimping or prostitution
zones, civil and administrative regulations usually follow, such as requiring specific brothel licensing, registration of the women involved in
prostitution activities, health monitoring, taxes on prostitution venues,
or other measures. Further criminal measures are often necessary to
stem the growth of organized crime in the prostitution sector.

After decriminalization, local councils are inevitably burdened with a host of regulatory measures. Council duties include dealing with complaints, including those alleging violence and abuse of women. However, local councils have neither police authority nor resources to investigate or penalize, and in most cases, they have no capacity to confront illegal brothel operators. Thus, unlawful sex venues proliferate in cities and countries that have decriminalized prostitution and the sex industry, and as in the Netherlands and Australia, the same pimp-entrepreneurs control the legal and illegal brothels.[24]

In pro-prostitution discourse, prostitution is *sex work*, not *sexual exploitation*. *Pimps* are *third-party business agents* who women choose to protect themselves and their interests, not *first-class exploiters*. In Victoria, Australia, pimps who are legal *brothel owners* are designated as *sex work service licensees*. *Prostitution users or buyers* are *customers or clients* who provide women with incomes, not abusers. *Brothels* are *safe spaces* for women to ply their trade, not *quarters where women are controlled and kept in check*. *Women in prostitution* are *sex workers*, not *victims of sexual exploitation*. And *victims of trafficking* are *migrant sex workers* whose passage from one country to another is *facilitated migration* by *helpful people movers*. Even the words "escort" and "escort agencies" make the system of prostitution sound more chic and safe.

A final word about language. I make a distinction in this book between *sex workers* and *survivors*. Both of these terms are self-designated by women who are or have been in prostitution (see chapter 1). Both "sex workers" and survivors claim to represent women in prostitution. As used in this book, the term "sex workers" describes those who are or have been in prostitution and who promote prostitution as work or as a commercial sexual service.[25] Survivors understand prostitution as violence against women and oppose the commodification of women inherent in the sex industry. I argue that it is time to differentiate "sex workers" from survivors (i.e., to distinguish between those women who actively support the sex industry by advocating for it and those who struggle against it). When "sex workers" argue for the decriminalization of pimping and brothel keeping, they do not act on behalf of the majority of women in prostitution but rather in the interests of the sex industry.

Sex work advocates have become the modern-day mythmakers who prop up the globalized system of prostitution. Through the myths generated by these apologists for sexual slavery, pro-prostitution ideologues have helped to launder prostitution and sex trafficking in many parts of the world.

# 1

## Myths and Mythmakers
## of Prostitution

Saying prostitution will always be with us is cynicism and hopelessness.

*—Trisha Baptie, Canadian survivor and journalist*

There are central fictions that bolster the system of prostitution and influence public opinion. These myths have been influential in media presentations of prostitution and have held sway in various sectors of society. A reason why these myths prevail is the intellectual veneer in which they are often couched. The most implausible argument is made to sound plausible. Take the commonplace that prostitution is inevitable. Declaring the system of prostitution to be rooted in a long history makes those who defend it sound serious, their maxim authorized by history.

Chapter 1 will analyze many of these falsehoods, including:

- Prostitution is inevitable.
- Only "sex workers" can represent women in prostitution.
- Abolitionism is moralistic, not pragmatic.
- Prostitution is a choice.
- There is a crucial distinction between forced and voluntary prostitution that should govern prostitution policy and legislation.
- Off-street is safer than on-street prostitution.
- Women in prostitution are not victims. They are agents of their own destiny.

All these myths are misconceptions about not only the women in prostitution but also the actual workings of the sex industry and its perpetrators of exploitation.

It is important to understand that these fictions are not freestanding but have been promoted by powerful constituencies. These include apologists who lobby for the normalization of prostitution and governments that fund NGOs whose goal is to legalize and/or decriminalize systems of prostitution and the sex industry. Intellectual, corporate, and political cadres, as well as journalists, are always ready to assert that prostitution is inevitable.

Unfortunately, progressive academics and activists have been slow to recognize and counter the effectiveness of those who defend the normalization of prostitution because the sex industry has been sheltered under a sacred canopy of human rights, i.e., by the arguments that prostitution is a human right. But at the onset of the twenty-first century, this situation is beginning to change. More and more people are recognizing that prostitution is not a human right but a violation of human rights, especially of women's human rights.

## PROSTITUTION IS INEVITABLE

Perhaps the most senseless argument in defense of maintaining the system of prostitution is the mantra that prostitution is inevitable. This cliché is invoked time and again, as if its repetition were an explanation. Claimed as a pragmatic statement, inevitability is really a moral fallacy that argues from "is" to "ought," from description to prescription. It declares that because prostitution has been part of societies for centuries, it ought to be for the future. Essentially, since crime has been with us forever and doesn't seem to be disappearing, let's do away with the criminal code.

The attempt to shore up a system of prostitution by resorting to its alleged inevitability appeals to a patriarchal history in which women are the objects, not the subjects. As with any argument that invokes historical validation, we must ask who its beneficiaries are. Prostitution is not the oldest profession. Pimping is. The only inevitable fact about prostitution is the pimps who sell women and children for the sex of prostitution and the men who demand it.

Who trumpets this nonsense of the inevitability of prostitution? Alan Young, the lawyer who argued the challenge to the prostitution laws in Canada that resulted in the decriminalization of pimps and brothels, has stated, "You do not have to read Freud to know that our species is always on the lookout for sexual outlets, and when the pleasure does not present itself, some will go to the marketplace to buy it. There is nothing the state can do about this. Every time a prostitute is arrested, two take her place. This is a bottomless market."[1] Inevitably the media often runs with this platitude.

Claudia Nielsen was the Zurich city councilor for health and environment in 2011 when the council proposed a drive-through brothel district, based on the German model. A buyer cruises by women displaying their bodies in an approved area, selects one, and backs his car into a private "sex box" where he can use the woman in prostitution. Councilor Nielsen acknowledges that the present regulatory regime in Zurich is untenable, but "we also know we can't forbid it . . . what can't be forbidden should be made feasible or not harmful to the population or to people in that situation. It is very pragmatic: what we can't change we have to live with."[2]

The obvious retort is why can't we change it? Zurich already has a regulatory regime that in Nielsen's own words doesn't work. Instead Nielsen wants to add another regulatory structure—drive-in brothels— to the mix because it is the alleged pragmatic way of dealing with the long-standing existence of prostitution. Nothing, however, is as pragmatic as change. Challenging the inevitability of prostitution by penalizing the prostitution users has proven to be an assuredly practical change in the campaign to eliminate prostitution in Sweden and Norway (see chapter 2).

Whether phrased as "historically eternal" or as "unstoppable," much of the inevitability rhetoric comes from powerful sources that are ideologically and politically opposed to eliminating prostitution and the sex industry. For them, inevitability serves as a convenient underpinning to normalize prostitution and the industry and to continue the violation of women in prostitution worldwide. If we accept there is nothing we can do about systems of prostitution, inevitability becomes a self-fulfilling prophecy. "The real culprits are those who by interest or inclination, declaring constantly that war is inevitable, end by making it so, asserting that they are powerless to prevent it."[3] As with war, so too with prostitution.

Legal regimes of prostitution cave in to the fatalism of inevitability, declaring that only a pragmatic approach reduces harm. The tobacco industry sold this harm reduction argument to the public when it promoted filtered and low-tar cigarettes, but smokers still became sick and died. Like the endorsement of filtered and low-tar cigarettes, making prostitution legal is defended as a harm reduction strategy. Harm reduction is a misnomer because regulated prostitution measures fail in their claim even to reduce the harm to women in prostitution. Take condoms, for example. Many prostitution users simply refuse to wear them although educated to do so, and women in prostitution are left with the burden of convincing them. Many prostitution users pay more for sex without condoms and are able to pressure women who need the money to put themselves in harm's way.

On the national level, countries such as Australia, the Netherlands, and Germany bear great responsibility for policies and practices that have reinforced the sex industry and the transfer of wealth to traffickers, pimps, recruiters, and brothel owners who are legitimized as respectable sex entrepreneurs in these countries. In normalizing prostitution, these countries practice a form of gender apartheid, whether displaying women behind picture windows in a legal, human, sexual zoo; mandating them to undergo tests for sexually transmitted infections when the prostitution users are not required to submit to the same monitoring; or segregating prostituted women into so-called tolerance zones. As journalist Julie Bindel writes, "Zones were not created to help the women, but to dump them somewhere away from 'respectable folk' . . . horrible, dangerous places with no proper protection."[4]

Sexual exploitation is not inevitable. Since when did political activists permit the claim of inevitability to stand in the way of social change?

## THE SEX WORK APOLOGISTS: LAUNDERING THE SEX INDUSTRY

The sex work apologists, also called the pro-prostitution lobby, are varied. Many are academics who define prostitution as sex work and argue that prostitution should be legalized or decriminalized. Others are NGO activists and women's rights advocates who defend prostitution as a woman's human rights rather than a violation of a woman's human rights. Some are active members of pro-prostitution organizations.

### Sex Industry Advocates

Writing in the British *Guardian* newspaper Rosie Campbell, chair of the UK Network of Sex Work Projects, promotes a sustainable prostitution system through harm reduction programs. Her message is that foreign "sex workers" need rights, more emphasis on harm reduction, and less focus on victimization and the need to exit prostitution.[5]

Sex industry apologists cite "sex workers," and often are "sex workers," as authorities for their views. The founder of the San Francisco Erotic Service Providers Union, Maxine Doogan, launched a petition to stop the city from providing social services for women in prostitution. In her opinion assistance programs are a moral condemnation of those who continue to work in the sex industry and reinforce the presumption that women in prostitution are rushing to leave their "jobs."

Doogan's petition also supported the termination of city-sponsored demand reduction activities, such as johns' schools. In lieu of a penalty, first offenders arrested for solicitation are given the option of attending a program where they learn about the harm of prostitution to women, to themselves, and to society. Doogan claims that "a whole cottage industry [of] interrupting the market, targeting the clients, trying to suppress prostitution" has organized around such anti-prostitution programs and profited from them. Instead, it looks as if Doogan herself, a former escort service owner who was prosecuted in Seattle and pled guilty to a misdemeanor, is really saying that these programs are interfering with her own profit-making.[6]

Carol Leigh, a self-described sex worker and longtime advocate of prostitution as work, states that "sex worker activists" are more concerned about "the harm done in the name of rescue and through anti-trafficking laws and policies."[7] This is a callous statement when we examine the amount of research that documents how prostitution ravages the lives of women subjected to it.[8]

Some academics prefer to debunk the numbers of victims of trafficking, saying that most statistics are highly exaggerated and most accounts of trafficking depend on the few gruesome accounts of trafficked women that are sensationalized in the media. Nick Davies has claimed that numbers of victims of sex trafficking in Britain have been hugely inflated.[9] Other apologists question the reliability of numbers of trafficked victims cited each year in the U.S. government's annual trafficking in persons report.

The debate surrounding numbers has been a mainstay of the pro–sex work position on trafficking. Sex industry apologists complain that the numbers of victims don't warrant the attention being given to sex trafficking and generate, as Laura Agustin argues, a "myth of trafficking." Agustin's homilies, in particular, trivialize the numbers. Her repudiation of the magnitude of victimization is comparable to Roman Catholic Church apologists for the sexual abuse scandal who also rely on the defense that the numbers of priest-abusers are insignificant— not a structural flaw for which the Church is accountable. Justifications such as these excuse the responsibility of perpetrators, no matter what the numbers are.

Persistent attacks on the validity of statistics implies that if we cannot obtain accurate figures on sex trafficking, governments and NGOs should not be devoting such attention and funding to anti-trafficking programs and policies. This attack on the numbers results in all incidents of trafficking being viewed with suspicion. Are we supposed to question the magnitude of trafficking because there are no agreed-upon statistics? Do we have airtight statistics on victims of torture or of those "disappeared" in the "dirty wars" of Latin America? What figures are too few to impel us to take action, and what numbers qualify as actionable? Are we supposed to feel "proportional revulsion" and to be three times more outraged if the numbers are 2 million instead of 800,000?

The sex industry apologists have been successful in influencing some UN agencies and programs, such as the World Health Organization and UNAIDS, to change their discourse on prostitution to that of *sex work* and *sex workers*. Apologists have also been influential within the European Union.

In 2004 European Parliament member (MEP) Marianne Eriksson from the Nordic Green Left party in Sweden held a public hearing at the European Parliament on *The Consequences of the Sex Industry in the European Union*.[10] In a report released at a press conference after the hearing, Eriksson stated that various NGOs were being funded by the European Union's anti-trafficking initiatives whose policies and sources of revenue are not clear and transparent. Specifically she singled out HIV/AIDS groups: "In an investigation into the HIV/AIDS programmes, it emerged that organisations taking part in these programmes and receiving considerable financial amounts often used the funds actively to campaign for the legalization and regulation of prostitution in and outside the Member States."[11] This was not the purpose for which the funds were awarded.

The Eriksson Report faults EU member states that have "accepted the prevailing situation and, through legalization and regulation of prostitution, have helped make what was previously a criminal activity part of the legal economic sector. The Member State then becomes part of the sex industry, yet another profiteer on the market." Finally the Eriksson Report voiced strong concern that no background checks are carried out in the European Commission when it appoints experts on trafficking and prostitution. "In view of the way in which organized crime operates, it is therefore possible that the Commission, the initiator of common legislation, is being advised by representatives of criminal organizations."[12]

## John Davies

An alleged expert on trafficking that the Eriksson Report may have had in mind is John Davies. In 1994 Romania accused Davies of bringing twenty-eight expectant Romanian women into Hungary to deliver their babies, after which the babies were sent to a private adoption service in the United States linked to the religious right wing and promoted by televangelists.[13] Americans paid $20,000 to adopt babies provided by Davies. In the aftermath of these accusations and investigations, both the United States and Romania issued exclusion orders banning Davies from coming into either country for five years.[14] In effect, Davies was accused of baby trafficking.

In 1995 Davies was jailed for two weeks in Zagreb, Croatia, after he was accused of coercing women to give up their babies—a charge he has denied. Many of these women had been lured to Zagreb and were raped Muslim refugees from the conflict region who became pregnant and subsequently dishonored in their culture. Davies claimed the women, rather than abort, asked him to find homes for the babies.[15] A court released him, and Davies threatened to sue the state for wrongful arrest. Although he was acquitted of engaging in illegal adoptions, the judges authorized prosecutors to continue the search for evidence against him.[16]

In 1997 the European Commission (EC) awarded Davies a grant of €140,000 to establish a "help center" for women in prostitution in Szeged, Hungary. Brussels investigators found that the funds had not been used to set up any services for women and may have been diverted for Davies's "personal enrichment."[17] In awarding the grant, the EC seemed unaware of Davies's past convictions of fraud and deception for using fake credit cards while working for a British charity in Romania. It is also the case that the EC may not have known that Davies had previously been placed on an Interpol watch list as a suspected baby trafficker.[18]

In 1998 Hungary attempted to deport him, and Davies appealed for support to the stop-traffic listserve, most of whose members were sex work advocates. The appeal was evidently successful, and Davies was allowed to remain in the country. However, even two major pro-prostitution groups, the Dutch Foundation Against Trafficking in Women (STV) and La Strada, announced they were withdrawing their cooperation with Davies and the foundations he was affiliated with—the Salomon Alapitvany Foundation (Hungary) and the Morava Foundation (Albania and Romania).[19] Davies responded, "There is no fraud investigation, the project in Hungary was audited after the unsubstantiated allegations last year and the audit did not uncover any misuse of funds."[20] On May 7, 1999, Davies sent another response claiming he had provided the EU with "a considerable file of material since those allegations and after several weeks. . . . The EU has not requested any repayment of the grant."[21] I know of no official EU or EC documentation confirming Davies's responses.

After the EC investigation and the exclusion orders issued against him, John Davies resurrected himself in 2002 equipped with Norwegian grant funding for anti-trafficking work in Bangladesh. In Dhaka, he worked as a chief technical adviser for the Ministry of Women and Children's project to stop trafficking. When allegations of trafficking and evidence of exclusion orders caught up with Davies, his relationship with government anti-trafficking programs was severed in 2002, his funding was stopped, and he left Bangladesh.[22]

To anyone attending anti-trafficking conference in the 1990s, Davies was a familiar figure. Davies continues to make vocal appearances at anti-trafficking conferences where he carries on his campaign to defend prostitution as sex work and opposes those who advocate that prostitution is violence against women. At a 2009 conference organized by the International Organization for Migration (IOM) in Palermo, Italy, Davies asserted, "The anti-prostitution lobby has hijacked the issue of trafficking and is profiting from it. . . . My mother was a prostitute when we were very poor. The only ones who gave her problems were policemen, never clients or pimps."[23]

Davies spent many years at an academic haven for pro-prostitution researchers—the Sussex Centre for Migration Research at the University of Sussex in England. In 2009 the university awarded Davies a doctorate. At various times the Sussex Centre has harbored students and visiting research fellows who define trafficking simply as "facilitated migration" or argue "trafficking is a myth." Passing through its doors have been sex industry apologists including Jo Doezema, Nick Davies, Laura Agustin, and Julie Vullnetari. These four writers have put a positive slant on women's experiences of trafficking and conclude that many women from developing countries who end up in the prostitution industries of western countries have chosen their destinies.

In 2009 John Davies went on trial in Britain for sexually abusing two girls, aged six and eight, during the years 1980–1981.[24] The trial lasted eight days at the end of which he was cleared. As with other accusations, hearings, and indictments, John Davies has managed to elude conviction, or the charges simply disappear. But the list of accusations is a very long one, spanning at least fifteen years.

## Milorad Milakovic

Among the traffickers promoting legalization of prostitution is Milorad Milakovic, a notorious sex slaver in Bosnia. When interviewed in 2003, "Milakovic said he was eager to promote his scheme to legalize prostitution in Bosnia 'to stop the selling of people, because each of those girls is someone's child.'"[25] His unctuous claim to care about "someone's child" is belied by the way in which he bought and enslaved hundreds of girls and women for his brothels in Bosnia. In November 2000 the UN-sponsored international police force (IPTF) raided Milakovic's nightclub-brothels in Prijedor. Thirty-four young women were freed. Milakovic's major complaint was that he had paid good money for the girls and that he wanted compensation. "He also spoke openly about the cozy relations he had enjoyed with the IPTF peacekeepers, many who had been his customers."[26]

Milakovic's words will come as no surprise to anyone who has seen the shattering exposé of sex trafficking in Bosnia depicted in the 2011 film *The Whistleblower*. With great courage and cost to herself, UN police officer Kathryn Bolkovac denounced fellow UN peacekeepers and police, charged with protecting the people of Bosnia, for their role in buying women and girls whom they knew were kept in sexual slavery. It is a travesty of justice that only in 2011 did local police finally raid Milakovic's brothel called Sherwood Castle and arrest him for engaging in human trafficking and sexual slavery.

Abolitionists not only have to challenge the sex industry, but they also find themselves having to do battle with human rights organizations infected by pro-prostitution myths and mythmakers. Many human rights advocates, intentionally or not, lend support to the sex industry by supporting its goal to normalize prostitution as work.

## ONLY "SEX WORKERS" CAN REPRESENT WOMEN IN PROSTITUTION

> I was a prostitute for 15 years and I have never met a sex worker. The name stems . . . from the people who support and benefit from the commodification of women. I know prostituted women— I have even been one.
>
> —*Trisha Baptie, Canadian journalist and survivor*

Two conflicting voices speak for women in prostitution. Both claim the authority of experience. One voice—survivors of prostitution and their supporters—maintains that prostitution is violence against women. It warns that decriminalizing the sex industry and regulating prostitution as work is normalizing sexual slavery. It asserts that defending the rights of women in prostitution requires prosecuting their perpetrators, including pimps and prostitution users, and giving assistance to victims. This means providing women in prostitution not simply with safe-sex education but also with life alternatives.

The second voice—"sex workers" and their allies—is louder, commands more media presence, and seems to enjoy more financial support. It proclaims that prostitution *is* a woman's right and a form of productive labor, and that the best way of protecting women in prostitution is to improve their "working conditions." Advocates of this model allege that prostitution is part of the service economy, providing sexual services to clients, and that women should be free to hire managers, otherwise known as pimps. Their message has focused on teaching prostituted women how to use condoms, not how to create a better future for themselves.

For many years COYOTE, which stands for "Call Off Your Old Tired Ethics," was the most influential group in the United States advocating decriminalization of the sex industry. Billed as an organization of "sex workers," it claimed to represent women in prostitution and presented itself to the media as a national organization of and for prostitutes. However, as Valerie Jenness in her sympathetic book on COYOTE writes, COYOTE has created an "organizational myth." "Contrary to COYOTE's public image, only a small percentage of its members have worked as prostitutes, and an even smaller percentage are active prostitutes who are also active in the organization. On occasion, [Margo] St. James has admitted that COYOTE is not an organization constituted by prostitutes."[27]

COYOTE became a public relations group in support of the sex industry. Margo St. James, founder of COYOTE, served as a witness for the defense at the bizarre 1982 trial of the Mitchell brothers, who founded the notorious pornography emporium called the O'Farrell Theatre in San Francisco. At the trial, St. James rebutted the accusations that the Mitchells promoted prostitution in their club. Instead, she testified that men didn't go to the O'Farrell to be aroused or gratified sexually. She asserted, "Arousal and gratification means [*sic*] more to me than a quick sniff."[28] COYOTE also actively lobbied for the repeal of laws against pimping, pandering, and solicitation. Historically, it has not provided direct services for women in prostitution but has seen itself as a public defender of normalizing prostitution.

COYOTE made prostitution look sexy, and it was always attractive to media and available for commentary. From 1974 to 1978, COYOTE launched the Hookers Ball in San Francisco with the slogan, "Everybody Needs a Hooker Once in Awhile." Each yearly ball garnered larger crowds and generated more money than the previous one. The 1977 ball grossed $93,000, a sizable amount of money for a small nonprofit organization in these years.[29]

Who speaks for women in prostitution—"sex workers" or survivors? Defenders of the sex industry or its opponents? It is difficult to distinguish those who identify as sex workers from those who are agents of the sex industry when many "sex workers" shill for the industry in the media and on their websites. For example, the website of the Vancouver Network of Sex Work Projects contained multiple links advertising all kinds of prostitution venues, even inviting sex businesses to advertise gratis.[30]

## Survivors Speak

To amplify the voices of survivors of prostitution and their allies, the CATW and the European Women's Lobby (EWL) organized a press conference at the European Parliament in 2005.[31] In contrast to COYOTE and the Network of Sex Work Projects, the conference issued a *Manifesto of Survivors of Prostitution* from Belgium, Denmark, Korea, the United States, and the United Kingdom. The *Manifesto*, based on a similar statement issued by seventy-five survivors of prostitution in the Philippines, proclaimed, "Prostitution is not 'sex work,' and trafficking is not 'migration for sex work.'" It called on governments to "stop legalizing and decriminalizing the sex industry and giving pimps and buyers legal permission to abuse women in prostitution."[32]

Korean American survivor Chong Kim stated at the EP conference, "There are individuals and agencies that claim to represent women in prostitution, that claim to sympathize with our pain, but they want us to stay in pain. They offer us condoms, but not the conditions for a better life outside prostitution. They make distinctions between trafficking and prostitution but believe me, there are none. I was both trafficked and prostituted."[33]

In 2005, other survivors testified before a Canadian House of Commons committee gathering opinions from individuals and community groups. Dawn Hodgins, formerly in prostitution in Edmonton, Canada, said, "Local prostitutes didn't care about decriminalization or legalization. That wasn't the problem. . . . The problem was that they are homeless, addicted."[34]

Canadian survivor and journalist Trisha Baptie exposes harm reduction strategies and prostitution users in many of her writings. "You can't make prostitution 'safer'; prostitution is violence in itself. It is rape, the money only appeases men's guilt. Do we really think they are unable to do without orgasm on demand?"[35]

Survivors are poles apart from the sex workers' message. Survivors experience prostitution as sexual exploitation; sex workers claim that foreign women who end up in local prostitution industries have "migrated for sex work," as if poor women, most from financially ravaged countries, paid their own way and obtained their travel documents for the trip. Survivors tell us that these women are victims of trafficking (see chapter 5).

This is not simply a debate about words. It is about the reality of women's lives. It is about the fact that women in prostitution do not wake up one morning and decide they want to be prostitutes. Instead, most women in prostitution make this "choice" when all else fails. The essential difference between these two views is that recognizing prostitution as work keeps women in prostitution and often in great danger. Understanding prostitution as a violation of women's human rights helps women out of prostitution and out of harm's way.

## ABOLITIONISM IS MORALISTIC, NOT PRAGMATIC

> Hanneke . . . walked me through the red-light district near the Central Station [in Amsterdam]. . . . I remember feeling as if I'd been hit in the stomach by the sight of women standing behind glass, naked or strung together in obscenely sexual clothes. It made me think of animal parts hanging off hooks at the butcher's stall. . . . This was exploitation: I recoiled from it. Hanneke couldn't persuade me that these women were doing it voluntarily, as an honest day's work.
>
> —*Ayaan Hirsi Ali, infidel*

Hirsi Ali's statement is one of moral revulsion, all the more powerful for the animal parts comparison that it evokes. Abolitionist arguments to eliminate prostitution and the sex industry have been characterized as moral—but not in a positive way. Sex work apologists use the word "moral" pejoratively to diminish those who work to abolish prostitution and the sex industry and to avoid what prostitution means at its core—the dehumanizing and degradation of women. What they call moral is any emphasis on justice, dignity, and bodily integrity for women.

It has become fashionable for the sex industry apologists to dismiss any argument that opposes the system of prostitution as moralistic. In their vocabulary, moral means moralism. They argue that in the rough-and-tumble real world, individuals and governments must make decisions and policies that suspend the ethical because it has no practical value. When prostitution was normalized in the Netherlands, the minister of justice explained the legalizing of brothels and pimping in this way: "That prostitution exists is a given fact, even for the government. That requires a realistic approach, without moralism."[36]

The great seduction of legal prostitution regimes is to believe that sexual exploitation can be made better through pragmatic legislation that claims to provide improved "working" conditions for women. The reality is these regimes provide first-class working conditions for pimps and brothel owners whose status is elevated to legitimate businessmen. By law, there are no pimps in the legal brothels of the Netherlands or Australia—only sexual entrepreneurs and licensed agents who are given the legal right to live off the earnings of "voluntary" women in prostitution.

As for the claim that legal regimes destigmatize women, those actually destigmatized are the men who buy and the pimps and traffickers who sell. Even in the Netherlands few women are legally registered because they want no record made of their prostitution. Interviews with women prostituted in the Dutch-licensed sector reveal that the most important aspect of their "work" is anonymity, and they rank it even higher than a regular income or salary.[37] The same reluctance to register or join unions is prevalent among women in prostitution in Germany.[38]

## Humanizing Systems of Oppression

Pro-prostitution NGOs participate in a long and dispiriting tradition of humanizing systems of oppression. During World War II the international Red Cross decided to distribute food packages to the Nazi death camp inmates, and to remain silent about the killing of Jews. Red Cross representatives were allowed into the camps, saw the "unbelievable," and documented it, but they kept the evidence in the organization's files. In March 1945 as the Allies were winning the war, Nazi officials allowed Red Cross representatives into the camps to ensure the "safety" of the prisoners, but only if they agreed not to try to remove them from the camps.

After their visit to the Theresienstadt (Terezin) camp—a visit completely orchestrated by Nazi officials—Red Cross officials praised the camp, confirming that most prisoners enjoyed good treatment, nutritious food, adequate housing, and cultural events. The Nazis, of course, wanted to deceive the world into believing that Jews were well treated.

When it finally released its World War II documents in 1997, the Red Cross defended its decision by saying that its efforts reduced harm and starvation and enabled the organization's continued monitoring of prisoner-of war camps.[39] NGOs such as Médecins Sans Frontières were founded to abolish this kind of collusion with criminals in the name of humanitarianism.

Similarly what we see in the harm reduction approach to prostitution is the decision to distribute condoms in the worst of brothels but to remain silent about the conditions that exist in them, including the prevalence of children used in prostitution. Most organizations can only access brothels with the permission of the criminals that control them. As early as 1996, HIV educators in Bombay agreed to the pimps' directives mandating that they could encourage condom usage in the prostitution sector only if they would not discuss "social issues," and if they would ignore the rampant child prostitution in the sector.[40]

In 2011, sex industry apologists defended this kind of collusion with pimps and brothel owners, wrapped in gentrified language and annexed in an official UNAIDS report on *HIV/AIDS and Sex Work*: "Alliances should be made with managers and agents of sex workers to encourage and support efforts to implement worker safety initiatives, such as requiring all customers to use condoms and posting signs to such effect."[41] What a devil's bargain this report proposes in the name of protection for prostituted women.

Likewise, the Netherlands, Germany, and Australia are state powers that cooperate with criminals redefined as sexual entrepreneurs and clients. In effect, the Dutch prostitution regime has turned criminals into cordial capitalists.[42] Dutch government officials consult with pimps, brothel owners, and buyers, all who have formed associations to promote their self-interests such as the "need" for expanding the legal system of brothels (see chapter 3). How is it that a government like the Netherlands can promote human rights around the world at the same time it whitewashes the sexual slavery of the world's women within its own prostitution nation? Perhaps because they are above the tiresome ethical concerns about exploitation and human dignity in favor of pragmatic ones, like good housekeeping in the brothels.

## Words that Demoralize the Harm and Make It Invisible

The sex industry and its apologists especially challenge the meaning of concepts such as "sexual exploitation," "human dignity," and "victim," which they relegate to the dustbin of morality. During the two-year process leading up to the completion of the Palermo Protocol on trafficking, apologists worked to expunge the words "victim" and "sexual exploitation" from the protocol as it was being drafted. They maintained such terms were moral concepts devoid of pragmatic content.[43] In place of "victims of trafficking," they proposed "trafficked persons," a more neutral term that conveyed little of the exploitation involved in sex trafficking. Transfer this passive adjective to "raped persons" or "tortured persons" to understand how it eviscerates the harm done to victims.

The rejection of using the word "victim" in a UN instrument meant to combat trafficking reminds one of the Bush administration's linguistic gymnastics during its wars in Iraq and Afghanistan. As the sex work apologists worked to replace "victims" with "trafficked persons," the Bush administration attempted to "demoralize" methods of torture as "enhanced interrogation techniques," making these "techniques" pragmatic means to use in the "war on terror." The "mere infliction of pain and suffering" did not count as torture. Only prohibited were pain and suffering that constituted a level ordinarily associated with "death, organ failure or serious impairment of bodily function."

In like manner, when violence is committed in legal sex industries by pimps who are certified prostitution entrepreneurs, and by prostitution users who are accredited consumers, violence is treated as an occupational hazard that *women* must work to reduce—not as a crime. Mary Sullivan has argued that some of the techniques that pro–sex work groups recommend to mitigate the everyday violence of prostitution sound like "crisis management in hostage situations,"[44] where the prostituted woman must negotiate with the buyer for her own protection. Also recommended are provisions for "sexual specialty safety" (e.g., training in the safe use of S&M equipment, including branding irons, whips and canes, hot wax, and piercing instruments).[45]

The best that can be said about this kind of "occupational" advice is that it backhandedly acknowledges the brutality women are subjected to in legal brothels. Tellingly, pro–sex work organizations take for granted that prostitution is a violent and dangerous practice and that women must assume more and more of the responsibility for risk management. Because the words "sexual exploitation," "sexual torture," and "victim" have all but vanished from the vocabulary of what happens to women in legal systems of prostitution, so also is the harm to women made invisible.

## Why a Moral Struggle?

Politics is always based on some kind of ethics, or some kind of values. During the civil rights struggle of the 1960s, Martin Luther King, Jr., pressed U.S. president John F. Kennedy to speak about civil rights in moral terms and to transcend the political considerations of north-south relations, states' rights, and public order. King knew that moral suasion had pragmatic consequences and that hearts and minds needed to be changed in order to transform laws. Wrapping Kennedy's proposed civil rights legislation in the language of what is right and just appealed to the moral sense of citizens. It helped prompt a civic response to oppose racial segregation and support civil rights legislation—especially as Americans watched television pictures of black nonviolent demonstrators in Birmingham, Alabama, get pounded by Bull Connor's high-pressure hoses, attacked by police dogs, and savagely beaten by police with billy clubs.

In his famous civil rights speech to the nation, Kennedy acknowledged institutionalized racism: "We face a moral crisis as a country and as a people. . . . Those who do nothing are inviting shame as well as violence. Those who act boldly are recognizing right as well as reality." Eventually, many U.S. citizens realized that institutionalized racism is built on a value structure that fails to accord African Americans dignity, respect, and rights.

### Whose Moral Panic?

When those promoting the abolition of prostitution "recognize right as well as reality," justice as well as pragmatism, and speak about the system of globalized prostitution as a moral crisis, they are attacked for being moralists. When abolitionists focus on what happens to victims, they are stereotyped as creating "moral panic," of using sensationalism, and of purveying "anecdotal horror stories." The debate over prostitution, however, is not filled with a surplus of moral wisdom but rather a scarcity of it.

Longtime apologist for prostitution as work, Ronald Weitzer, writes that anti-trafficking campaigns create "moral panic" and are the "institutionalization of a moral crusade." Weitzer has been yammering about moral panics for years, using this term repetitively in many of his articles to create linguistic sensationalism. Comparing feminist and other campaigns to abolish prostitution with historical moral crusades, Weitzer inveighs against this "far-reaching attack on commercial sex." "Moral crusades . . . typically offer anecdotal horror stories and . . . photos of young victims. . . . Such depictions dramatize human suffering and are designed to cause alarm and outrage and to stoke popular revulsion and support for draconian solutions."[46]

So now it is feminist abolitionists whose challenge to the sex industry is labeled a "moral panic" at the same time that pimps and brothel owners are welcomed as allies by a UN committee report, and by numbers of academics, NGOs and some governments. As Gail Dines and Julia Long have noted about the application of the term "moral panic" to anti-pornography feminists, "No one in progressive circles would suggest for a moment that criticism of the corporate media is a moral panic . . . yet those of us who organize against the corporations that churn out sexist imagery are regularly dismissed as stirring moral panic."[47] Much of the academic literature attacking abolitionists reads as its own panic about the success of those who have thwarted state-endorsed prostitution policy and instead created legislation penalizing demand.

One effect of this linguistic sensationalism is that human rights advocates and progressives shield pimps, traffickers, and prostitution users. In doing so, many progressive activists and organizations help strip the sex industry of any legal accountability and whitewash its history of the sexual exploitation of women and children. Others may hesitate to condemn systems of prostitution because they fear being tainted as moralistic and as condemning sex.

## Moralism and Morality Are Not the Same

Moralism discourages thoughtful decision making and is a passive stance. Morality is the sphere of "moral intelligence," in Andrea Dworkin's words, actively searching out the common values on which a politics is based.

Values do matter. The promotion of human rights for women in prostitution is twofold. On the one hand, prostituted women need safety, security, and services. On the other, they need dignity, respect, and equality. Prostitution is particularly objectionable because of its personal degradation of body and spirit, and the gender subordination on which the system is built. If women in prostitution cannot have a future where their lives have value, their prospects are bleak.

Unfortunately the whole vocabulary of values has been ceded to the religious and conservative right. But the right wing and institutional religions have no monopoly on ethical thinking. Many people believe that war is immoral, not just that we should fight it better and smarter. Likewise, many concerned people believe that prostitution is a moral issue that must be addressed within a framework of freedom from exploitation, justice, human dignity, and bodily integrity. People need to hear about this moral framework for why prostitution should be abolished versus normalized in order to make legal and policy judgments. As Ellen Goodman has written, we should vote our values. "It's time to parse what we believe in."[48]

The legal status of prostitution is essentially an ethical and political inquiry and cannot be solved by reducing it to a pragmatic and economic calculus that is value-neutral. It is deceptive for states such as the Netherlands to pretend that its system of legalized prostitution is built on a benevolent pragmatism that is protective of women. Rather the Dutch system is built on a pragmatism that is instrumentalist and materialistic—instrumentalist in the sense that it utilizes women as instruments of male gratification and materialist in that it provides revenues not only for the sex industry but also for the state coffers. Ethically speaking the Dutch system is immoral, reinforcing the position of prostituted women in society as sexual objects and instruments of pleasure to be bought, consumed, and discarded by pimps, brothel owners, and buyers. Missing is a deeper inquiry about what kind of a society institutionalizes sexual exploitation as sex work.

A legacy of twentieth-century feminism is its critique of the historical sexualization of women, including the "sexual liberation" movement of the 1960s. In this twenty-first century, we seem to have returned to a resexualization of women, passing as post-feminist liberation. Women's bodies, clothing, magazines, and self-image are saturated in a culture of pornography that also ennobles prostitution as sexual liberation. Tolerance has replaced protest against what passes for the sexually liberated woman, who is too often the *sexualized woman.*

It is not fashionable to criticize anything that is deemed sexuality, including prostitution and pornography. Too many people seem to believe that anything that passes for sex is off-limits to criticism, because they do not want to be identified as old-fashioned, moralistic, and/or censorious. This mind control has shaped dominant academic and popular cultural discourse on prostitution as sex, not sexual exploitation.[49]

The net effect of the pro–sex work narrative of prostitution is that a lower value is set on the women in prostitution, which accepts that they can have things done to them that are not done to others. The presumption prevails that prostituted women are inured to the violence and violation of prostitution, and can be subjected to the daily sexual servicing of multiple prostitution users and the criminals who control them. This is a familiar form of dehumanization.

We need to remove criticism of pornography and prostitution from the zone of derision to a frank discussion of the difference between sexuality and sexual exploitation. Even if women "choose" prostitution under conditions that are informed and totally voluntary (which most do not), that decision would not be morally defensible. An ethical choice forces us to consider the conditions of inequality under which prostitution is "chosen" and legally institutionalized for the world's women.

## PROSTITUTION IS A CHOICE

Women's silence and "consent" can be bought—I remember how much mine cost . . . allowing a minority of women in prostitution to argue "choice" on the backs of the majority who are out there, in a perfect storm of oppression, neglect, abuse and human trafficking.
—*Trisha Baptie, Canadian journalist and survivor*

From oral history testimony and interviews with women in prostitution, it is known that some women enter the sex industry because they have been forced, coerced, or deceived. Others enter because offenders abuse their vulnerabilities, including past and present sexual abuse, poverty and economic disadvantage, marginalization, and loss of self, and use predatory recruitment tactics that can include peer or family pressure. Those who enter the industry knowing they will engage in prostitution often have no idea of the conditions that await them. No matter whether women experience forced entry or initial "choice," they are still used and used up by an industry that exploits them to the hilt.

When a woman continues in an abusive relationship with a partner who batters her, or even when she defends her partner's actions, concerned people don't assume she remains voluntarily. They recognize the complexity of her compliance. Yet many well-intentioned persons who would recognize battering as violence against women see only an occupational hazard when they look at the same abuse of women in prostitution. Supposedly if women choose to stay in prostitution, there is no exploitation. Like battered women, which they are, women in prostitution often deny their abuse if provided with no meaningful alternatives.

It is one thing to endorse a notion of personal choice as necessary to women's freedom but quite another to claim that women can make meaningful choices within a system of prostitution that represses women's freedom. It is one thing to argue that women need sexual freedom but quite another to claim that prostitution provides it within a global sex industry where prostituted women must service five to fifteen men a day, and most need drugs or alcohol to do the "job."

Choice has come to replace what is actually a *strategy of survival* for most prostituted women. It is a "choiceless choice." Paying someone to have sex with you when your motivation is to get enough money to survive, or to buy the next bag of groceries or drugs, is not voluntary intercourse. It's a transaction based on her disadvantages and his power of purchase. It's *compliance* to the only options available.

## In the Receding Background of Choice

The presumption of women's consent effectively means that it doesn't matter what men do when they buy or sell women's bodies. The presumption of consent, and the fact that this issue engages most of those who debate the status of prostitution, absolves men from responsibility. It begs the question of why any man would achieve sexual pleasure over the bought bodies of women and children. The emphasis on choice in the politics of prostitution has reduced prostitution to a question of a woman's consent, sprung free from the context of male dominance and the commercial power of an international sex industry. Both forces are allowed to recede into the background because whether or not it is her choice takes over the foreground.

If we are simply free to choose cigarettes, foods that put us on the road to obesity, and assault rifles that kill, the corporations that create these "products" retreat from view. If people are convinced that they willingly choose their poisons, then markets in poisons will prevail and profit. The public opinion game promises greater consumer freedom and convinces people that choosing anything in a free market is good. But there are many situations in which defending choice is deceptive and dangerous, and prostitution is one of them.

The sex work ideologues use a minimalist definition of choice as freedom from coercion. However, the ability to choose depends on many determinants such as emotional and physical health, education, and financial standing. Moreover, women who initially make the alleged choice to engage in prostitution cannot be said to remain there by choice when the sex industry and its legions of pimps, brothel owners, and buyers hold women in a vise of control, violence, debt bondage, and drug-induced endurance.

In 1990 at a UN Economic and Social Council (ECOSOC) meeting, the Dutch government argued for a woman's right to choose prostitution, including her right to choose her pimp: "The right to self-determination, enjoyed by every independent adult man or woman who has not been subjected to any unlawful influence, implies the right of that individual to engage in prostitution and to allow another individual to profit from the resulting earnings."[50] These words could have come out of a sex industry playbook.

Another factor that makes the focus on choice problematic is that women in prostitution develop coping techniques, some of which involve minimizing the harm and exploitation they face day after day in prostitution. Coping can also generate denial or rationalization of one's own actions, or those of one's abusers, in order to save face. Survivors understand what Trisha Baptie tells us that, when in the sex industry, she would have told people "it was empowering and liberating—how could I look at myself in the mirror otherwise?"[51]

## Who Has the Real Choice in Prostitution?

If women really choose prostitution, why is it mostly disadvantaged and marginalized women who do? If we want to discuss the issue of choice, let's look at who is doing the actual choosing in the context of prostitution. Surely the issue is not why women allegedly choose to be in prostitution, but why men choose to buy the bodies of millions of women and children worldwide and call it sex.

Philosophically, the response to the choice debate is *not* to deny that women are capable of choosing within contexts of powerlessness, but to question how much real value, worth, and power these so-called choices confer. Politically, the question becomes, should the state sanction the sex industry based on the claim that some women choose prostitution when most women's choice is actually *compliance* to the only options available? When governments idealize women's alleged choice to be in prostitution by legalizing, decriminalizing, or regulating the sex industry, they endorse a new range of *conformity* for women. Increasingly, what is defended as a choice is not a triumph over oppression but another name for it.

## THE FALSE DICHOTOMY BETWEEN FORCED AND FREE PROSTITUTION

Sex work ideologues drive a wedge between sex trafficking and prostitution, conveying the impression that trafficking is forced and prostitution is voluntary. Thus, there arises the confusion of anti-trafficking NGOs and governments who are pro-prostitution, promoting the illusion that sex trafficking can be stopped without challenging prostitution itself.

The severing of forced and voluntary prostitution has proven to be a powerful legal tool for perpetrators of sexual exploitation. In systems of both legal and illegal prostitution, prostitution is only actionable when women can prove that their prostitution was coerced, almost at the barrel of a gun. Sex work apologists put the burden of proof on the woman to prove she was forced. Forced prostitution is like shrinking the legal definition of rape, torture, or battering to only forced rape, forced torture, forced battering. As opinion writer Maureen Dowd has noted in one of her insightful columns, "What on earth is forcible rape? It's like saying nonlethal murder. Why define acts of aggression against women as non-acts of aggression?"[52] Because, in the case of prostitution, the act of aggression is wrapped in the cloak of consensual sex?

Legislation that makes only forced prostitution unlawful practically guarantees that the number of indictments and prosecutions will be minimal. If victims must prove that force was used in recruiting them into prostitution or keeping them there, very few women will have legal recourse, and very few offenders will be prosecuted.

## The UN Protocol on Trafficking

The line between voluntary and involuntary was vigorously debated during the negotiations that led up to the passing of the UN Protocol on trafficking, also called the Palermo Protocol. Whether to make the definition of trafficking exclusively dependent on the victim being forced was the most contentious part of this two-year drafting process that took place at the United Nations in Vienna. On the one side was a small group of NGOs that promoted the view that sex trafficking is forced prostitution. They fought to make force the basis of the definition of trafficking and to saddle posterity with the tautology of "forced trafficking."

On the other, the Coalition Against Trafficking in Women organized 140 NGOs into the International Human Rights Network that was instrumental in elaborating a definition of trafficking that protected all victims of trafficking. The network argued that a narrow definition of force does not protect large numbers of trafficked victims for whom the burden of proof of force or coercion will be too high. For example, many women who are trafficked into the sex industry have had pornography made of them, where they are portrayed as smiling and seductive. Many victims of trafficking do not fit the classic picture of those who are forced.

The Human Rights Network argued that consent is irrelevant. Trafficking can occur with or without the victim's consent. A human rights definition of trafficking should focus on *exploitation*, which is the core of the crime. Whether trafficked women consent, they are still exploited. Further, there are many vulnerabilities leading women and children into the sex industry that cannot easily be brought under a narrow definition of coercion or force. Feminist abolitionist organizations succeeded in expanding the conditions of trafficking to "abuse of a person's vulnerabilities."[53]

These organizations were also successful in promoting a definition of trafficking that included the provision that trafficking could occur "with or without the consent of the victim." Grounded in a human rights approach to trafficking, this definition draws no distinctions between deserving and undeserving victims of trafficking. It takes the burden of proof off the exploited and places it on the exploiters. And it provides the strongest support to international efforts to end trafficking because it is clear, unambiguous, and offers fewer loopholes for traffickers.

The problems associated with basing a definition of trafficking on force, rather than exploitation, are illustrated by several actual situations. In March 2007 Japanese prime minister Shinzo Abe announced there was no evidence that the Imperial Japanese Army had coerced thousands of Asian women into Japanese military brothels during World War II.[54]

Abe's statement was followed by a full-page advertisement in the *Washington Post* signed by a group of Japanese lawmakers who wanted to share "the truth with the American people" about those called "comfort women." The ad claimed that no historical document proves that these women were forced, but rather it alleges they were "embedded with the Japanese army . . . working under a system of licensed prostitution that was commonplace around the world at the time." Although the ad acknowledged there were some "breakdowns in discipline," it asserted many of these women "made more money than field officers and even generals."[55]

In this ad the Japanese government concealed its conscription of Asian women into military prostitution by "embedding" them within a system of legal prostitution that distinguishes between women who are forced and women who choose to be in prostitution. Additionally, it resorted to a smoke screen of women's financial gain to deny that the "comfort women" were forced and exploited. A 2004 ILO report stated "that victims of trafficking have been perceived in Japan as voluntary participants in illegal immigration, which thereby removes them from protection,"[56] another example of the Japanese legacy of victims as voluntary.

A further irony of this situation is that pro–sex work advocates argue that most trafficking *is* voluntary migration, playing into the hands of countries like Japan that would deprive women of protection because they are seen as voluntary illegal migrants, not as victims of trafficking. Much of Laura Agustin's work can feed into this perception of confusing victims with criminality. Reviewing her book, *Sex at the Margins*, in the *New Statesman*, Brendan O'Neill cited her position:

> Most migrant women, including those who end up in the sex industry, have made a clear decision to leave home and take their chances overseas. They are not "passive victims" who must be "saved" by anti-trafficking campaigners. . . . Rather, frequently, they are headstrong and ambitious women who migrate to escape "small-town prejudices, dead-end jobs, dangerous streets and suffocating families." . . . Some poor migrant women "like the idea of being found beautiful and exotic abroad, exciting desire in others."[57]

When trafficking is seen as migration for sex work, it reinforces the idea that prostituted women are victimizing society, not that they are the real victims.

## South Korea and U.S. Military Prostitution

Force takes many faces not limited to physical coercion. In the aftermath of the Korean War, South Korean lawmakers used official "persuasion" to encourage women to prostitute for the good of the country. In a system of "kijich'on" (military camp town) prostitution that was sponsored and regulated by both the South Korean and U.S. governments for the benefit of the U.S. military, thousands of women were designated "bar girls," "hostesses," "special entertainers," and "comfort women." Koreans called the women "Western whores."[58]

In the early 1990s when political scientist Katharine Moon set out to document kijich'on prostitution, she found that many South Korean activists and academics "never placed the kijich'on prostitutes in any framework of exploitation or oppression. . . . Even those who advocate on behalf of the former Korean 'comfort women,'" conscripted for Japanese military abuse believed "kijich'on prostitutes . . . voluntarily want to lead a life of prostitution, because they are lacking in moral character." In the context of U.S.-Korean foreign policy where Korea was a client state, these women were induced into prostitution as "personal ambassadors" for improving U.S.-Korea relations by keeping U.S. soldiers "happy." In any meaningful sense of choice, it was not the kijich'on women who chose to satisfy the sexual demands of U.S. soldiers but rather the government's "willingness to accommodate the U.S. military's interests."[59]

In 2009 a group of former prostituted women in South Korea accused their government of blatant hypocrisy. They pointed out the government's criticism of Japan's lack of responsibility for prostituting thousands of Korean women in military brothels during World War II but contended the Korean government directly implemented its own state-sponsored system of prostitution for the benefit of the U.S. military in Korea from the 1960s through the 1980s. "Our government was one big pimp for the U.S. military," stated one woman interviewed. "Whether prostitutes by choice, need, or coercion, the women say, they were all victims of government policies . . . to meet what one called the 'natural needs' of allied soldiers."[60]

The South Korean and U.S. governments were actively involved in ensuring that a supply of women existed for the U.S. military; that these women were medically examined for sexually transmitted diseases but not the men who used them; and if found infected, women were detained in so-called monkey houses in which they were guarded until cured by forced medications.[61] These actions replicate the system of Lock Hospitals set up for prostituted women in Britain during the era of the Contagious Disease Acts.

One Korean woman prostituted for U.S. military use articulated the way in which prostituted women were "sacrificed" in Korea's regulated system of prostitution. "Women like me were the biggest sacrifice for my country's alliance with the Americans. . . . Looking back, I think my body was not mine but the government's and the U.S. military's."[62]

It may be easier to understand that meaningful consent does not exist within a military context where women of another country are used in prostitution by the dominant power. However in a non-military context, governments can also be persuasive promoters of prostitution in countries that have legalized or decriminalized systems of prostitution. These countries become nations in which women are officially encouraged to prostitute *because* it is legal; men are given legal permission to buy women *because* prostitution is rebranded as a "sexual service"; and pimps preying on the vulnerabilities of women and children are transformed into acceptable business agents who assist women in their chosen occupational goals.

## Social Consequences of Distinguishing Between Forced and Free Prostitution

When the city of Budapest, Hungary, established a legal tolerance zone for those in prostitution, hotline workers reported that many more phone calls seeking help came from girls whose fathers and brothers were pushing them into prostitution for financial reasons. The girls didn't know how to defend themselves against the pressures of their male relatives. Activists fear that full legalization being debated in Hungary—a country with consistently high unemployment—will create hundreds of these requests for help, and that family members will have no compunction about requiring that daughters enter prostitution because it will be fully legal.[63] Advocates also fear that they will not be able to provide women with help from the criminal justice system, since police will no longer be able to prosecute pimps and brothel owners.

The weight of government approval of legal prostitution cannot be underestimated in giving the ethical and social go-ahead to women and families in need and to men to become prostitution users, all encouraged by government policy to participate in the sex industry. Active government complicity in the sex trade is just as present in the Netherlands, Germany, and Australia as it was in Japan and South Korea during the periods documented above. And the scope of what gets defined as voluntary is significantly enlarged in legal systems of prostitution.

An Israeli journalist writes that he once separated the women trafficked into Israel for prostitution into the good, who were forced or tricked, and the bad, who knew they would be in prostitution. In interviewing foreign women in prostitution in Israel, he asked if they knew what they were getting into. One woman, Natasha, responded, "They told me it was prostitution, but they didn't tell me the conditions." She went on to describe her horrendous experience of being transported across the Sinai, inspected like merchandise by pimps, sold to these pimps by her recruiters, subjected to ten buyers per day, assaulted by both buyers and bosses, kept in the brothel and not allowed out, phoning her father who cared nothing about her plight, and finally escaping. The journalist concluded, "Did Natasha 'choose' to become a prostitute? Does any girl who grows up desolate—without love, money, prospects, or self-esteem—really 'choose' that destiny?"[64]

## The U.S. Trafficking Victims Protection Act

U.S. policy has made clear that prostitution and trafficking are intimately connected. Likewise, UN Special Rapporteur Sigma Huda writes, "For the most part, prostitution as actually practiced in the world usually does satisfy the elements of trafficking. It is rare that one finds a case in which the path to prostitution and/or a person's experiences within prostitution do not involve . . . an abuse of power and/or an abuse of vulnerability."[65]

Under the leadership of Amb. John Miller, former director of the U.S. Office to Monitor and Combat Trafficking, the 2004 *Trafficking in Persons* report emphasized that legalized prostitution regimes do not curb trafficking. "The United States Government takes a firm stand against proposals to legalize prostitution. . . . When law enforcement tolerates or communities legalize prostitution, organized crime groups are freer to traffic in human beings. . . . Legalized prostitution is therefore a trafficker's best shield, allowing him to legitimize his trade."[66] The policy originated in an earlier 2002 National Security Directive "based on evidence that prostitution is inherently harmful and dehumanizing and fuels trafficking in persons, a form of modern-day slavery."[67]

A contradiction remains, however, between U.S. policy that rejects legalization of prostitution and the U.S. Trafficking Victims Protection Act (TVPA) passed initially in 2000. Ever since the TVPA came into force, the U.S. government is mandated to publish an annual Trafficking in Persons report. Countries that have legalized or decriminalized prostitution are ranked in the report's Tier 1 category, the best ranking. Obviously this classification does not square with U.S. policy asserting "prostitution is inherently harmful and dehumanizing and fuels trafficking in persons." The culprit is the definition of trafficking in Section 103 (8) of the TVPA, which makes only "severe forms of trafficking" actionable and requires "force, fraud or coercion."

Previous examples illustrate the difficulties with basing any remedies for the exploitation of prostitution on policies and legislation that make force a requirement for proof. The U.S. TVPA has many good points but prosecutors must *prove* that "force, fraud or coercion" was used in carrying out the trafficking. This requirement—a condition of criminalizing the trafficker—is very challenging to substantiate. Even when the traffickers have used force, fraud, or coercion, the burden of proof rests on the victim. Prosecutors depend on victim testimony, but victims may be reluctant to give evidence because their testimony can retraumatize them and endanger them or their families.

Dorchen Leidholdt, cofounding director of the Coalition Against Trafficking in Women, in her testimony before the U.S. House of Representatives committee considering reauthorization of the TVPA in 2007, described the cases of two Korean trafficking victims assisted by her organization. "These traffickers preyed on their victims' poverty and undocumented status, made them endure 14 to 16 hour days of sexual servitude, deprived them of sleep and food, and demanded that they endure sexual intercourse with as many as ten customers a shift."[68] Although these victims were subjected to physical and psychological torture, their traffickers were not prosecuted under the federal Trafficking Victims Protection Act because the prosecutors could not meet the proof requirements of force, fraud, or coercion. Instead, the traffickers were prosecuted under another statute—the Mann Act—that metes out much less of a penalty.

It is unusual that U.S. federal prosecutors use the Mann Act to put traffickers on trial. The Mann Act is an older interstate trafficking law that has no force, fraud, or coercion requirement. Instead, it establishes that victims can be "persuaded, induced or enticed" into prostitution. As a stand-alone piece of legislation, this older and less punitive law is reluctantly used because trafficking cases consume much time and are costly to investigate. Prosecutors say that it isn't worth the time and money to achieve a small penalty for a big-time trafficker who is guilty of gross human rights violations. A solution to this problem would be to incorporate the Mann Act's broader definition of trafficking into the TVPA and give prosecutors the ability to inflict greater penalties on international and domestic traffickers.

In 2007 abolitionist anti-trafficking organizations worked with Rep. Carolyn B. Maloney and others to revise the U.S. federal anti-trafficking law. An amended version of the TVPA deleting the force requirement passed almost unanimously in the U.S. House of Representatives but was stonewalled in the Senate by a coalition of groups, including the Justice Department, that convinced legislators it would divert the federal government "from its core anti-trafficking mission against crimes involving force, fraud or coercion and child victims."[69]

The Heritage Foundation, relying on the separation between trafficking and prostitution, argued the amended bill "trivialize[s] the seriousness of actual human trafficking by equating it with run-of-the-mill sex crimes—such as pimping, pandering and prostitution—that are neither international nor interstate in nature."[70] A coalition between conservative and liberal groups—including members of the Freedom Network and certain governmental authorities, including then senator Joe Biden's office—appeared not to believe that prostitution is a serious crime, nor pimps serious criminals, nor that most prostitution is in fact domestic trafficking. Unfortunately, Senators Joe Biden and Sam Brownback refused to support the amended anti-trafficking bill that had already passed the House of Representatives by a vote of 405 to 2.[71]

Legislation dictates how victims and perpetrators are treated. When anti-trafficking legislation and statutes rely only on force, fraud, or coercion requirements, victims suffer. The trafficker's defense often includes evidence of women having signed prostitution "contracts."

When victims become dependent on their traffickers, sometimes marrying them, these actions seem to demonstrate consent.

Thus, the number of trafficking prosecutions in the United States remains low, as evidenced by the number of charges and convictions over the last five years (2004–2008) for which statistics are available. The highest number of those charged was 120 in 2005, and the highest number of those convicted was 103 in 2007.[72] Many of these convictions were for labor trafficking, not sex trafficking.

In 2002 T-visas, which allow victims of trafficking to stay in the country, became available. As reported in 2011, only an estimated nine-year total of 2,300 out of an available 5,000 a year had been granted to victims.[73] This means that law enforcement is not certifying victims for various reasons, including the requirement that victims must cooperate with authorities, the legitimate fear that women experience, and the inexperience and lack of knowledge among law enforcement agents who either don't understand the anti-trafficking law and program or are reluctant to certify.

Research shows that there is no clear boundary between those who are forced or trafficked and those who "consented" to prostitution. Perhaps the most telling admission of this lack of a dividing line between voluntary and involuntary prostitution is the comprehensive 2007 report, *Prostitution in the Netherlands Since the Lifting of the Brothel Ban*, commissioned by the Dutch Ministry of Justice. This evaluation stated, "It is virtually impossible to pronounce on possible developments in the number of prostitutes working under some kind of duress. In this context, it is worrisome that there seems to be no decrease in the number of prostitutes with pimps."[74] This is a significant finding because, of course, the foundation of the Dutch legalized system of prostitution is the distinction between voluntary and involuntary prostitution.

## OFF-STREET IS SAFER
## THAN ON-STREET PROSTITUTION

Advocates of legalizing or decriminalizing the sex industry argue that violence is noticeably reduced or eliminated in most indoor settings. They claim that off-street prostitution venues are safer for women. Nevertheless, even proponents of decriminalizing prostitution, as well as some self-defined sex worker groups, admit the dangers of off-street prostitution when they distribute "occupational health and safety" tips to mitigate the violence to women in off-street prostitution locations.

Other pro–sex work groups admit the violence against women in their studies. In 2005 the Sex Workers Project (SWP) of the Urban Justice Center in New York City published a report on "indoor sex work" entitled *Behind Closed Doors*. The report includes interviews with fifty-two persons in "sex work" who operate independently or in other off-street locations such as brothels, escort agencies, dungeons, and private clubs in New York City. The report found that 46 percent of the respondents experienced violence from buyers; 42 percent had been threatened or beaten; and 31 percent were robbed by buyers. Fourteen percent experienced violence at the hands of police. Eight percent of the respondents, who had been trafficked into the country, told of being threatened, beaten, raped, and having money withheld by traffickers.[75]

A Transcrime report commissioned by the European Parliament, in its examination of the effects of prostitution legislation in eleven European countries, found, "The wide-spread view that the exploitation of victims of trafficking is always more violent outdoors than indoors does not seem to be confirmed. The level of violence is quite homogenous between outdoor and indoor trafficked prostitution in the selected countries and furthermore, in some countries (such as Austria and Spain), the level of indoor violence is also greater than the level of outdoor violence."[76] The Transcrime report also noted that prostitution in Germany takes place almost exclusively indoors, with 96.3 percent exploited in bars, brothels, private services, and by escort services that go to private homes and hotel rooms. The report states, "The *indoor* market seems to be a little more violent than the *outdoor* one."[77] Austria and Germany have legalized prostitution; Spain has decriminalized aspects of the sex industry. The prevalence of violence against women in both systems refutes the claim of sex work advocates that legal off-street prostitution venues are safer.

Jody Raphael and Deborah Shapiro in their 2004 article on "Indoor and Outdoor Prostitution Venues," reporting interviews with 222 prostituted women in Chicago, found that the prostitution location made minimal difference to the violence women experienced. Fifty percent of women in off-street locations such as escort services reported forced sex; 51.2 percent of women in the strip clubs reported threats with weapons; and one-third of women engaged in prostitution in their own residences reported rape, unwanted fingers inserted into vaginas, or forced sex.[78]

Esohe Aghatise, president of the IROKO Association, has provided direct assistance to women and girls trafficked and prostituted in Italy since 1998. A large number of victims of trafficking for prostitution in Italy comes from Nigeria and Eastern Europe and is made to prostitute for pimps and madams along the roadsides in various areas of the country. Aghatise reports that the decriminalization of off-street prostitution venues in Italy would mean that traffickers would have the possibility of legally importing women to fill brothels or sequester them in private apartments where already isolated women from other countries could be further cut off from assistance. Currently the women in on-street prostitution that IROKO serves often meet people who may be willing to help them, including police, members of the public, or organizations on the road. Were it not for the fact that victims are out in the open, NGOs and others would find it difficult to offer assistance and intervention.[79] This is not an argument for off-street prostitution but rather a challenge to the myth that indoor prostitution is safer for women.

In the studies I have directed, and in my international experience speaking with women in prostitution, the majority of women in prostitution come from marginalized groups with a history of sexual abuse, drug and alcohol dependencies, poverty or financial disadvantage, lack of education, and histories of other vulnerabilities. These factors characterize women in both off- and on-street locations. A large number of women in prostitution are pimped or drawn into the sex industry at an early age. These are women whose lives will not change for the better if prostitution is decriminalized. Many have entrenched problems that are best addressed not by keeping women indoors but in establishing programs where women can be provided with an exit strategy and the services that they need to regain their lost lives. There is little evidence that decriminalization or legalization of prostitution improves conditions for women in prostitution, on or off the street. It certainly makes things better for the sex industry, which is provided with legal standing, and the government that enjoys increased revenues from accompanying regulation (see chapters 3 and 4).

Legal expert and writer Catharine MacKinnon's insight that the distinction between indoor and outdoor prostitution is "an inapt proxy" for the class structure of prostitution rings true. "The indoor/outdoor distinction basically functions ideologically to feed the illusion . . . that the women in prostitution who appear classy really have upper class options," such as choice and ability to leave anytime, and they are not subject to the same level and rates of violence as their outdoor sisters.[80]

This "inapt proxy" was at work during the Eliot Spitzer exposé, when the media made much of the fact that Spitzer used a high-class escort from an upmarket agency in New York City. The prices he paid for his sexual activities reinforced this picture. Nevertheless, we learned that the former governor of New York State subjected women to acts that "you might not think were safe."[81] Men with money, whether rich or not, have the funds to spend on women who are mostly poor or poorer than they are, whether indoors or outdoors.

The Canadian decision to decriminalize brothels claimed that indoor prostitution would make it better for women in prostitution who would then be able to own their own businesses. In welcoming indoor prostitution, the court left the poorest and most marginalized women out in the cold. Those who will profit most from the Canadian decision are the current owners of brothels who will be transformed from criminals into comfortable capitalists overnight. Alan Young, the lawyer for the applicants, when asked during oral arguments whether it would be acceptable to the three "sex workers" he represented if street prostitution remained criminalized, responded yes.[82] He said, "I'm here representing the intelligent, independent and well-informed sex worker."[83] Despite their rhetoric about how street prostitution is more dangerous than off-street prostitution, Young and the threesome he speaks for were as good as telling the street prostituted women they were dispensable.

## WOMEN IN PROSTITUTION ARE NOT VICTIMS: THE VICTIM DENIERS

For the sex industry apologists, the world of prostitution is a world of post-victimism where the sufferings of women are rationalized away as choice. The victim myth can only prevail by denying the gravity and prevalence of the exploitation experienced by women in prostitution, which apologists minimize. They denounce those who want to "rescue" (i.e., help and assist) women from a life of prostitution as extremists and ideologues. The actual extremists and ideologues are those who let the women continue to suffer.

Victimitis is a trivializing term used by sex work advocates who promote the "myth of the woman as victim." It is a term used almost in sneering disbelief by those who deny that women in prostitution are victims. This denial of women's victimization is illustrated in Phelim McAleer's commentary on the "Happy Hookers of Eastern Europe" in which she maintains that anyone "who isn't infected with victimitis" knows, "The overwhelming majority of girls going to the West understand before they leave that they will be working in prostitution." McAleer continues: "The sex slave myth also portrays Eastern European women as idiots." Those who accept this "myth," she argues, assume that women from the East have never read a newspaper or seen a TV program on sex trafficking.[84]

In response to McAleer, certainly a number of women enter the sex industry knowing they must prostitute but have no idea of the abuse they will have to endure. Also many trafficked women believe that their experience will be different from the media exposés and that they will manage to avoid the traps of traffickers. In interviews with trafficked Nigerian women who were asked whether they and their families were familiar with the dangers of being trafficked into prostitution in Europe, many responded they believed these accounts to be exaggerated (as the sex work apologists maintain), or these harmful consequences could not happen to them or their relatives.[85]

Victim deniers make it sound as if pimps and traffickers are a girl's best friend. "The truth about human trafficking is that for desperate people it is usually a good bet. . . . Asylum seekers and migrants rely equally on traffickers and a crackdown impedes those fleeing persecution just as much as those fleeing poverty." The poor human traffickers are "always demonised, but most help desperate people."[86]

In his research on *Prostitution, Politics and Policy*, British criminologist Roger Matthews has found that women in prostitution are not only among the most victimized groups, but many are multiple victims. Thus, the term "victim" can be especially applied to women in prostitution. According to Matthews's research, women in street prostitution are eighteen times more vulnerable to being killed than other women.[87]

Victim deniers reject the abuse done to women in prostitution claiming the abuse is sensationalized, particularly in the media. There is some truth to media sensationalism, most notably in cases where a victim is mutilated or killed in gruesome ways, and where the focus is a voyeuristic preoccupation with the sexual graphics of her victimization. In U.S. TV shows like *Criminal Minds* and the proliferating *CSI* and its derivatives, we are treated to the autopsies that reduce victims to their organs extracted in the morgue. Victimization of women has become mass entertainment, and the CSI experts and criminal minds' profilers function as the "good guy" actors in a serial killer entertainment industry. Psychopathology and the idealization of scientific crime experts marry well, and the visual slaughter of women in all its gory details—especially of those in prostitution—captivates viewers.

One consequence of sensationalizing prostitution and its victims is that persons come to identify only women who resemble those in the crime shows as the "good victims." The victim deniers contribute to this perspective by insisting that the real victims of prostitution are few and far between, and most women in the sex industry have chosen to be there.

Opposing the victim deniers, Suki Falconberg, a survivor of prostitution, states, "I only faced two acts of violence the whole time I was in prostitution. . . . No one hit me. No one slammed my head against a dashboard. I was not broken and controlled by a pimp. I could leave my apartment at any time I wanted. . . . I worked as a prostitute under optimal circumstances—compared to most of those . . . in the sex industry." Yet, "it was so damaging that I didn't have any will or commonsense or intellect or brain left—to fight or make other decisions for myself."[88]

Another set of victim deniers limit the agency of women only to their choices to remain *in* the prostitution industry. The sex work apologists romanticize "empowerment" for women in the sex industry and locate female power in the very behaviors that feminism has rejected—sexual objectification, acceptance of the use of women's bodies as commodities for male pleasure and for profit, and misrepresentation of this as rebellion.

Agency under oppression is usually found in those who *resist* their oppression in large or small ways. However, sex industry advocates locate women's agency in conformity to their roles in the industry, not in their resistance to them. Sex industry advocates argue that prostituted women are shrewd and savvy deciders of their own destinies who perform needed sexual services, and that many of the "bad guys" help them along the way, serving as trusty business agents and protecting women's interests.

Sex industry apologists use women's agency to rationalize and empower the victimizers, not to show how survivors of prostitution have resisted those who exploit them. The point is not to deny a prostituted woman's agency but to locate agency in the right places—in surviving and opposing a dehumanizing sex industry. A prostitution industry that objectifies and commodifies women is not a culture in which women are effective agents. It is a culture in which women are deceived and made satisfied with the pretexts that pass for empowerment. Trisha Baptie knows through experience how women in prostitution justify what they do to themselves: "What I remember about my years as a prostituted woman was how much I tried to find something empowering in what I found myself doing. That by choosing who raped me, based on their ability to pay, I was empowered. That by consenting to the abuse, I was free from it."[89]

What I constantly learn, in my discussions with survivors of prostitution and trafficking, is the human resilience that women possess and the innumerable ways they endure the worst of conditions. When you talk to women personally and hear what they have withstood and how they have done it, there is no essential victimization. Victims battle oppression in remarkable ways. Many women who have been abused in the sex industry act constantly to survive, resist, and rebuild their lives. But the victim deniers locate agency not in women's resistance but in their conformity to the sex industry.

Victim denial influences governmental views not only of women but also of young girls in prostitution. The legal system in most U.S. states criminalizes young girls caught in prostitution. This means that girls found prostituted on the streets and exploited by pimps and buyers can be charged with prostitution and sent to a juvenile detention center, rather than protected as victims of child sexual abuse. It was not until 2008 that the passage of the Safe Harbor law in New York State mandated that juveniles would be treated as victims the first time they are arrested for prostitution and offered services and protection from pimps.

In trumpeting the agency of women in prostitution, the victim deniers reinforce the view that women choose their own oppression. By reiterating that women are agents and make rational choices to enter prostitution, they ally themselves with a patriarchal culture of blaming women who "make their own beds and therefore must lie in them." This coincides with the view of conservative moralists, whether religious or secular, who hold women responsible for being pimped, exploited, and abused.

The conservative view of prostitution is to blame women and girls for their alleged choice to be in prostitution; the liberal view is to romanticize women's "choice" as self-determination and use it to normalize prostitution as "sex work." Both succumb to the belief that whatever happens to a woman in prostitution is normal because it's her choice. Both these views have facilitated the expansion of sexual slavery in many parts of the globe and the extensive ways in which women themselves become "goods and services"—as prostituted women, as trafficked instruments of exchange, as objects of sex tourism, and as indentured domestic workers who are often sexually exploited as well.

Denying or minimizing women's victimization in prostitution reverses decades of feminist activism that finally broke through the wall of societal denial that women *are* victims of male violence. Now that headway has been made in the campaign that domestic battering is violence against women, *whether women choose to stay in an abusive relationship or not*, it comes back to haunt us in the prostitution debate, not only from those who want to suppress women's rights but also from those who claim to enhance women's rights.

When violence happens to women in prostitution, it is called sex; but when violence happens in a context that is not sexual, it is called a crime. Men's prostitution abuse is tolerated as inevitable and unassailable.

# 2

## Prostitution on Demand: The Prostitution Users

The streets of Italy put on a display of enslaved women coupled with a demand for sex on payment, which involves millions of Italians. . . . Anyone buying a pirate CD in Italy is liable to criminal charges; anyone exploiting a slave, instead, feeds into the trafficking of humans, and is not liable to sanctions of any kind.

*—Stefania Prestigiacomo*

The former equal-opportunities minister of Italy spoke these words in 2005, when she proposed legislation to penalize the prostitution users who solicited women for prostitution on the streets of Italy. Nevertheless, Minister Prestigiacomo was attacked for daring to suggest that buyers be penalized. "I am still having to defend my position on that stance because . . . someone sneaks in amendments which would have the slaves jailed and the clients just rapped over the knuckles."[1]

Civil society in many countries has yet to decide the legal status of prostitution users, the buyers who purchase women and children for the sex of prostitution. Even fining the buyers is suspect because opponents will argue, among others, that boys will be boys, prostitution is consensual sexual activity, or they will offer other excuses that rationalize what men do to women in prostitution.

This situation is beginning to change. Most of the Nordic countries have passed legislation criminalizing the buying of sex. It is this model that is creating a paradigm shift in many countries and jurisdictions. The United Nations, as well as the militaries of a number of nations, has prohibited their troops, peacekeepers, and other personnel from using women in prostitution, even in jurisdictions where prostitution is legal.[2]

In 2000 the first UN instrument to address demand for sexual exploitation was passed.[3] Together with Sweden's 1999 legislation criminalizing the purchasing of a person for prostitution,[4] the 2000 Palermo Protocol gave impetus to other national legislation penalizing the prostitution users. These two groundbreaking laws also promoted public awareness that those who buy women and children for the sex of prostitution are collaborators with the criminals running the sex trade. Prostitution users contribute the funds that keep sexual slavery alive and well.

NGOs and governments are also devising other methods of discouraging demand. It is true that men must be educated not to participate in the sexual exploitation of women and children and enlisted as catalysts for change. At the same time, it is also true that men should be held liable for the criminal acts they commit. Historically, it has been acceptable legally for men to beat their wives. "Heightened awareness and an increase in reports of domestic violence has led to a widespread legal response since the 1980s. Once thought to be a problem that was best handled without legal intervention, domestic violence is now treated as a criminal offense."[5] Although the rates of woman battering are still high, few persons would openly defend it, not only because both men and society have been educated to the fact that violence against women is a harmful, mostly male practice, but also because men are legally accountable for committing a crime.

If you're found buying heroin or stolen goods, you are legally liable, as Stefania Prestigiacomo pointed out. The principle is that the buyer creates the market for these drugs and goods and abets the organized criminals who supply the products. Claiming lack of knowledge that an item is stolen is no defense to being charged with handling stolen goods. Abuse of women and children ought to command the same legal accountability as facing prosecution for buying illicit drugs or "hot" DVDs.

## WHO IS THE MALE DEMAND FOR PROSTITUTION?

There are studies that estimate the prevalence of men who, as buyers, engage in prostitution activities. Various numbers come from different countries, and any of these studies can be disputed. In Asia an early study on Thailand conducted by the former U.S. Agency for International Development (USIA) reported that 75 percent of Thai men were prostitution buyers, and almost 50 percent had their first sexual intercourse with women in prostitution. In Cambodia 60–70 percent of men have purchased women for sexual activities.[6]

Figures that range from 10 to 25 percent are cited for numbers of European prostitution users. A 1997 UK study estimated that 10 percent of London's male population buys women for the sex of prostitution.[7] Before the law penalizing buyers came into force in Sweden, about one in eight men (or 12.7 percent) used women and children in prostitution; after the law, national population samples indicate the number of those purchasing sex dropped to 7.6 percent in 2008.[8] According to German criminal psychologist Adolf Gallwitz, 18 percent of German men regularly pay for sex.[9] A survey by Spain's National Statistics Institute found that one in fourteen Spanish men bought women for prostitution at least once during 2003, the year the interviews were conducted. And 27 percent acknowledged paying for a prostituted woman at least once during their lifetime.[10]

In the United States the numbers are wide-ranging. Earlier studies, such as Kinsey and others' (1948), estimated half of the adult male population were frequent prostitution users.[11] In 1964 Harry Benjamin and Robert E. L. Masters estimated that a whopping 80 percent of U.S. men used women in prostitution.[12] Later, in 1994 a study found that 16 percent of U.S. men engaged in the sex of prostitution.[13] In a more recent 2011 study *Comparing Sex Buyers with Men Who Don't Buy Sex*, Melissa Farley and others had a great deal of trouble finding men to interview who had never bought sex.[14]

During the late 1990s and the first decade of the twenty-first century, articles, studies, and more qualitative reports about the sex buyers began to appear in the work of some researchers, journalists, and writers.[15] At the same time, numerous websites such as the *World Sex Guide* emerged, encouraging men to trade information about their preferred kind of sex, the "quality" places to buy, and the most accommodating women to seek out.

The Internet has spawned a virtual brotherhood of buyers who traffic in information about their experiences in using prostituted women, and who bond with one another over the bodies of women they treat as commodities. One study found that the men gain "status and respect" from their virtual peers for the sexual savvy they bring to such forums about past and present experiences in using women in prostitution. These sites foster a cyber-culture of buyers enabling men to ratify their use of women as "normal and nondeviant"—a hobby rather than a crime. In examining the postings of these "hobbyists" and "mongers," as they refer to themselves, it is clear that they view women in prostitution "as goods rather than human beings."[16]

In the next section of this chapter, the buyers speak for themselves. Their narratives are organized into thematic responses culled from media features and research reports, as well from the words of men who trade information about prostitution and the sex industry on Internet sex sites. These themes, although not exhaustive, are typical responses that recur in the interviews. The buyers' narratives are provided without commentary. Each quote is a revelation within itself.

The traditional question asked by many about prostitution has been, Why do women do this? The information in the men's narratives redirects this question to its proper target, Why do men do this? All of these accounts give us a picture of the buyer. All provide some information about why men *say* they buy women for the sex of prostitution.

## The Buyers' Narratives

### The Biological Determinism Narrative
"It should be legalised over here [UK]. This is the way God created us." (British)[17]

"The people who made this questionnaire [about why men buy women in prostitution] do not understand how strong men's physiological needs are. Men with high spirits have been struggling with their sexual needs every day since they were fifteen years old. Men looking like gentlemen have the same mindset." (Japanese, media, age 60s)[18]

### The Men Will Be Men Narrative
"It's just a lust for life, a quest for pleasure—there's not many men who are (faithful) you know." (Australian)[19]

"It's a boys' thing, and you never tell what happens with the boys." (Australian who never visits a brothel alone)[20]

### The Women as Scum Narrative:
### Getting Off on Humiliation, Degradation, and Violence Against Women
"I think a lot of them [women in prostitution] are disgusting." (Dutch)[21]

"At just the right moment I leaned forward and shot my load on her face! Good amount on her lips, cheeks and an eye shot as well! She was suprised [*sic*] and shocked, this got me more excited than the act. I left her there with nothing to wipe the cum off with and her exclaiming to get something. Yeah right!" (American, Internet buyers site)[22]

*The Thrill of Transgression Narrative*

"Men who want to buy sex aren't deterred by police. The fear adds to the thrill." (Canadian, business professional, age 40)[23]

"But one of the main reasons I enjoy prostitutes is because I enjoy breaking the law—another reason I don't want brothels made legal. There is a charm about the forbidden that makes it desirable . . . crime and risk are part of the texture of life. . . . Risk is what separates the good part of life from the tedium." (British, age 41)[24]

*The Making My Fantasies Real Narrative*

"I've been leading up to it; using pornography and looking at various websites. Rather than being a fantasy it was someone you could have sex with." (British, management consultant, age 40)[25]

"I want my prostitute not to behave like one. I want them to role play to be a pretend girlfriend. . . . She should enjoy her business. I actually want her to be genuinely attracted to me." (British)[26]

*The Unsatisfactory Wife, Partner, or Girlfriend Narrative*

"I was quite elated afterwards. From the sexual side, which was better physically than what I would get at home, and also the conversation with the woman." (British, IT worker, age 50s)[27]

"I find it hard for her [his wife] to turn me on . . . and in truth she doesn't want it regularly anyway—but I have developed a sexual feeling for women that look different in some way . . . exotic beauties." (Australian)[28]

*The Having It Both Ways Narrative*

"The thing which in some way bothers me the most is my almost boundless capacity to just simply ignore what I have done, and fully plan to do it again." (British)[29]

"I know I love her [his wife] and I don't want to leave. It's not like I'm having an affair. I've been using the girls at the parlours for over nearly 20 years. . . . It's not really about the person. It is just about a sexual release. My wife is still my best friend." (Australian)[30]

*The Service Like Any Other Narrative*

"I see us as adults. I want to pay and someone wants to sell." (British, IT worker, age 50s)[31]

"If I am satisfied with what I am buying, then why should I be violent? I will be violent when I am cheated, when I am offered a substandard service. . . . Sometimes [violence] is because the prostitute wants

the client to use condoms. They force it on the client. . . . He will natu-
rally be disgruntled, and there will be altercations." (Indian, bank clerk,
age 54)[32]

### The Traveler's Narrative
"Truck driving is not an easy task. . . . We miss our wives. . . . Yet we
need comfort." (Cameroonian, truck driver, 38)[33]

"[It] would be a walk of shame in your own backyard. . . . But when
you're on the other side of the world man, who cares?" (undesignated
john)[34]

### The No Emotional Strings Narrative
"I am attracted to prostitutes because there are no emotional entan-
glements, and I like the idea of sex with different women." (American,
PhD, inventor, philanthropist, age 52)[35]

"No big deal, it's just like getting a beer." (British)[36]

### The I Don't Like What I'm Doing, But I Still Do It Narrative
"I do not like myself engaging in prostitution. I am selfish in that I
cannot live without engaging in prostitution." (Japanese, public official,
age 40s)[37]

"See, I understand that the prostitute is there in the first place
because she has no choice. . . . I feel bad about this, especially if she
is forced or sold. But the fact is that she is in the flesh market. . . . It
may sound bad, but the fact is that she is a commodity offering a service and she should accept that. We should all." (Indian, civil servant,
age 39)[38]

### The Male Bonding Narrative
"You go out for a few beers with your mates after work and then like,
someone'll just mention it, 'Let's go get a brass,' 'finish a good night
off.'" (British)[39]

"Here in Australia, we think nothing of going to a strip bar for a
business luncheon. . . . It's just something you do with your mates. . . . If
you're in the mood for a little lap dance for dessert or want to head off
to the VIP room for a quickie, no one really gives a damn." (Australian)[40]

### The Easy Option Narrative
"After a working day of 8–9 hours, I am not interested in looking for
vague company in a bar. . . . It is the easiest option in my life situation

for satisfying my sexual needs." (Finnish, education professional, age 50)[41]

"It's like going to McDonald's; most people are looking for a good quick cheap meal. It's satisfying, it's greasy, and then you get the hell out of there." (McSex)[42]

## The Welfare Narrative

"These girls gotta eat, don't they? I'm putting bread on their plate. I'm making a contribution. They'd starve to death unless they whored." (American military, Philippines)[43]

"Maybe it is true. Maybe these women have horrible, depressing lives. If they do and to the extent that they do, I'm a few hours of easy money. I'm a free meal." (American, sex tourist)[44]

## The Man as Victim Narrative

"How would you feel, waking up the next morning thinking 'I can't get laid unless I pay for it?' The harm is done to men, too . . . the women are doing as much harm to the men." (Canadian, business professional, age 40)[45]

"MEN are the ones being exploited by these whores. . . . While men can control their actions, they cannot control the urge. This leaves men open to abuse and exploitation." (undesignated john)[46]

Studies indicate that prostitution users come from all walks of life, all classes, and are usually not men deprived of sexual contact with women. A significant number are married or have partners. At the most publicized end of this spectrum, there is Eliot Spitzer, the former governor of New York, caught buying women for prostitution from a New York City escort service and having them transported to his hotel in Washington, D.C.; and there is also Dominique Strauss-Kahn, the former director of the International Monetary Fund, whose marauding sexual activity includes the use of many prostituted women in France and the United States.[47] In 2012 the elite U.S. Secret Service detail assigned to guard President Obama purchased at least twenty women for prostitution in Cartagena, Colombia, the nights prior to the president's arrival.[48]

Martin Monto and Nick McRee found that 40 percent of U.S. buyers are married (38 percent who reported their marriages were very happy, and 40 percent said pretty happy).[49] A Danish study found that 71 percent of prostitution users had a steady partner, 20 percent in marriage. Discrediting the lonely or deprived sexual buyer theory, the study stated, "Only a few of the sex customers go to prostitutes because it is their only means of having sex."[50] There is also the living testimony of survivors of prostitution. An Irish survivor relates her experience as a child in prostitution being used by up to ten men a day.

> Do not for a moment think that the men paying to abuse here are not "ordinary men." I could not count the number of wedding rings and babies' car seats I encountered. The men who pay to debase and degrade women and girls in prostitution are the same men who play out the pretence of being happily married family men. I wonder sometimes at the amount of women who would be shocked, not only to know their husbands are visiting prostitutes, but also to know the depth of their own husbands' contempt and misogynistic hatred of women.[51]

The men's narratives are contested and interpreted differently through the eyes of the women who are bought. The women's opinions of the buyers deliver a powerful reality check and counterweight to the self-interested rationalizations provided by the men. "Were it not for the wreckage they leave behind, the self-delusion of the average sex buyer would be laughable."[52] The myth that prostitution is a mutual, consenting, and pleasurable act experienced by both parties, promoted by the sex industry and its apologists, is at odds with most of the women's statements that follow.

## Women's Assessment of the Buyers

Answers to the question of *why* men buy women in prostitution depend on who is asked. As with the male interviews, the accounts that follow are taken from research studies and media interviews. Unlike the men, however, women in prostitution do not trade titillating information about the buyers on Internet sex sites. Women do express many opinions about the prostitution users, but these are often related to the violence, the injuries, and the illnesses that women are subjected to in the sex industry.

### The Violence Narrative

In a study of trafficking and prostitution in five countries, a woman from Thailand who had been trafficked to Japan described the violence from male buyers in a karaoke bar/brothel in Shinjuku:

Our clients were all Japanese between the ages of 20–70. . . . Most of my clients were very insensitive and rough. . . . They would beat us before intercourse with sticks, belts or chains till we bled. . . . There were some clients who inserted coke bottles into the girls' vaginas . . . and poured boiling water into it; gave the nipples electric shocks. . . . If girls came back traumatized after going out with a sadistic client, and reacted hysterically or had nightmares, they would be beaten by the mama-san and told that they must have provoked the client to be violent. . . . If we cried on the job or resisted a client, we were beaten even more. (Nu, Thai, age 28)[53]

Mon, another Thai woman in prostitution, stated,

Before each sexual encounter, I am seized with the fear of client violence or of contracting disease. I block these thoughts out and think of the hardship of my family, especially my mother who is a nervous wreck, and the income needed to sustain them.[54]

Women in the Venezuelan study of prostitution in five countries offered the following opinions about the men who bought them for sex: Men are dirty; incapable of getting a woman to have sex without paying; sexual perverts; crazy, sick, swinish, and unsatisfied; not worthwhile; insatiable, full of fantasies and repressed; and cruel and mean but could be more human if they knew themselves and if they knew women; have no shame and are hopeless; do not acknowledge women as persons; have problems and empty lives. Only one interviewee offered that each person has a reason for his behavior, and she does not judge the men.[55]

Even a report of the Sex Workers Project at the Urban Justice Center in New York City, a pro–sex work group, found that 46 percent of women experienced violence from buyers in the course of being in prostitution. One woman, Sara, said,

[The buyer] . . . came in and had a knife. . . . I was cornered and I was about to be attacked and raped.[56]

Marie, a client at Ruhama—the well-known Irish center providing assistance to women in prostitution—remarked that the men who seek sex are increasingly getting younger and more physically aggressive.

They come in groups of twos and threes and will egg each other on for more aggressive and violent acts.[57]

The link between the most violent acts experienced by women in prostitution and the acts depicted in "gonzo" pornography is hard to ignore. As sociologist Gail Dines has written, "'Gonzo' . . . depicts hard-core, body-punishing sex in which women are demeaned and debased."[58] Gonzo pornography permeates the Internet and brings in millions of dollars to the pornography industry. Likewise, Gonzo prostitution pervades the sex industry. In her interviews with women in the legal Nevada brothels, psychologist Melissa Farley was told that only a small part of the violence done to women in the legal brothels is ever reported.[59] Farley learned that the question women found most difficult to answer was how many customers they had to service. One woman said,

> "I don't want to add it up. If I thought about it as much as you, I wouldn't be doing it. But then, I'd be in a car starving." Others refused to answer with one woman underlining her words, "*I do not count.*"[60]

Physician and writer Alexa Albert lived in the Mustang Ranch for three weeks to undertake her study of a legal brothel in Nevada. She depicts it almost as a benevolent home for women (and men) that provided them not only with income but also with "friendship, compassion, trust and hope."[61] Her conclusions fundamentally differed from Farley's and seem even naive at times. The Mustang "home" was the same brothel that in 1990 and 1999 was shut down for racketeering crimes, including tax evasion, payoffs, money laundering, and fraud.[62]

Despite her assessment of the cozy brothel environment, Albert quoted Daisy who "let loose" about how she really felt about being used in prostitution and about the buyers.

> The first words that come to mind are degraded, dehumanized, used, victims, ashamed, humiliated, embarrassed, insulted, slave, rape, violated. . . . 99% of them fit these words: pig, dog, animal, uncaring, user, slave owner, asshole, mean, thoughtless, rude, crude, blind.[63]

After Daisy released these scathing opinions on an Internet site called Cyber-Whore Mongers—a site for men trading prostitution information—other women followed with equally caustic comments about the men. In the aftermath of the women's postings, buyers sent apologetic messages, changed the crude tenor of their own postings, and turned on one another in "shows of gallantry."[64] Regrettably Albert treats these messages as redeeming the buyers.

## *The Younger, the Better Narrative*

Women in prostitution also verify that more and more buyers want younger women, and these women serve as the drawing card, for example, in the legal brothels of Canberra, Australia, where about 25 percent of the prostituted women are university or senior high school students. According to one woman,

If you don't have those young girls you do get a drop in customers.[65]

One young girl who found help and acceptance at Girls Educational & Mentoring Services (GEMS) in New York City described her exploitation in this way:

I'm 14 years old. Emotional. Angry. Hurt. Alone. I'm in the life and getting abused by a grown man who has tricked me into having sex for money with strangers—other grown men. (Martha, American, age 14)[66]

In interviews with girls who were prostituted at a truck stop, one young girl said,

"I hate having sex. I have nowhere to sleep unless I find a man. Sometimes I don't have money and food for two days. A man without a condom will pay more, so obviously I say O.K. because I need money." When asked what she needed most, she said, "Someplace to be a girl. Someplace where I won't have to have sex with men anymore." (Mbali, Swaziland, age 16)[67]

Writing in the *Red Light Dispatch* published by the Indian NGO, Apne Aap, Meena Sheikh told of being kidnapped from home when she was eleven or twelve and brought to a brothel in Bihar.

I was raped by many men every day. I hate the people who bought me and pushed me into this as much as I hate the men who were my clients.[68]

The moment of enlightenment came to thirty-three-year-old Debbie when she was asked by one of her buyers if he could have sex with her infant daughter. She knew then she had to get out.

> I was so disgusted by how he must have perceived me to be. . . . I felt like I had violated my daughter even by having him in my house.[69]

### The Male Fantasies Narrative

Women in the Nevada brothels tell of men who pay the women to pretend, dress up, and say they are little girls. Some of these men demand the exact script.

> "Fuck me, Daddy. I won't tell Mommy."[70]

A woman formerly in Seattle prostitution described the obvious "cognitive dissonance" that buyers undergo when they ask women in prostitution to enact their fantasies of young girls but don't ask themselves the obvious question,

> If we were that innocent, why would we be working in a place where we made money by watching men masturbate to us?[71]

Male fantasies and delusions trump common sense.

> Every customer wanted to pretend that his cock was the only one we'd ever seen. But at the same time, they had to know that if we'd take their money, we'd take anyone's.[72]

One young Australian woman, Ashley, from a legal brothel in Brisbane said,

> The girls I know don't like men. Their perspective of men has changed from this [prostitution], they do it because they can get a dollar amount at the end of the day . . . it's about how much you can get out of him . . . whether they're a nice person or a bad person, it does not matter.[73]

Kylie, another Australian woman from a legal brothel in Sydney, revealed that many men are insecure about the size of their penis. When she tells them they are average, they point to the porn that is playing endlessly on the TV screens and say, "What about him?" She also stated that the buyers' "biggest fantasy is still lesbians. Men want as many girls in the room as they can afford."[74] It is probably more accurate to say that prostitution users want women to engage in the same-sex activities that they fantasize as stereotypically lesbian, with the man at the center of alleged lesbian sex acts.

### The Good Guy Narrative

There are also more positive accounts from women in prostitution about the buyers, but some are mixed with contradictory statements. For those women who give their buyers a passing grade, it is qualified by their dependence on the men for money, food, and drugs.

From a woman in Hong Kong who spoke about one "really nice" and "caring" man:

> He . . . gave me several thousand dollars as pocket money. . . . He would go to the supermarket with me to do the shopping and carry all the stuff we bought to my apartment. . . . He was the only client who was indeed concerned about me. . . . I once misinterpreted his care as love, and found myself in love with him. I stepped back. . . . I always think at most I can only accept the clients as good friends, but they can never be my partners. (Suen Yi, Hong Kong, age 30s)[75]

A self-described "Ivy League Callgirl," now a university lecturer, wrote a book about her positive experiences in prostitution but ended with a complex epilogue.

> I am aware . . . that many women are not in this profession because they hold doctorates and want to pay off their student loans. Many women are in fact forced, raped, lied to, torn from their homes and lives and given nothing in return . . . treated as morally inferior beings because they have been used to satisfy both the sex and monetary appetites of supposedly morally superior beings. . . . Many women experience what I describe briefly in this book: the slavery of drugs that was imposed on them deliberately so that they in turn could serve as slaves in a business that regards their lives as cheap.[76]

It is all the more puzzling that she ends her book with a call to legalize prostitution, asserting "regulation means safety." But even this prescription is qualified with ambivalence.

I have a positive story to tell. I'm not sure that my experience is that of the majority of the women involved in this business.[77]

Likewise, the same incongruity is expressed by Brigitte, a woman who testified for legalizing brothels in Brussels and services a handful of buyers yet believes prostitution should not exist.

[Prostitution] kills you. . . . I am not a woman who can say I hate men. It's not hate. But I cannot have respect anymore for a man. . . . I know a lot of women suffering in that business. . . . For me, even though I'm making good money, it should not exist.[78]

### The Denial and Recognition Narrative

Women in prostitution develop protective mechanisms, sometimes built on denial, that allow them to separate themselves from the humiliation, violence, and degradation experienced. It is not until most women leave prostitution that they admit the damage that has been done to them.

You tell the lie—"I like it"—so much that you believe it yourself. You make it OK by saying, "I haven't been beat up today . . ." Women have to justify it: they can't tell themselves or anyone else the reality of it or else they'd die.[79]

Another woman added, "You can't be mentally present in this business or you'll go crazy."[80]

Elena, a young Moldovan woman living in Paris, spoke to Hubert Dubois who interviewed her for his film *The Client*. When Dubois told her that no women he interviewed up to that point admitted to being forced into prostitution, Elena responded,

I too would have given you the same answers if you asked me back then when I was a prostitute. I would have told you, "Yes, I do this voluntarily." I would have been incapable of telling you otherwise. I had resigned myself to my fate. And furthermore, I would have never been able to say to the man that each of his acts was in fact a rape.[81]

Survivors' accounts show how statements made when "in the life" are quite different than the realizations that come after they have left prostitution.

In acknowledging that "choice" is a factor for some women in prostitution, Marie, a survivor of prostitution in Ireland, defined the "choice" as a choice for the money, not the prostitution.

> These women are not happy with what they are doing but happy with the money they get. . . . The problem . . . is that they discover only in later years how degraded and broken they have become.[82]

It is not surprising that women in prostitution articulate different opinions than the men who buy them. Women in general have a more critical attitude about prostitution than men in general. For example, a Finnish researcher who has studied sexuality in his country found that most Finnish men approve of prostitution in contrast to a minority of women who approve. These varied findings about Finnish society have remained constant over a long period of time.[83] Also leading up to the passage of the law criminalizing the purchase of sexual activities in Iceland, a study showed that 70 percent of the population was in favor of the law. Eighty-two percent of Icelandic women were in favor compared with 57 percent of Icelandic men.[84]

## Prostitution Users: Interpretation and Advocacy

Pro–sex work researchers have criticized studies documenting buyers' violence and exploitation of women in prostitution as one-dimensional, biased, and more advocacy-oriented than evidence-based. For example, Canadian researcher Chris Atchison launched a website called Johns' Voice: Providing a *Safe Space* for Sex Buyers to be Heard (italics mine), in which he states,

> The picture of sex buyers has mainly been painted by religious, moral, political and social interest groups who's [*sic*] sole interest is in the abolition of prostitution in Canada. We believe there is another side of this story to be told—we wanted to give the opportunity to clientele of sex workers to represent their own stories in a non-judgmental, anonymous, and confidential environment, without fear of being subjected to oversimplified generalization about their values, beliefs, and behaviors.[85]

Atchison and his colleague, sociologist John Lowman, offer not simply evidence but an interpretive picture of their data favorable to the buyers. If you believe Johns' Voice, most of the men are decent

fellows who care about the women. This is an interpretation at odds
with numerous evidence-based studies and interviews. Many women in
prostitution, in addition to those quoted earlier in this chapter, contend
that the men who use them are at best exploitative and degrading and at
worst violent and pathological. For those women who rate their buyers
more favorably, their opinion is often circumscribed by dependence on
these men for their livelihood.

Johns' Voice has created a haven for prostitution users. The site is
not simply accumulating objective research but is based on the opinions
of researchers who are known advocates of decriminalizing the sex industry. In 2008 Lowman drafted an affidavit in support of a challenge to
Canada's prostitution laws to eliminate the criminalization of the country's buyers, pimps, and brothels. As previously stated in the introduction to this book, there is no problem in using research for purposes of
advocacy. However, Lowman faults abolitionist researchers for engaging
in advocacy to eliminate prostitution. Yet he and other pro–sex industry activists such as Ronald Weitzer use their own research to publicly
campaign for the opposing view.[86] At the same time they accuse others
of being advocates who are "unscientific, ideological . . . biased."[87] Both
Lowman's and Weitzer's studies have been widely criticized for not meeting evidence-based standards. For example, Lowman was strongly faulted
for the unreliability of his findings presented in support of the Canadian
legal case in favor of decriminalizing prostitution and the sex industry.

> The opinions and purported facts contained in the affidavit of Dr.
> Lowman are based on a highly fragile edifice of substantive and
> methodological assumptions They are of highly questionable va-
> lidity and reliability. Further, they have been stripped of the con-
> text and precautions provided in their original sources. . . . The
> conclusions of his affidavit are thus more in the nature of argu-
> ment and opinion, in the common rather than the legal sense of
> that word, than they are of research findings. . . . They are not em-
> pirically substantiated, nor commonly accepted facts or findings
> that are susceptible of informing judgment.[88]

Weitzer's work has also been faulted, especially for his reliance on
unpublished authors. For example, political scientist Max Waltman in-
dicts Weitzer for citing an "unpublished author's work to support his
statement that 'independent assessments indicate that Sweden's law has
not had the salutary effects claimed by advocates.'"[89] Yet Weitzer is especially fond of derogating writers with whom he disagrees for their

alleged lack of peer-reviewed or unpublished sources; and in the case of the authors he faults, these "offenses" are largely incorrect.

Chris Atchison has been actively involved in research with the "sex buying community" since 1995. As an advocate, Atchison has also participated in a number of pro–sex work organizations in both Vancouver and Toronto over the past fourteen years.

Compare Atchison's research presumptions cited above with that of well-known Swedish researcher Sven-Axel Månsson's overview of Scandinavian research on the buyers. Månsson is at pains to portray a picture of the buyers that is complex and multifaceted. Who are the buyers? What are their motives and how can these motives be understood in the context of changing gender relations in our society? Månsson's interpretation of research in Scandinavia concludes with the need for advocacy, which he states upfront: "Challenging this [global sex] industry is of major importance." Instead of concluding that male behavior in prostitution should be decriminalized, Månsson recommends transforming masculinity in a political sense, "such as the new Swedish law prohibiting the purchase of sexual services."[90]

The point of briefly contrasting the positions of Atchinson and Månsson is to understand the interpretive and advocacy function of research. Divergent interpretations can be made of similar studies that look at similar behavior, particularly when formulated in the discussion, conclusions and recommendations of any study. The issue is not that abolitionist research studying men's behavior in prostitution is one-dimensional and biased, as Atchison claims. The reality is that studies of similar populations can come to quite different conclusions about how the research is interpreted and used in the policy realm.

Contrary to the popular saying, the data does not always speak for itself. Statistics particularly are supple, and one can always question the reliability of statistics by criticizing inadequate numbers of those interviewed, how samples of interviewees were chosen, methodologies, and time-bound data. The significance of any data depends on how it is construed. In interpreting their data, Atchison and Lowman downplay the violence perpetrated by prostitution users.

Other Canadian researchers at the University of Ottawa go further in minimizing the violence of pimps in their research on "Rethinking Management in the Adult and Sex Industry." The Ottawa objectives include contributing to a "better understanding of: Management practices and . . . Specific problems engendered by the criminalization of certain aspects of sex work." Their research is part of a body of academic studies that transform pimps into managers by "transcend[ing] the traditional focus of deviance and/or violence."[91] They are members of the chorus of advocates who chant for full decriminalization of the sex industry.

Starting with a biased goal of "transcending the violence" of pimping, they insist their project is based on "solid research methodology." The Ottawa team maintains that pimps have been critically examined in the past, and much of what we know about them is shrouded "in myths, racial, class and gender stereotypes, and misconceptions." They offer no evidence for these claims. Instead, they claim to shed more diverse light on "management," along with "a self-conscious attempt to inform justice and social policy." The Canadian researchers from the get-go are predisposed to whitewash pimps. They also put the cart before the horse, placing advocacy before evidence. Their intention is "inform justice [for pimps?] and public policy."[92]

Perhaps the findings of the Canadian sex industry research will bolster the role of pimps who seek to be accredited as expert witnesses in court. A pimp in his New York rape and robbery trial asked to be qualified as an expert witness so that he could explain his "profession" to the jury. He added, "It would be helpful . . . to understand the relationship between pimps and prostitutes," claiming that "beatings were part of the pimp-prostitute relationship and that this kind of sex was consensual." Thus, he asked not be prosecuted as a criminal but taken seriously as an expert witness who was testifying to the normative nature of beatings as part of the management structure of prostitution. His request was unsuccessful.[93]

## HOW NOT TO ADDRESS DEMAND

Increasing numbers of people now understand it is nearly impossible to combat sex trafficking and prostitution unless we address the demand. However, there are still too many people, especially in high places, who do not understand or do not want to challenge men's role in the chain of sexual exploitation. Instead, they take refuge in the myths that prostitution is inevitable: that men who purchase sex are fulfilling their alleged biological needs and that prostitution is a necessary sexual service for lonely men, frustrated men, men whose wives or partners do not perform according to the male fantasy script, military men on tours of duty, businessmen who have stressful jobs, migrant laborers who are away from wives and family, and for men who because of disability or dysfunction do not have the usual number of women available to them—in short, all kinds of men. These myths assume that we must not challenge the demand because there is always some population of men who need sex and must get it, although that means they buy the bodies of women and children.

Other responders say that we must address demand, but they offer measures that appease prostitution users, such as "ethical buying" programs. Journalist Brenda Power goes to the heart of this absurdity. "Asking men to phone a confidential number if they've had sex with a foreign prostitute who seemed troubled or reluctant is one such stunt. When has any 'john' given a flying curse about the real feelings of a prostitute?"[94] These "stunts" undermine efforts that truly address demand and leave prostitution users free to continue buying women "responsibly."

The following are some examples of how *not* to address demand.

## "Ethical Johns" Campaigns

At a conference in Iceland in October 2010, a representative from CARE International spoke about his organization's initiative to educate young men about gender-based violence. Another speaker at this conference, Ruchira Gupta, director of India's Apne Aap, asked if CARE taught these young men that prostitution was gender-based violence and encouraged them and their peers not to buy sex. The representative responded that CARE International had not decided whether "sex work" was gender-based violence.

Gupta replied that, in practice, the CARE programs in India and Bangladesh have indeed decided that prostitution is *not* violence against women, because they have been teaching young men that *if* they buy women and girls for sexual activities, they should use condoms. The message becomes that it is acceptable to be prostitution users as long as you use protection.[95]

The irony of the CARE program is that in the name of reducing violence against women, men are given permission to increase violence against women in their exercise of behavior deemed off-limits to being acknowledged as violence. In the name of opposing violence against women, young men are sanctioned to engage in the sexual exploitation of prostitution more "ethically" without being called on to understand that prostitution *is* violence against women.

*Providing Affirmation and Anonymity for Buyers*
The tenets of "ethical johns" campaigns were set out in an article titled "Non-Discriminatory Approaches to Address Clients in Prostitution."

The essay described several projects in European countries where prostitution has been normalized, and it listed the importance of the following guidelines in undertaking campaigns to address the male buyers. First, acceptance of buyers is important, and men should be given "*a sense of being 'allowed' to be a client.*" The article continued: never register disapproval or violate the men's anonymity. A prerequisite for a successful campaign is to offer an affirmative and tolerant approach to the buyers. Not only will women in prostitution benefit from the avoidance of "moral judgment" about the buyers, but "clients will also gain because only a fair business relationship can provide the basis for a more agreeable service."[96]

The "Don Juan Project" in Switzerland, the brainchild of Swiss AIDS Control, was highlighted as a model project. Don Juan exhorted men to reduce the harm of sexually transmitted diseases by practicing safe sex—not prevent the harm by refraining from using women in the first place. The organizers set up a tent that was filled with "erotic pictures" and messages on printed beer mats "as a means of starting a conversation" about sexually transmitted diseases and safe sex.

The project was based on the unfounded assumption that men who are buyers will be "more successful educators," because they possess empathy combined with a basic tolerance of the clients. Was the project successful? The wording of the Don Juan report is interesting. Of the eight hundred prostitution users who came into the tent and were found not to use condoms regularly when buying women in prostitution, about two-thirds said, "They would *consider* changes in their behaviour."[97] What they weren't asked to consider was to stop buying women in prostitution.

The 2006 World Cup Games in Germany provided advocates of "ethical sex tourism" with another version of simply "pondering" the demand. The National Council of German Women's Organizations (Frauenrat) set up stalls around the football stadiums and urged male sports fans to "think about" the fact that the women they might have sex with are coerced. Henny Engels, its executive director, made clear they weren't against men purchasing women for the sex of prostitution. "We have nothing against prostitutes or prostitution. But we are against people trafficking and forced prostitution."[98]

During the Games, German women's organizations conducted a campaign called "Responsible Johns." In literature translated into four languages and distributed around the stadiums, the campaign encouraged men to abstain from sex if the prostituted woman says that "she has extremely high debts with the owner of the brothel," or "she is being exploited," or she "tells you that she is being forced into prostitution." In case there might be some translation problems with foreigners, the literature even advised men to bring a dictionary with them when they go to a brothel. Finally, the organizations recommended that the buyer give the abused woman his cell phone to call the authorities before he left. There is no record of how many, if any, buyers reported abuse.[99]

It is a mockery of women's rights that women's organizations would set up "thinking stalls" for men to muse that some women might be forced into prostitution, so that these men can proceed with a clear conscience to use alleged voluntary women in the "sex stalls" of twelve cities in Germany. These campaigns succeeded in putting a German-grade stamp on the body of every woman in prostitution, certifying that some can be bought but others cannot—in the name of women and human rights.

### Cooperating with the Buyers to Report Abuse

Two European governments have baptized initiatives that seek to enlist prostitution users in the fight against trafficking by encouraging them to report abuse. With funding from the German Agency for Technical Development (GTZ), the German Federal Ministry for Economic Cooperation and Development (BMZ), and the Federal Ministry of Family and Women Affairs, the NGO Terre des Femmes launched a campaign billed as "Men Show the Way." The campaign "presupposed that customers are prepared to help women in enforced prostitution, if they are informed about the practical steps they can take."[100] This is a mistaken supposition.

In 2006 the Netherlands launched a special Crimestoppers Campaign that encouraged buyers to report abuse (presumably not their own) of the women they might use in prostitution. The campaign posters "Guaranteed Anonymity." Through a special hotline, men were urged to report to their local police signs of force, cruelty, and degrading treatment of women. The police advised that signs of force include bruising, fearfulness, and "little responsiveness to the client." However, if one reads the postings on the *World Sex Guide*, where men complain about the "unenthusiastic bitches" who don't meet their standards of a "good fuck," male prostitution users are more likely to report unresponsive women to their pimps rather than to the police. And force has been a classic turn-on for prostitution users, as attested to in the women's comments about the buyers cited in the earlier section of this chapter.

The organizers of the Crimestoppers Campaign developed a video titled "Forced labour in prostitution is a crime." It shows the silhouette of a woman rubbing her naked body in sexual motion, accompanied by the audio of her screams as a man chokes her; he hits her to her knees where she promptly simulates a posture of anal intercourse, after which he puts a gun to her head; it ends with the woman continuing to posture seductively. The text states, "It could be deception."[101] Effectively, the one-minute film succeeds in eroticizing violence against women. It is a primary example of a new pornography of crimestopping in which the violence itself is sexualized allegedly in the interests of preventing it.

The police placed advertisements of the Crimestoppers Campaign on the Dutch sex site hookers.nl in the hopes of enlisting more buyers who would report abuse. Thousands of men, who seek to purchase women in prostitution worldwide but mostly in the Netherlands, use this site. The police paid the sex site hookers.nl €1,200 to run the campaign ad. When critics complained that the government was subsidizing the pornography industry, the police retorted that the site reaches forty thousand "visitors" a day and enthused that "the sum of €1,200 is a piece of change compared with what is normally paid for such an advert."[102] And the director of the UN Office of Drugs and Crime quickly welcomed the launch of this campaign and said he hoped other countries would follow the Dutch example.[103]

### Results of the "Ethical Buyers" Campaigns

Do such campaigns have any effect on the buyers? In 2009 a small study was funded by the Amsterdam City Council to sample the views of seventeen Dutch men who used the Internet sex sites of hookers.nl and ignatzmice.com. Not surprisingly, the report concluded, "When customers do come across signs of forced prostitution, they tend not to take any action."[104] When asked about a potential Dutch regulation to criminalize buyers of illegal prostitution, the interviewed men offered a self-interested response: "Customers believe that making customers criminally liable for illegal prostitution will lead to fewer offenses being reported to authorities."[105] No contradiction was noted between this conclusion and the fact that the same customers acknowledged that they do not *now* "take any action."

In a Finnish interview with customers of prostitution, buyers said they would call authorities if they encountered women who had been trafficked. One respondent stated, "If I ran into human trafficking, I would call the police." However, none of the men interviewed admitted that they had met trafficked women in their prostitution encounters.[106]

In one U.S. chat forum for prostitution users called Utopiaguide, the men discussed whether they would come forward if they had any information about a Long Island, New York, serial killer of prostituted women. Most said they wouldn't say anything. "Are you guys nuts? I wouldn't step up and give information in a million years. You'd really compromise yourself like that?"[107]

Farley and others' study of two hundred men in Boston, Massachusetts, both sex buyers and non–sex buyers, logged similar opinions from men who continued to use women in prostitution, despite knowing that women were abused. "The knowledge that the women have been exploited, coerced, pimped, or trafficked failed to deter sex buyers from buying sex. Many of the sex buyers had used women who were controlled by pimps. . . . Sex buyers in this study seemed to justify their involvement in the sex industry by stating their belief that women in prostitution are essentially different from non-prostituting women."[108]

In Denmark the Ministry of Social Affairs set up a hotline for men who use women in prostitution to help them modify their behavior. The Socialist People's Party said the campaign had been a "complete flop." "The fact is that a lot of men like to buy sex—and they aren't interested at all in the government's programme to change that." When asked about the dismal results of few men even contacting the hotline, the minister responded by saying there was no goal for the number of calls the hotline should receive.[109]

In 2002 Dutch buyers who regularly used women in prostitution succeeded in organizing themselves into a group called the Man/Woman and Prostitution Foundation, which promotes equal legal treatment for the buyers. Its aims, continuing to this day, have been to make buying persons in prostitution more acceptable and openly discussable, to clarify the buyers' own rights and responsibilities, and to promote a nondiscriminatory prostitution policy especially that protects the interests of buyers.[110]

The Netherlands has gone further than any other country in dignifying the demand for prostitution. Sex buyers and brothel owners enjoy a special advisory role and have been consulted in reviewing the country's prostitution system. In 2007 buyers reported in an official government-commissioned report that the Dutch prostitution sector lacks "innovation," and thus sex establishments boringly stay the same. Buyers regret that the Dutch market has not improved to meet their ever-changing "needs" for other possibilities of "relaxation," for example, in saunas that are not legal. Thus, they warn Dutch men will continue to travel to other countries for the sex of prostitution, attracted by the more exotic and varied offerings in the German sauna clubs.[111]

Ethical johns' campaigns are cynical, not ethical. They are based on the supposition that buyers will report abuse when they are trained to see it and that regulating the sex industry will limit its reach. But buyers want more services rather than fewer, and, it appears, they leave the legalized countries when the services on offer fail to meet their needs. Such demands for an ever-increasing variety of sexual services reveal that these campaigns gloss over the harm of those who use and abuse women and children. Should rapists or torturers be given the right to continue raping or torturing if they report other rapists or torturers?

Likewise, the same hypocrisy infects websites such as punter.com/ punternet.com, which freely advertise brothels in the U.K. where buyers can go for gangbangs, for obtaining alleged virgins, and for sex with women who will forgo condoms. Almost mockingly, these sites publish small-print warnings about sex trafficking and its "dark side." These advisories are opportunist in that they protect the company rather than its victims, similar to those put on cigarette packages that smoking is dangerous to a person's health, but "we'll sell them to you anyway." Warnings allow prostitution-promoting websites to continue facilitating sexual exploitation, at the same time they appear to be ethical in the small print. However, in the large print, they promote a trade in women and children that depends on more and more provocative and grotesque information to men about the "dark side" of prostitution.

The attitudes of many buyers interviewed in magazines and studies reveal that they don't believe that most women in prostitution are abused and often trivialize abuse, trafficking, and coercion in prostitution as fabrications. They especially deny that their own use of women is exploitative. In one media interview with several men who were asked if they thought women in prostitution were victims, all found "irritating" the view that a significant number of women were coerced. Two of the men stated,

> "The figures bandied around for the numbers of trafficked women are absurd." (British, business consultant, age 31)
> "I've never come across one. All the people I've seen, they have always been happy, we have talked beforehand." (British, IT worker, age 50s)[112]

A study done by the Chicago Coalition for the Homeless interviewed 129 prostitution users in nine popular bars in Chicago. The men were asked "If you knew that the majority of persons in the sex trade experience homelessness, are victims of violence, and start at very young ages, would that change your attitude about paying for sex?" Forty-two percent said yes, but 44 percent said no. Fifteen percent [sic] did not respond.[113]

Other interviews and studies document similar attitudes. One buyer stated, "I asked if they are forced into it and most say no and that the money is better than another job that don't pay shit."[114] Another buyer contended, "I think it's all a myth that they're all slaves and things."[115] Perhaps these buyers had read works by Ronald Weitzer, Laura Agustin, and Nick Davies, all who have written about the myth of trafficking (see chapter 4).

In her 2006 United Nations report on the demand for sexual exploitation, the former UN Special Rapporteur on Trafficking in Persons, Sigma Huda, concluded, "Prostitute-users are typically incapable of distinguishing and/or unmotivated to differentiate between prostituted persons who have been subjected to . . . illicit means . . . and those who have not."[116] Sometimes, the buyers *state* for the record that they would report such abuse but their behavior proves otherwise. At more honest times, they will tell the truth, as does this man interviewed by Antonia Crane on the *Rumpus.*

> **Max:** I think the thing I am most ashamed of is that I've been to Asian massage parlors. . . . Many of these women are victims of sex trafficking. . . . Thing is, they are not glassy-eyed robot slaves sobbing under their oppressor like you see in movies about this kind of thing . . .
> **Rumpus:** But it's not consensual. It's coercion. It's sex slavery.
> **Max:** And I felt very remorseful when I learned this. And then I did it again.[117]

## Taking Men Out of the Picture: Making the Demand for Prostitution Abstract

The Swedish Law Prohibiting the Purchase of Sexual Services clearly articulates that demand has a gender and this gender is male—not as in male biology but as in male behavior. Some commentators write as if demand is abstract and that prostitution is not driven by live men but by "market forces."

A 2003 report commissioned for the International Organization of Migration (IOM) maintains there is no direct and unilateral relationship between "consumer demand" and any specific form of sexual activity. More than male demand for the sex of prostitution, the authors cite three reasons for the rapid expansion of the sex industry: a market that is poorly regulated, widely stigmatized, and partly criminalized.[118]

Of course many scholars and advocates who work against trafficking and prostitution, and who see "consumer demand" as a root cause of prostitution and trafficking, know that male demand is not the only propeller of prostitution. National and international economic policies;

globalization; countries in financial and political crisis; female poverty that is preyed upon by recruiters, traffickers, and pimps; military presence in many parts of the world; racial stereotypes and practices; and women's inequality all contribute to the rise in global sexual exploitation. At the same time, many scholars and activists see the male demand for the sex of prostitution as the most immediate cause of the expansion of the sex industry. A prostitution market without male consumers would go broke.

A major theme in the IOM-commissioned report appears to be that "sex work" is much too complex an issue to limit demand simply to the consumers of sexual services.[119] It is true that factors promoting the expansion of global commercial sexual exploitation are complex. Complexity, however, seems used in this report as an academic excuse for inaction, or as a non sequitur from which few answers can then follow. Indeed, we must not simplify the complexity, we must confront it. Complexity should be conducive to clarity, not confound it.

If we want to discuss demand in a more nuanced way, let's borrow the concept of a "limiting factor" from environmental science. A limiting factor is one that controls or inhibits the growth of an organism or entire population. Other environmental factors can also influence the growth, but scientifically, only one is limiting. Male demand is the limiting factor, the sine qua non, of prostitution. It controls all the other factors, such as globalization and poverty in the sense that without its presence, other factors alone or together could not sustain the system of prostitution. Although the complexity theorists of prostitution may not understand this, the sex industry certainly does.

The authors of the IOM report are greatly reluctant to penalize the buyers. They write,

> Even when focusing only on the sex sector, it is not clear that calls for punitive policies against customers would lead to the desired outcome. . . . Given the political and moral problems posed by a policy of legal suppression . . . we would argue instead that those who wish to see the commercial sex market shrink rather than continue to expand . . . need to come up with more creative, less punitive and longer-term strategies.[120]

Although their report was published in 2003, the authors may not have been aware of the 2003 Swedish National Rapporteur's report documenting that in the first three years after the Swedish law prohibiting the purchase of sexual services was passed, street prostitution declined dramatically.[121] Of course, the authors of the report could not have known then about the more long-term 2010 Swedish government evaluation of the legislation penalizing demand, which reported that the law had been influential in decreasing prostitution by 50 percent over a period of ten years and in creating a chilly climate for international traffickers.[122] Sweden appears to be the only country in Europe where trafficking has not increased.

The IOM authors cite another disincentive for targeting the male "consumers" of prostituted women. They claim that the same argument would be "rarely applied to any other sector—for example, consumers who buy the product of the labour of 'trafficked' women, children and men in the form of T-shirts, diamonds, processed meat, etc."[123] The authors omit that these "products" of other trafficked persons do not involve the exploitation of their bodies both as "product" and as "labor."

In T-shirt making, the consumer buys the T-shirt, not the person making it. In prostitution, the woman or child is the product. In T-shirt making, one can separate the products of forced labor from the abuse of persons forced into it. One survivor of prostitution exposed the superficiality of this comparison when she stated in response to the claim that prostitution was no better or worse than flipping burgers at McDonald's, "In McDonald's, you're not the meat! In prostitution, you are the meat."[124]

In academic literature on prostitution, demand often reduces to market forces that promote prostitution and trafficking, as if there are no actual men who are the driving forces. Men once more become invisible. It is not market forces or genderless persons who, as British MP Denis MacShane has written, "insist on a right to put money down and insert their penises into women's bodies."[125] Economic rhetoric distances us from the fact that most buyers are ordinary men who may be our fathers, brothers, husbands, partners, and friends.

## EXPOSING MORE MYTHS
## AGAINST PENALIZING THE DEMAND

### Penalizing the Demand
### Drives Prostitution Underground

Some critics have alleged that, since the introduction of the law penalizing demand in Sweden, prostitution and the women in it have gone underground. This claim followed early official Swedish reports that the law has reduced prostitution by 40 percent.[126]

In a letter criticizing a 2011 U.S. State Department document that strongly endorses policies that address the demand for "commercial sex,"[127] a group of researchers and policy advocates states, "If the well-being of those who sell sex is the goal of this document, where is the evidence that making purchasers of sex into criminals will actually benefit sex sellers, rather than divert sex work underground, where it can be much more dangerous to the sellers, the majority of whom are women?"[128]

What is the meaning of "underground?" What critics usually mean is that prostitution has been driven to an indoor site or to the Internet, which they imply are more clandestine and dangerous situations for women. Both of these sites are hardly underground. Advertisements for prostitution on the Internet are very visible. In fact, one could argue that advertising there for prostitution is more visible than in other places. Police also report that they can monitor prostitution sites on the Internet as well as they can monitor it outdoors. The 2010 report of the Swedish National Police Board reveals, "Exposure on the Internet makes it easier for the police to reach the people who are organizing the trade and to locate purchasers of sex and victims."[129] Additionally, at some point prostitution requires that a buyer and a seller come together at a time and location for the sexual act to happen. These locations are no more hidden than current off- and on-street contact sites.

Sweden has no more Internet prostitution than neighboring Nordic countries,[130] or, for that matter, than countries that have legalized prostitution. Internet advertising for prostitution has increased worldwide, but this is a result of the availability of the technology in all countries, not of a law penalizing the buyers in one country. Nor does any evidence suggest that the law has caused prostitution to migrate to indoor locations. Organizations working to assist victims report there has been no overall increase in indoor prostitution since the law penalizing the buyers went into force in 1999 and since the dramatic reduction in street prostitution.[131]

There is a blatant contradiction in critics' claim that the Swedish law has driven prostituted women into more clandestine and dangerous locations such as indoor sites. For the most part, these critics are advocates of normalizing prostitution and are longtime opponents of the Swedish law. When they promote legalization/decriminalization of prostitution and the sex industry, they argue that indoor prostitution is safer than on-street prostitution. When their aim is to discredit the

Swedish law, they contend that indoor locations are more dangerous because they are more "underground." The critics of the Swedish model cannot have it both ways.

Sex work advocates not only work to discredit laws against the buyers, but they also give media interviews misrepresenting evidence. Some have a bent for reporting unaffected by any concern for the truth. In June 2012 the Pro Sentret organization in Oslo that provides resources for "sex workers" alleged that the Norwegian law penalizing the buyers had made women vulnerable to increased violence and less inclined to seek help at the center. Pro Sentret's report was based on its interviews conducted with prostituted women working on the streets, out of apartments, and in massage parlors. Oslo politician Annike Hauglie of the Conservative Party, who said she was appalled by the findings, called for the law to be repealed.[132]

The Pro Sentret report spread through the international media and was listed in the Brussels UN Regional Information Centre (UNRIC) resources online. Several days after the report was published, the police issued a statement denying any increase in violence. Pro Sentret was forced to retract its statement that violence against women had increased, and their representative stated the data in its report provided no foundation for its earlier statements. The group admitted its findings could prove the opposite: violence against prostituted women had decreased.[133] Pro Sentret had been the main opposition to the passage of the Norwegian law and appeared to be grabbing at anything that might undermine it.

## Penalizing the Demand
## Forces Women to Take Bigger Risks

Another argument against penalizing the prostitution users maintains that women will be pressed to make hurried judgments about buyers on the street who are impatient to arrange the price and the "services" to escape detection. For example, Pye Jakobson, founding member of Sex Workers and Allies, is much opposed to the Swedish law on these grounds. According to a BBC News article, "she says the criminalization of clients has actually made sex workers' lives more dangerous. She says that a woman working a deal on the street used to be able to assess the client before getting into his car. Now because he fears arrest, she [the woman in prostitution] has to get in and do the deal afterwards."[134]

Survivor Trisha Baptie maintains this argument is a myth. "I had five minutes, I had two minutes, I had ten minutes . . . it didn't matter.

It's the luck of the draw. There was no real way for us to know who was going to be a good date and who was going to be a bad date."[135]

Many women in prostitution already have little ability to assess their potential buyers. In numerous prostitution venues, women are put on display and have no choice about the men they are pressured to service. Men always do the choosing—whether in the legal window brothels of Amsterdam or along the rural roadsides of Tuscany where I have witnessed them drive up to solicit the African women who take up positions there. The woman must jump into the man's car quickly after he has cruised by several times deliberating *his* choice. The woman's pimp lurks in the background as he monitors that she gets into the car, drives off with the buyer to a less visible spot, and ensures that she returns to her roadside spot after which he collects her earnings.

Prostitution per se forces women to take bigger risks than women who are not in prostitution. Women cope constantly with dangerous buyers. However, in a legal and social culture where the buying of women and children for the sex of prostitution is not tolerated, the possibilities for protection are greater since the number of buyers is reduced, mainly because they fear being caught and exposed. Even after a protracted negotiation between a buyer and woman on the street, the potential for her to be abused, harmed, or killed is as real as from a more hurried transaction. For this reason, pro–sex work groups in the legalized countries write manuals on how women can "protect" themselves even from aggressive and violent buyers who pay for sex in state-sanctioned brothels where they are supposed to understand and abide by the house regulations.

It is the prostitution industry, not the law penalizing the buyers, that forces women to take bigger risks. In a financial recession, for example, women must service more customers whom they might not take in better economic times, perform more risky sexual activities as demanded by the buyers, and allow more men to treat them more aggressively and violently.

Women in both legal and illegal systems of prostitution report that many men pressure them to engage in sexual activities without a condom, and many women comply. Because women are monitored frequently by their pimps and/or brothel owners who trawl the Internet sex sites used by buyers to learn how "their" women are being reviewed, the women have to satisfy more and more demands of customers who complain that women refuse to perform certain acts or don't offer "quality services."

The prostitution industry is a dangerous business. Buyers are a major part of that risk. Women in prostitution everywhere have to make risky choices, even endangering their lives when they cannot use condoms or control the buyers' demands.

## Penalizing the Demand
## Deprives Women of Making a Living

The Durbar Mahila Samanwaya Committee (DMSC) in India has testified that legislation criminalizing the buyers will put "sex workers" out of business, and women will find it difficult to earn needed money.[136] The DMSC is a group of "sex workers" and its allies that explicitly campaigns for the recognition of prostitution as an occupation. Its members not only advocate for the "right to work" and the "right to form trade unions," but they have also expanded their demands for "the right to pleasure"—for the buyers.[137]

The argument that stifling the demand will financially hurt prostituted women is comparable to the welfare narrative of johns who perpetuate prostitution by claiming they are "distributing . . . wealth to people who don't have it."[138] In effect, the DMSC is claiming that women in prostitution are better off when men continue to buy them, than when men are prohibited from doing so.

Closing nuclear power plants raises a similar claim. If we shut down nuclear power plants, we reduce jobs in the nuclear industry. In my own backyard, over the border of Massachusetts in Vernon, Vermont Yankee is living out its last days as an aging nuclear power plant that is leaking radioactivity and has had a series of accidents, including a cooling tower collapse in 2007. A tri-state citizen group called Safe and Green is campaigning to get the plant closed, decommissioned, and the workers provided for. Entergy Corporation, which owns the Vermont Yankee plant, has claimed, "The best way you can be concerned about the employees is to continue to support the operation of Vermont Yankee."[139] The corporation has accused Safe and Green of pretending to care about the workers while its real interest is in shutting down the plant. A spokesperson for Safe and Green said there is nothing underhanded about the campaign's stance on closure since it has publicized this position for many years on its website. The campaign also works to provide new opportunities for the workers who are its neighbors "through conservation, efficiency and renewable solutions."[140]

Likewise, in the face of accusations that laws penalizing the buyers will endanger women's income, abolitionist advocates maintain the best way of protecting women is to stop demand. Although the state should not criminalize persons in prostitution for their own exploitation, the state has no obligation to facilitate the buying of women and children for the sex of prostitution in the name of allowing women to make a living. The state does have the duty to protect those in prostitution from being exploited and to provide resources for them.

The law's immediate goal should be to stop the sexual exploitation of women by penalizing the demand, thus making it more difficult for buyers and other perpetrators to exploit women. The priority of any activist for social change should be "do no harm" by withdrawing from danger those who are vulnerable. Drawing the blueprint for "what after" comes next.

In Sweden many survivors of prostitution have been encouraged by the passage of the law stating that the legislation gave them moral support to exit prostitution and to seek the resources now available.[141] When the law went into force in 1999, part of the larger Violence Against Women Bill provided additional funding to help women out of prostitution and assist them in finding other alternatives. Since then Sweden has increased the budgetary aid to victims several times.

In Korea when legislation was passed in 2004 that penalized the buyers and provided added means to assist women in prostitution, hundreds of women left prostitution. In 2008 when I met with feminists in Korea who had been monitoring the new law, they reported that its most gratifying part was the 56 percent decrease of women in prostitution reported from 2004 to 2006.[142]

## Women in Prostitution
## Don't Want the Buyers Penalized

Over the last decade India has been debating changes to its prostitution and anti-trafficking law (ITPA). A proposed amendment to the ITPA provides for penalizing a person who visits a brothel for sexual exploitation. A group called the National Network of Sex Workers in India held a press conference in 2005 protesting the amendment. "How will we survive if they start punishing our clients?"[143] Punishing the client, in their words, is "unfair."

The DMSC has also been a major force in India for decriminalization of the sex industry. Its leaders, who appear to front for the pimps of Sonagachi as gatekeepers of the area, claim to serve the interests of thousands of "sex workers" and buyers there. A part of Kolkata, Sonagachi is the biggest outdoor brothel area I have seen within the smallest plot of land that measures one-half of a square mile, and is teeming with prostitution users, pimps, and thousands of young girls and women in prostitution. Everything takes place in the open, where pimps roam like lords of their sexual fiefdoms, overtly offering their young sexual slaves to grown men, and girls as young as eight years old are made to service these men in the alleys and gutters of this sexual sewer.

In September 2006 I walked the Sonagachi area with staff members from Apne Aap. Visitors like us—not out to buy women and girls—had to check in at the DMSC office, since the organization seems to monitor the comings and goings of strangers in the area and has good relationships with the pimps. As we walked, I heard about typical practices ordered by the pimps and implemented by the madams to season young girls into prostitution. The most abhorrent practice was one used in training ten- to fourteen-year-old girls. To prepare them for being sexually penetrated by adult men, dildos were forced into the girls' vaginas. The girls were then submerged in tubs of water for hours during which the dildos expand and, with excruciating pain, enlarge their vaginas.

The DMSC cooperates with the pimps of Sonagachi in its campaign to promote "safe sex practices" in the area. Yet the organization is silent on the "unsafe sex practice" of torturing young girls with water-expanded dildos to make their vaginas more sexually pliant for buyers. With the former help of massive and long-term funding from the Bill and Melinda Gates Foundation, the DMSC instead focuses on the HIV/AIDs issue and uses its safe sex funding to promote normalization of prostitution and to oppose any measures to criminalize the prostitution users. The DMSC repeatedly emphasizes that any attempt to criminalize clients "would be detrimental for sex workers" and that "sex work is as much of an art as dance is."[144]

The argument that women in prostitution don't want the buyers penalized depends on which group of women is queried—those who define themselves as sex workers or survivors. It is quite evident from the survivors cited previously that most do want the buyers penalized. In representing the opinion of the thousands of survivors of Apne Aap, Indian survivor of prostitution, Naina, who was prostituted when she was thirteen, stated, "We must punish those who buy us. Their punishment will protect us from new buyers who will fear punishment too."[145]

Building on Naina's comments on behalf of survivors of prostitution, Apne Aap director Ruchira Gupta told the 2009 UN General Assembly:

> Victims and survivors of human trafficking . . . want no ambiguities in laws and international instruments on criminalizing trafficking and addressing the demand. They want both justice and

accountability, and they want those responsible for trafficking to be punished and stopped. They want interventions to focus on the responsibility of those who buy trafficked people such as buyers of prostituted sex and those "entrepreneurs" (traffickers, procurers, pimps, brothel owners, and managers, owners of plantations and factories and money lenders) who make a profit off trading in women and girls, boys and men.[146]

The Apne Aap centers are providing prostituted women the kind of support that gives them a different future than remaining in prostitution and enables their children to get an education.

## Penalizing the Buyers Harms their Wives, Partners, and Children

Any person who commits an illegal act exposes his family and friends to the consequences of his crime. It is the responsibility of the man who purchases women and children for the sex of prostitution to safeguard his family and friends from the hurt visited on them by his actions. The best way of doing this is to refrain from committing the offense in the first place. It is not the responsibility of the criminal justice system to protect the prostitution user and his relations from the private and public consequences of his act of using women in prostitution just as it is not the state's responsibility to shield the perpetrator of any other crime and his relations from the results of his offenses.

Sheltering the buyers from exposure and penalties does *not* in fact save their wives and partners from harm. Common sense dictates that these women have the right to know what their male sexual partners have been doing, including the knowledge of possible exposure to sexually transmitted infections and disease. As women's equality theorist, Twiss Butler, has stated, "The disingenuous threat that 'women will be hurt' by any change that would truly benefit them can only be disarmed by providing a clear picture of the way that women are hurt by the status quo, who is responsible for that harm, and how the proposed change will end it."[147]

The arguments against penalizing the demand do not hold up. Prostitution users are shielded by the paradox that any measure to restrict them provokes yet one more argument from the pro–sex work lobby that penalties levied at men will mainly harm women—whether in prostitution or not. Men's continuing ability to abuse women in prostitution is made invisible by these claims and by those who repeat them, many who will not condemn these deeds for fear of being labeled repressive, moralistic, or judgmental.

## HOW TO ADDRESS DEMAND

The laws are not made to change the heart but to restrain the heartless.

—*Martin Luther King, Jr.*

The Nordic model of legislation is a powerful antidote to the myths about prostitution users that pervade legalized prostitution regimes. The model is both legislative and normative. It makes prostitution users legally accountable for their actions while at the same time sends the message that there are societies that do not accept the buying of women in prostitution as normal. By recognizing that prostitution is violence against women, a human rights violation, and a crime, the legislation educates other countries, as well as NGOs, on how to challenge male sexual exploitation and violence.

It is no accident that the Nordic countries have been the first to challenge legalization of prostitution and, instead, take legal action against the buyers. Studies confirm these countries lead the world on most indicators of gender equality.[148] Gender equality experts and advocates have long pointed out that in economics, politics, and social services, the Nordic countries top the charts. A less noticed equality indicator is that Nordic countries outpace others in legal action to stem the sex trade by addressing its anonymous perpetrators.

### Sweden

As human trafficking became an increasingly global problem in the 1990s, Sweden took a critical look at its prostitution policy. Thinking outside the conventional box of legalization of prostitution favored by several countries in Europe, Sweden acknowledged that prostitution is a form of male violence against women and children, and in 1999 it criminalized the purchase of sexual services.

Legislators sometimes promote legalization proposals because they believe there are no legal alternatives, but there are. Rather than sanctioning prostitution, states could confront the demand by penalizing the men who buy women for the sex of prostitution. The Swedish law clearly articulates that prostitution is *men's violence* against women, and as such, it prohibits the purchase of sexual services within the larger framework of a Violence Against Women Bill that addresses other forms of violence against women. The law does not penalize the victims and provides victim assistance.[149]

In July 2010 the government of Sweden published an evaluation of the first ten years of the law.[150] While the report acknowledged that much remains to be done, its findings are very positive: street prostitution has been cut in half, "a direct result of the criminalisation of sex purchases"; there is no evidence that the decrease in street prostitution has led to an increase in prostitution elsewhere, whether indoors or on the Internet; extensive services exist in the larger cities to assist those exploited in prostitution; and fewer men state that they purchase sexual services. More than 70 percent of the Swedish population supports the law.[151] Superintendent Jonas Trolle, operational head of crime and narcotics surveillance with the Stockholm police department, has stated, "Today it is impossible to run a brothel in Sweden."[152]

The success of the Swedish model is not only in penalizing the men. The penalties—mostly fines—are modest. As of July 2011 the maximum prison sentence for those buyers convicted has been raised from six months to a year.[153] Since a higher penalty usually means that police give higher priority to these crimes, perhaps this will raise the conviction rate. As of 2009 only 5 men have been sentenced to anything more than fines, but 714 have been fined during this same period. As political scientist Max Waltman states, "Tellingly, a Supreme Court Justice himself was convicted in May 2005 for purchase of sex from a male prostituted person, then fined approximately US$6,000. . . . The justice managed to keep his appointment. . . . The fact that the law's application leaves much to ask for is not an argument against criminalizing purchase of sex, of course, but an argument for interpreting the Swedish law more strongly."[154]

The success of the Swedish model is mainly that it removes the invisibility of men who are outed when they get caught. In addition to the fines that purchasers incur, police report that buyers are more worried about the revelatory effect of being discovered as prostitution users. This, in turn, makes it less appealing for pimps and traffickers to set up shop in countries where the customer base fears the loss of its anonymity and is declining.[155]

If a buyer in Sweden is fined, it is always official, and anyone can contact the prosecutor's office or the court to obtain the information. Also if a buyer seeks a job where police and court records are checked for verification of his status, they can find out if the applicant is charged with buying sex, just as with other offenses such as domestic violence or speeding.[156]

Key to the success of the Swedish model is the reduced numbers of women in prostitution. In 1999 before the law was passed penalizing the buyers, there were about 2,500 prostituted women in Sweden, 650 on the street. Three years after the Swedish law came into force, it was estimated that the total number of women in prostitution had decreased to 1500.[157] By 2008 assessments, there were 300 women in street prostitution, and 300 women and 50 men who advertise on the Internet.[158] This total count of 650 may be overestimated since pimps often advertise women under different names in these online ads.

Compare these statistics to neighboring Denmark, where purchasing persons for prostitution is legal. Sweden has a total population of 9.4 million juxtaposed with Denmark's population of 5.6 million. Yet, numbers of those in prostitution in Sweden are about one-tenth of those in Denmark—650 in Sweden versus 5,567 in Denmark, of whom 1,415 are subjected to prostitution on the streets.[159]

## Norway

The Swedish legislation became the Nordic model in 2009 when Norway outlawed the purchase of women and children for sexual activities,[160] the result of years of feminist activism by the Women's Front (Kvinne-fronten), the Women's Shelter Movement, the Feminist Group Ottar, and other organizations. In 2005 the Norwegian Confederation of Trade Unions joined the campaign to criminalize the buyers. Their support was crucial to mainstreaming this law proposal and in influencing public opinion. In 2006 the newspaper *Aftenposten* published a survey reporting that 60 percent of Oslo residents supported the proposed law.[161]

Results were immediate and dramatic one year after the Norwegian law came into force. During 2010 all known brothels were closed in Oslo; fines have been increased against buyers, resulting in fewer men hunting for women on the streets; outdoor prostitution is down by 50 percent; and indoor prostitution has decreased by 30–40 percent.[162] An earlier Bergen municipality survey studying the first results of the law from January to June 2009 confirmed that the number of clients also had dropped; the number of women observed in outdoor and off-street prostitution had decreased by 50 percent; and advertisements for off-street prostitution declined by 60 percent.[163] Effective monitoring of the telephone numbers of buyers who respond to such ads not only enables police to identify and charge buyers but also exposes a wider network of criminal groups involved in child prostitution, pornography, and drug trafficking.

Unfortunately, the Norwegian model does not allow the police to reveal names of buyers who agree to pay a fine. Thus, the deterrent power of the law is diluted. If the prostitution users receive a larger penalty in a Norwegian court, only then are their names made public, and media can publicize them. The Oslo police do, however, take the media with them on patrol as often as possible. Although the journalists cannot reveal the buyers' identities, they can document that the law is being enforced and buyers are being arrested.[164]

All charges and fines should be a matter of public record. The penalties that most deter the buyer are those that remove his invisibility. According to online websites, chat rooms, and message boards frequented by men who are buyers of women in prostitution, the prostitution users agree. In Farley's study comparing men who are sex buyers with non–sex buyers,

> Both sex buyers and non-sex buyers agreed that the most effective deterrent to buying sex would be to be placed on a registry of sex offenders. Other effective deterrents included public exposure techniques such as having their name or photo publicized on a billboard, newspaper, or the Internet. Spending time in jail was considered an effective deterrent by 80% of sex buyers and 83% of non-sex buyers. Educational programs were considered the least effective deterrent by both groups of men.[165]

## Iceland

Also in 2009 Iceland passed landmark legislation criminalizing the purchase of sexual services. The law was passed with no legislator opposing it and only two abstentions. Anyone who purchases or promises to purchase sexual services can expect fines or up to one year in jail. If he purchases a young person under the age of eighteen, he risks two years in jail.

Mainly owing to the work of feminist groups that put pressure on parliamentarians who paid attention to what they said,[166] Iceland has declared that women are not for sale. The push for legislation was the result of the committed and arduous work over almost a decade led by the feminist group Stígamót and other women's organizations. The new legislation shows the connection between pornography, prostitution, and human trafficking by outlawing strip and lap dancing clubs in the country. Of the thirteen clubs that were in operation before the law, two remain open in 2013.[167] These actions were taken for feminist reasons. Kolbrún Halldórsdóttir, the politician who moved the law through the parliament, stated, "It is not acceptable that women or people in general are a product to be sold."[168]

In an age when some governments have legalized prostitution, most of the Nordic countries have rejected this model. They have done so based on principles of gender equality. The Nordic countries have become a chilly climate for prostitution users, for traffickers, and for the sex industry.

### France

A major political milestone took place in the French parliament on December 6, 2011. All political parties in the National Assembly signed a resolution that "Reaffirms the abolitionist position of France, the objective of which is ultimately a society without prostitution." Significantly this means that France does not recognize prostitution as "sex work," nor does it support legislation legalizing brothels and pimping. Legislators resolved that legal acceptance of prostitution is incompatible with French policies that promote gender equality and human rights. In supporting the resolution, legislators spoke about the failure of legalized prostitution systems in other European countries, which have become magnets for organized crime and violence against women, and about the success of the Nordic model.[169]

The most far-reaching recommendation of the mission headed by Danielle Bousquet, Socialist member of the National Assembly, and expertly detailed by rapporteur Guy Geoffroy from the UMP party, was a law proposal whereby prostitution users could face penalties of six months in jail and/or a fine of €3000. The cross-party resolution was the follow-up to a yearlong French parliamentary information mission that heard testimony from various groups and individuals relating to prostitution law reform in France. Author and historian Malka Marcovich, who testified at the hearings, remarked that the strong report of the committee "shows that the cultural stereotype of the French male's irrepressible sexual needs, enshrined in an archaic vision of French culture, can be opposed in the name of a revolutionary French vision of human dignity, equality and liberty."[170]

If the law passes holding prostitution users accountable for their commercial sexual exploitation, France will be the first country on the continent to penalize the demand for prostitution. The parliamentary resolution has set the groundwork for a future vote on the proposal.

## The United States

The U.S. government has supported statements, policies, and programs to fight sex trafficking by restraining demand for prostitution. In 2005 the U.S. anti-trafficking act (TVPA) was amended to enhance U.S. efforts to combat trafficking by including measures to reduce the demand for commercial sex acts (Sec. 108b). A grant program was also established to boost state and local efforts to combat trafficking in persons by making funds available to states and local law enforcement agencies to establish, develop, expand, or strengthen programs "to investigate and prosecute persons who engage in the purchase of commercial sex acts" (Sec. 204 [1] B). In 2011, the U.S. Office to Monitor and Combat Trafficking issued a strong fact sheet entitled "Prevention: Fighting Sex Trafficking by Curbing Demand for Prostitution." "Strong policies are critical for ridding countries of all forms of modern slavery, but ultimately for encouraging a broader cultural shift in order to make meaningful progress in reducing demand for sex trafficking. This can only be achieved by rejecting long-held notions that regard commercial sex as a 'boys will be boys' phenomenon, and instead sending the clear message that buying sex is wrong."[171]

## Nordic Model-lite

Some countries have passed an anemic version of the law penalizing purchasers of sexual activities, covering only prostitution users who buy trafficked, forced, or unlicensed persons in prostitution. Take the example of Finland that in 2006 passed a lackluster version of the Swedish law. The Finnish law was a compromise and "penalized the buying of sex only from 'involuntary' prostitutes, where it must be proven that the customer knew the prostitute was being forced."[172] Police and magistrates must produce evidence of buyers' knowledge that the women they used were forced into prostitution.

The question remains, why would a buyer ask a woman he uses in prostitution if she's been forced or trafficked—and why would she tell him? It obviously is not in the self-interest of either to ask or tell.

The most recent official results of the law from Statistics Finland state that from 2007 to 2009, thirty-seven men were sentenced to pay fines for the offense of buying sex from a person abused in the sex trade.[173] Finland has a population of 5.3 million in which we may reasonably assume that about half are male. Compare Finland's numbers to the neighboring country of Sweden with a population of 9.4 million where, in the same three years, there were 261 convictions.[174] This means 86.6 men per year were convicted in Sweden as opposed to 12.3 per year in Finland. Taking into account that Sweden's population is almost twice as large as Finland's, the comparative statistics would be approximately 43 men convicted annually in Sweden vs. 12 in Finland, reflecting very negatively on Finland's law.

The data shows that Nordic model-lite, as it operates in Finland, is one of the most ineffective policies for addressing the buyers. There is encouraging news from Finland, however. Because the 2006 version of the law penalizing only buyers of persons forced into prostitution has been so unsuccessful, Finnish legislators are considering a "general criminalization of the purchasers of sexual services."[175] Justice Minister Ann-Maria Henriksson has announced that she is planning to submit a bill that would bring Finland's legislation in line with Sweden's and is optimistic that the Finnish parliament will pass it.[176]

## Treating the Buyers as Conspirators in a Crime

In the United States, prostitution law is the province of the states. In most states it is a misdemeanor, not a felony, to buy a woman for the sex of prostitution. Tellingly in a study of arrest as a deterrent for buyers, Devon Brewer and others estimate, "Only 7–18 percent of clients in a community are ever arrested for patronizing over periods as long as 5 years."[177] Because of these weak arrest rates, prostitution users enjoy legal impunity. Brewer's research also found that "apprehending clients decreases their patronizing behavior substantially." Arresting buyers reduced the likelihood of a subsequent arrest by approximately 70 percent in one specific community that the authors studied. Also, "evidence from other parts of the US indicates little displacement of patronizing to other jurisdictions or sectors of prostitution following an arrest for patronizing a street prostitute."[178]

In the United States prostitution is illegal except in ten rural counties of Nevada. However, laws in most U.S. states against solicitation of prostitution have historically been enforced primarily against the women. Even when a man is found in the act of patronizing a woman in prostitution, he most often goes free. When a prostitution venue is raided, for example, the police seize the women but not the male buyers. The men who purchase the women are not viewed as criminals, but they are the demand side of the crime.

There is a simple solution to this situation. Police should be trained to arrest the men, which is their legal responsibility, and not be permitted to turn a blind eye to the demand. Arguably, a mainly male police force identifies with the "poor man" who may be caught, and the personal and professional consequences that may result from his detention and exposure. It will require focused education of police forces around the country to change this situation. When New York Police commissioner Raymond Kelly shifted his department's efforts to cracking down on prostitution users, arrests of women decreased by a quarter and arrests of buyers increased by a third.[179] But such efforts cannot be a one-time occurrence, and arrests of buyers must be consistently enforced.

In testifying before a U.S. congressional committee in 2009, police lieutenant Derek Marsh, co-director of the Orange County Human Trafficking Task Force, highlighted this failure to arrest buyers for solicitation in most states and proposed that buyers should be made more accountable. "Perhaps it is time to move johns from solicitors to conspirators." Noting that the crime of conspiracy requires no new laws and is familiar to investigators, prosecutors, and judges, as well as the success of its long application, Marsh maintains that "the crime of conspiracy has a real chance, based on research and best practices, of making these demanders of inhumane services cease their demands."[180] Making buyers actionable as conspirators would also be a powerful deterrent strategy.

At the very least, prostitution users should be treated as colluders in the crime of prostitution. The buyers prop up pimps, traffickers, and organized crime by contributing the funds that keep sexual slavery alive and well. Prostitution users are the men whose continuous pursuit of easy and abusive sex forges the grooves in women's continuous disintegration in prostitution.

Countries and organizations that want to be effective in the fight against trafficking, not havens of sexual exploitation, are beginning to understand that they cannot sanction pimps as legitimate sexual entrepreneurs and must take legal action against those who use women in prostitution. Of course, any law or policy is only as good as its implementation and consistent enforcement. The evidence from the first countries to penalize the buyers shows the law works if it is taken seriously by authorities and scrupulously enforced.

# 3

## Prostitution Nation:
## The State of Prostitution
## in the Netherlands

> The idea that a clean, normal business sector has emerged is an
> illusion. In the licensed window prostitution sector . . . human
> traffickers, pimps and bodyguards had free reign for years.
> —*Dutch National Police Service Report, 2008*

The Netherlands has become the model country of legalized and regulated prostitution in the world. However, no critical examination has
been done of the way in which the Netherlands arrived at its legal position. Nor has a serious scrutiny been conducted of the consequences
of the 2000 Dutch prostitution law. Although Amsterdam, Rotterdam,
and The Hague have closed their legalized municipal prostitution tolerance zones, and Amsterdam has shuttered one-third of its brothels
owing to the takeover of organized crime, the Dutch government keeps
intact a failed legalized prostitution regime. As the Dutch National
Rapporteur on Trafficking in Human Beings acknowledged in 2007,
"We have tried to decriminalize the prostitution sector by legalizing it,
by making it liable for permits and we have seen that it really doesn't
work that way. Many of these women in the legalized sector are being
forced and violently treated so the Dutch government is now thinking
are we on the right track?"[1]

   This chapter explores the history of the prostitution regime in the
Netherlands and its effects. It looks at the way in which the Dutch government institutionalized a long-standing tolerance for brothels and
pimping in its legalization law of 2000. It investigates the dearth of
public debate that led up to the new prostitution legislation and the way
in which women's NGOs and the state coalesced to bring about a "state
feminism" that substituted for democratic deliberation and consent.

In looking at the failures of the legislation, this chapter tests claims for the legislation measured against its results: the closure of the tolerance zones and many of the window brothels; the continuing presence of organized crime in the legal sector; the special advisory status accorded to prostitution users and pimps; and the legislation's impact on trafficking and child sexual exploitation in the Netherlands. Finally, this chapter documents the way in which Dutch prostitution policy has been exported mainly throughout Europe but also in developing countries.

## DUTCH PROSTITUTION POLICY: A HISTORY OF PRAGMATIC TOLERANCE

### Early History

The Dutch legislation that legalized brothels and pimping was built on fifty years of pragmatic tolerance of prostitution and the sex industry. Although earlier legislation forbade the organization of brothels and profiting from prostitution, brothels were tolerated and pimps were largely left alone. In 2000 the Dutch government officially struck brothels and profiting from prostitution from the criminal code and accepted the system of prostitution as legitimate work. Together, the changes in the penal code are generally known as "Lifting of the general ban on the brothels."

Like many countries in Europe, the Netherlands has experienced a legislative seesaw history of prostitution from criminalization of women, policing of brothels, and organizers of prostitution (seventeenth and eighteenth centuries); to abolition and later tolerance of prostitution (nineteenth and twentieth centuries); to regulation/legalization (twenty-first century).

As early as the end of the eighteenth century, tolerance was gaining ground. In a preview of later Dutch policy, defenders of tolerance praised the "sensible statesmanship" of the Amsterdam city fathers who countenanced prostitution as the "lightning conductor of male lust."[2] Male lust was depicted as a force of nature, capable of causing a cosmic cataclysm, unless channeled into a lesser evil, which was prostitution. The current prostitution policy of the Netherlands is built on the country's historical tradition of pragmatic tolerance and its historical concern with "conducting male lust" through legal channels of gratification.

Napoleon annexed the Netherlands for a short period of time in 1810. During the remainder of the nineteenth century, the norm in the Netherlands and the rest of Europe became known as the French system. This system mandated registration of women in prostitution and regulation of their activities, and also compelled them to submit to weekly medical exams for syphilis. When certified as "clean," they received cards that effectively licensed them to practice, without which they could be imprisoned.

In 1869 Josephine Butler condemned this system of enforced medical exams, inspiring a coalition of feminists, socialists, and Protestants to abolish them in Britain and to campaign in Europe against the regulationist system of prostitution as degrading to women. Reversing the essentialist view that prostitution was necessary for curbing male lust, abolitionists won the legal battle in Holland, and in 1911 the government adopted a legal system outlawing brothels and criminalizing organizing of and profiting from prostitution. Engaging in prostitution was not defined as a criminal offense, although active solicitation was forbidden. In Amsterdam, all the brothels were shut down as early as 1897.

Gradually the brothels returned. In the 1930s, Amsterdam saw its first window brothels within which women sat passively, thus avoiding the charge of active solicitation. Red lights, made possible by the advent of electricity, were used to attract men.[3] These brothels, known simply as the windows, also created the illusion of prostituted women as independent entrepreneurs, technically to comply with abolitionist legislation prohibiting brothel keeping and pimping.

In the 1950s the red-light district in Amsterdam, commonly called De Wallen, grew and became a tourist attraction. Prostitution, sex clubs, pornography shops, and drugs were openly tolerated. The government unofficially reverted to regulation of certain brothels and limited prostitution to specified areas, thus prohibiting prostitution de jure while permitting it de facto.

The 1980s saw an influx of women from other countries trafficked into Dutch prostitution, a trend that continues today. Despite all attempts by the pro-prostitution lobbyists to label this trend as migration for sex work, numerous reports attest to the legalized trafficking permeating the window brothels.

In 1985 the Red Thread (Rode Draad) was founded to advocate for the rights of women in prostitution. The Red Thread maintained these rights could only be achieved if pimps and brothels were decriminalized. The Mr. A. de Graaf Foundation, originally an abolitionist Christian research institute for the study of prostitution, reversed its mission and began promoting the acceptance of prostitution as normal work.[4] Supported by generous state subsidies, the foundation and its studies helped to inspire and lobby for the legalization legislation that was ultimately passed in 2000.

## The Dutch Campaign to Legalize Prostitution

Since the 1980s international feminist abolitionist organizations have found it very difficult to find partners in the Netherlands who would challenge the legalized prostitution system. Most of the criticism of the Dutch system has come from outside the country until recently. Examining the history of the modern Dutch campaign to legalize prostitution helps to explain why this is the case.

Preceded by very little public discussion, debate, and media attention, the "Lifting of the general ban on the brothels" passed the Dutch First Chamber in October 1999. It was supported by a "state feminism" orchestrated over a period of years by the government, with the result that women's non-governmental groups and governmental agencies overseeing women's issues became inseparable.[5] Effectively, the government created its own constituency for repeal by funding the women's organizations to fight for dismantling the 1911 abolitionist legislation.

The collusion between women's organizations and state agencies culminated in the year 2000 when legislation came into force lifting the ban on brothels, abolishing the penalties on pimping, and recognizing prostitution as work. The legislation was promoted in the name of protecting the rights of "sex workers," removing organized crime from the sex industry, and giving more control to the police to battle "forced" prostitution, international trafficking, and the sexual exploitation of children. The distinction between forced and voluntary prostitution, which came from the governmental women's policy network, became the philosophical foundation of the new law. It provided the basis for the separation between sex trafficking and prostitution that the Dutch government was soon to internationalize.

No Dutch municipality can prohibit a brothel within its jurisdiction. Even if a city or town opposes establishing a brothel, it must allow at least one because not doing so is contrary to the basic federal right to work.[6] Two years after the legislation came into force, 43 of the 348 municipalities were found to be in violation of the law because they were following a "no-brothel" policy.[7]

If a woman possesses an official work permit as an EU citizen, fulfills the age requirement of eighteen years or older, and pays taxes, she can be employed in the legal prostitution venues. In 2013, Amsterdam

increased its legal age for prostitution to twenty-one and stated that
the new age requirement is meant to fight the abuses of the sex industry and "strengthen prostitutes' position."[8] Women from other countries have to obtain a valid residence permit and "work" in the licensed
venues.

## A Sex Work Framework and a Market Scaffolding

The initial moves to revoke the older abolitionist legislation came
from the municipalities that framed repeal as a law-and-order measure.
Municipal initiatives to change Dutch law on prostitution paralleled
those of the governmental women's policy group. In 1982 the wom-
en's policy group organized a conference on prostitution in The Hague
where participants demanded a dismantling of the brothel ban, alleging a regulated brothel system would improve conditions of women in
prostitution.[9]

The governmental women's policy group called the Department
for Coordination of Equality Policy (DCE) took over the campaign to
engineer repeal within the government and the introduction of "decent
business practices" into the sex industry. The DCE became the leader
in setting up and organizing feminist and "sex worker" groups into a
policy network that would endorse the government's emerging position
for a legalized prostitution regime. In turn the DCE ensured the support of non-governmental organizations.[10]

In 1985 the First World Whores' Congress in Amsterdam brought
together international groups claiming to represent "sex workers." This
meeting was funded by the DCE,[11] and it served as the first international showcasing of the emerging Dutch prostitution policy. In 1986
the DCE subsidized the Red Thread,[12] which was intended to be a trade
union for prostituted women but by 2004 had only garnered about a
hundred members.[13] Women's groups became cash-flush lobbyists for
the passage of proposed Dutch legislation on prostitution, all the while
appearing as non-governmental actors exerting independent pressure
on the larger government apparatus for abolishing the ban on the sex
industry.

In 1987 the DCE funded the official creation of the Foundation
Against Trafficking in Women (STV). Perhaps the most influential
group in advocating for Dutch prostitution policy, the STV was specifically funded to "professionalize" its activities, conduct research on
trafficking and prostitution, and set up a support service for trafficked

women.[14] Over the years, the STV became the starting point for statistics and data on victims and possible victims of trafficking in persons in the Netherlands.[15] In 2007 the STV changed its name to Coordination Centre Human Trafficking (CoMensha) and is now part of La Strada International. Currently, CoMensha/La Strada must be notified when any victim of trafficking is suspected and found.

On the legislative front, the Liberal minister of justice submitted a bill to Parliament in 1983 to modernize the criminal code and remove what many regarded as the outdated penalties for pimps and brothels. In 1985 he institutionalized the division between forced and voluntary prostitution, arguing that it would uphold the right to self-determination of women in prostitution. The minister introduced the concept of "the emancipated and assertive prostitute who sees herself as a sex-worker . . . later developed to mark the difference between Dutch prostitutes and prostitutes from non-EU countries who by implication then emerge as unemancipated and meek."[16]

The political parties vacillated. From the mid-1980s until the law was passed in 1999, there were three parliamentary debates. Initially, several of the parties viewed prostitution as a form of sexual domination, but they also recommended a pragmatic approach, claiming it would improve the situation of the women in the sex industry. Building on the forced-free distinction, the political parties argued that women had the right not to be predetermined as victims but rather to be recognized as independent agents who made their own decisions about whether to engage in the sex market as in any other job sector.[17]

The Socialist and right-wing parties in Parliament kept their eyes fixed on the financial prize of the legislation—increased tax revenues—a powerful propellant of the legalizing legislation. Capitalizing on the traditional Dutch talent for creating new markets, many politicians reportedly envisioned the potential windfall of a 19 percent value-added tax (VAT) that could be collected once prostitution became a legal industry.[18] Revenue was the elephant in the room that became hugely invisible during the parliamentary process.

Three discussions in Parliament took place during which there was almost no public debate about the core of the issue—whether prostitution should be recognized as sexual exploitation or as "sex work." What was remarkable about the state of Dutch women's activism on prostitution was how quickly the violence-against-women perspective disappeared from the Dutch feminist and political agenda. In the final parliamentary discussion leading up to the bill's passage, the minister of justice declared that once the legislation was passed, regulations would make prostitution "healthy, safe and transparent, stripped of criminal side-issues."[19]

Market tradition helped turn the sex industry into a business to be regulated like any other. Prostitution users were transformed into customers and prostituted women into providers of sexual services. Both were regarded as *equal partners* in what became a commercial sexual transaction. This false symmetry meant that prostitution users were gradually drawn into the government's repeal campaign and treated as associates. Ultimately, buyers formed organizations to promote their interests and were consulted as advisers to governmental reports. The recognition of buyers as policy consultants would set the stage for the "ethical johns" campaigns that would occur during the first decade of the twenty-first century (see chapter 2).

In the early 1990s the DCE moved Dutch prostitution policy into the international arena, helping to place its state feminist partners in key United Nations and European Union venues and positions. During this period, the government also began funding the Global Alliance Against Traffic in Women (GAATW),[20] founded in 1994 partly in opposition to the Coalition Against Trafficking in Women, whose international abolitionist politics were antithetical to the Dutch position.

Given international credibility by a global NGO that promoted Dutch prostitution policy, the Dutch government and state feminists began to actively export their position. In concert with the STV and other Dutch organizations, the GAATW helped set the stage for internationalizing the key Dutch distinction between trafficking and prostitution. In turn the success of the NGO lobbying efforts on the international stage strengthened legalization efforts on the national front that were finalized when the law came into force in the year 2000.

State feminists generated the sex work framework, and municipalities and sex industry entrepreneurs constructed the market scaffolding. Each accommodated the other. Of course the women's policy agenda never would have been successful unless it joined with powerful constituencies, such as municipalities promoting regulation of prostitution, the association of "sex workers," sex entrepreneurs (formerly known as pimps and brothel owners), and male buyers who became governmental policy consultants.

## Normalizing Men as Sexual Consumers

Dutch prostitution policy regularized men as respectable consumers of "sexual services." The parliamentary debates did not challenge alleged male need, male rights, and male appetite for the sex of prostitution. As opponents of the law alleged would happen, Dutch legalized prostitution did not control demand. Instead, it gave men blanket entitlement to buy women and children for the sex of prostitution wherever men can be satisfied. Dutch men who are not content with the legal offerings can easily gratify their fantasies of more stimulating and exotic women and/or sexually abuse vulnerable children in both the legal and illegal prostitution venues that now flourish in the Netherlands.

Legalization of prostitution also increased demand by bringing to the Netherlands hordes of sex tourists who indulge their whims in the legal brothels. Consisting of three districts, the red-light area is reported to draw as many visitors to Amsterdam as its museums and canals.[21] The city's 450 window brothels are the main appeal for male tourists, who not only ogle the women on display as if they are animals in a zoo but also take advantage of the easy purchasing of sexual activities with women exhibited in the windows.

Women in the windows have not only complained about tourist harassment, particularly by men from Britain who arrive en masse in Amsterdam on stag parties, but from those who take photos of them. Photographing the prostituted women has become such a spectator sport that women have put stickers on their windows with the message that taking photos is prohibited. Because the red-light area is a public space, the tourists can ignore these stickers and take home pictures as souvenirs.

Volunteers from the Prostitution Information Centre conduct excursions through the prostitution area. One tour guide is reported to have said of a live-sex theater in the district, "We have a family show. We show you how to make families."[22] In 2005 Thomas Cook, a respected worldwide tour and travel agency founded to promote ethical and educational tourism and with the reputation of being a family company, launched a night walking tour through the red-light area.[23] Building on tours organized by the Prostitution Information Centre, it offered outings—free to children under three—jovially described on Thomas Cook's website: "The Red Light District is an unmissable experience, as attested by the packs of roving young men, couples holding hands, giggling groups of women, and Japanese tourists toting cameras. Spectacle notwithstanding, real business is done here at a steady pace, and those seeking a slightly more authentic experience, should head for the area on a weeknight."[24] Apparently, Thomas Cook was not reluctant to promote the view that prostitution is a legitimate "real business" and an "authentic [tourist] experience" in the very Amsterdam brothels later closed for perpetrating violence against women.

By 2008 when it became clear to the government that "Lifting of the general ban on the brothels" had failed in many of its aims, a series of measures was proposed. One was to prosecute the buyers of illegal prostitution—what the press called, "Taking a step in the direction of how Sweden has been approaching the problem."[25] This proposed measure to prosecute prostitution users who were reportedly flocking to *illegal* sex venues pitted the owners of brothels against the self-interests of the buyers. The Association of Operators of Relaxation Businesses (VER) said it welcomed the possibility of prosecuting the clients of illegal prostitution, because it would send a distinct signal to buyers "not to choose the prostitute offering the lowest price."[26] In other words, it would get rid of the competition—all the venues that in the view of owners offered cheap sex and were not quality controlled.

The new Dutch model of prostitution began to crack even in the immediate post-legislative years when the failures of legalized prostitution became evident. Local politicians increasingly recognized that a culture of impunity prevailed in the prostitution areas. By legalizing prostitution, politicians had opened up their cities further to international organized crime, trafficking in women and children, and drug cartels.

## THE FAILURE OF
## DUTCH LEGALIZATION LEGISLATION

The legalisation of prostitution did not bring about what many had hoped. We are still faced with distressing situations in which women are being exploited. It is high time for a thorough evaluation of the prostitution act.

—*Job Cohen, former mayor of Amsterdam*

Amsterdam's prostitution district is not a pretty picture. It is a breeding ground of ruthless pimps and traffickers who have historically dominated the area and continued to do so particularly after legalization came into force. In 2003 Amsterdam closed many of its sex bars and clubs, with the mayor also limiting all-night hours for brothels. Along with these first moves to mitigate the culture of prostitution in the city, several commercial TV stations stopped showing pornography. The manager of SBS television, launched in part as a major pornography channel, acknowledged that the situation "was getting out of hand."[27]

## Closing the Tolerance Zones and the Amsterdam Window Brothels

Most major Dutch cities have terminated their prostitution tolerance zones—restricted areas where men could buy women legally and, allegedly, where women could sell sex safely. These zones quickly became unsafe and sordid places for women. In spite of police presence, organized crime infiltrated the sex districts and operated there with impunity. Amsterdam eliminated its tolerance zone in 2003 and later prohibited street prostitution in all areas of the city. Former mayor Job Cohen stated, "It appeared impossible to create a safe and controllable zone for women that was not open to abuse by organised crime."[28] A Labor Party city councilor added, "The council must seriously ask itself if it still feels called upon to practise the trade of brothel manager."[29]

Rotterdam followed suit in 2005 and The Hague in 2006 with the closures of their prostitution zones. Eindhoven suspended its tolerance zone in 2009, originally set up as a street area for drug-addicted prostituted women. In the words of alderman Mariet Mittendorf, "We do not want to facilitate these women in remaining in their dead-end situation. We would rather offer them a dignified existence."[30] Official policy on legal prostitution zones had radically changed.

Also beginning in 2006 the Amsterdam City Council refused to renew the licenses of thirty-seven prostitution entrepreneurs in the red-light area. Using the Public Administration Probity Act (BIBOB) law that gave power to municipalities to investigate and close venues where possible illegality exists, the council concluded that many of the brothels were in the hands of organized crime. Among the charges were human trafficking, drug trafficking, fraud, and money laundering.[31]

Earlier in 1996 a parliamentary inquiry had already determined that sixteen persons with backgrounds or associates in organized crime controlled Amsterdam's prostitution area. In 2006—ten years later and six years after legalized prostitution went into effect—criminals dominated the Amsterdam sex industry even more. Europol confirmed that local Dutch pimps and brothel owners had formed online links with pimps and traffickers who bring women into the country and treat them as "a piece of garbage," often resorting to violence and murder.[32] Faced with this situation, the city ultimately closed down one-third of the window brothels in the Amsterdam red-light district.

One of the first to be shut down was Charles Geerts, the biggest prostitution capo in the district. He controlled sixty window brothels in twenty different buildings. In past times the city had granted Geerts several permits for new brothels in the heart of the city. However, Amsterdam changed course when, through the BIBOB, it acquired the means to investigate closer. When Geerts was suspected of money laundering, the city shuttered his windows.[33]

The other brothel owners, who altogether ran half the windows in the sex sector, appealed the city council closure decisions, but their appeal ultimately failed. During 2007–2008, the city shut down one-third of the windows by purchasing the former brothel buildings and turning them into shops for fashion designers. Geerts was not charged with any criminal activities but was instead bought out by the city. At the same time, Amsterdam announced that escort services, which had operated illegally since the legalization of prostitution, would have to apply for licenses.[34] The same year, the Dutch minister of justice also announced that all escort services would have to be registered and licensed.[35]

Former mayor Cohen announced, "The romantic picture of the area is outdated if you see the abuses in the sex industry and that is why the council has to act."[36] He also vowed to close more of Amsterdam's windows in the future. The closures of the tolerance zones and the window brothels within the red-light district give vivid proof that the aims of the prostitution legislation are not being met.

## Unfulfilled Goals of Legalized Prostitution

Public policies should be assessed by how they fulfill their goals. In the years immediately following passage of the legislation, official opinion claimed that lifting the ban on brothels had been successful. The 2004 governmental National Action Plan on Trafficking in Human Beings alleged, "The licensed and monitored sectors of the sex industry have now been cleaned up considerably."[37] In 2004 an annual police publication stated half the police forces reported that the licensed prostitution industry "was (as good as) free of any abuses."[38]

This optimism was short-lived. Authoritative reports in 2007 and 2008 were instrumental in signaling the unfulfilled goals of the Dutch legalized regime of prostitution. The 2007 Daalder report gave moderate signals of abuse within the licensed prostitution sector. Entitled *Prostitution in the Netherlands Since the Lifting of the Brothel Ban*, the report was commissioned by the Dutch Ministry of Justice. Although

Daalder stated there had been modest success in implementing the legalization legislation, he revealed many failures of the legislation in fulfilling its goals. Tellingly, the report found, "The prostitutes' emotional well-being is now lower than in 2001 on all measured aspects, and the use of sedatives has increased."[39]

The 2008 National Police Service report went further in highlighting "the illusion of a crime-free licensed sector."[40] Entitled *Beneath the Surface* (Schone schijn), the report was commissioned by the National Prosecutors' Office. It chronicled the results of an inquiry begun in 2006 that tracked gangs of traffickers in the prostitution districts of three cities in the Netherlands. Criminal gangs working as pimps and bodyguards were found to have violently victimized dozens of women in prostitution over many years within the *licensed sector*. "The prostitutes were totally in the power of the gang. They were never left alone or left unobserved. They were beaten and terrorized. They had to work long hours and to hand over all of their earnings, and some were forced to abort . . . or to have their breasts surgically enlarged."[41] Pimps even specified the women's bra cup size to the doctors.[42]

The report had two aims: 1) to describe the ways in which the criminals operated in the legal sector and how they were able to accomplish their control of the women in plain view and not be detected; 2) to more broadly analyze whether the current prostitution and trafficking policies were capable of identifying the abuses in the brothels.[43] With the publication of *Beneath the Surface*, "There appears to be an emerging national consensus that the law of 2000 has been a failure."[44] Following is an examination that lays bare the unfulfilled goals of the legislation.

*Legalization Would Distinguish the Real Victims—Those Who Were Forced—from Those Who Were Voluntarily in Prostitution*
The philosophical cornerstone of the "Lifting of the general ban on the brothels" was the distinction between forced and voluntary prostitution. From the beginning, the government and its NGO partners acted as if the distinction between voluntary and forced prostitution was clear-cut, self-evident, and discernible in the real lives of prostituted women. However, the 2007 Daalder report admits, "It is virtually impossible to comment on developments in the number of prostitutes who are working in the sex business under some degree of coercion."[45] Municipalities, authorities, and brothel owners indicated they found proving coercion and confronting it difficult.

The 2008 National Police Service report put this acknowledgment more strongly. "How is it possible that forced-prostitution, i.e., human trafficking, was able to take place in the *licensed* window-prostitution sector in the three municipalities under investigation?"[46] The report provided several answers to this question.

First, women's "bodyguards" operated very publicly and even enjoyed friendly interactions with the police inspectors in the prostitution areas.[47] Some victims, who were completely in the power of the gangs, had been in prostitution for years—some in the same window brothels—and their abuse went undetected.[48]

Second, brothel inspections provided little concrete evidence of victimization. There are several reasons for this, all of which are fairly obvious. Many victims were scared to report their exploitation, and some may not have identified as victims, especially if their pimps were their boyfriends. Inspectors failed to recognize that a woman's external behavior, such as a cheerful and inviting manner, did not necessarily mean a woman was free from being victimized, but rather that she may have hidden evidence of it in a brief inspection interview. Further, the minatory presence of pimps and bodyguards at the inspection sites reduced the likelihood of women reporting the truth of their violent situations.[49]

Third, the National Police Service report concluded that the process of checking women's papers did not prevent "forced prostitution." Possession of the right papers "does not preclude being a victim of human trafficking." Women who register with the municipal authorities are "rarely recognized as victims," and "it is also doubtful as to whether these administrative obligations form a real obstacle to underage/illegal prostitution."[50]

Fourth, that a prostitution business is licensed is no guarantee it does not abuse prostituted women.[51] A brothel keeper may also close his eyes to the exploitation of the women because of the negative effect it would have on his business. Similarly, the buyers have no incentive to expose themselves by reporting a woman's victimization.

Tragically, the current Dutch prostitution and human trafficking policy is based on the assumption that administrative measures will serve to detect—and the brothel operators and customers will be willing to report—exploitation and criminality. The 2008 National Police Service report concluded all points of control failed and, most of the time, did not detect what mattered—the exploitation of the women involved. Women were rarely recognized as victims, even in situations where exploitation permeated the venues.

*Legalization Would Free Women from*
*Pimp Control and Make Them Independent Agents*

The 2007 Daalder report found that the "great majority" of women in window prostitution have pimps or so-called boyfriends. Prostituted women's dependence on pimps appeared to be the norm in many legal prostitution venues. In visiting the windows, the researchers noted that many of the prostituted women "involuntarily" handed over their earnings to their pimps.[52] Some women interviewed stated that they had to change their "workplace" at the behest of their pimps, for example, when the pimps thought they did not make enough money at a particular brothel. Other women indicated that they themselves changed their location to escape from their pimps.[53]

Prostituted women in the Netherlands are also subject to double domination by both business owners and their manager-pimps. Initially procured for the brothel owners by pimps, many women remain subject to pimp control of their behavior and their earnings. "Pimps are still a very common phenomenon. . . . The fact that the number of prostitutes with pimps does not seem to have decreased is a cause for concern."[54] Brothel owners as well exert control over the women's performance and take-home pay.

The National Police Service report also specified the ways in which prostituted women were subject to pimp control in the window brothels of Amsterdam, Alkmaar, and Utrecht. The women were "snatched" from other pimps, "induced to 'switch' voluntarily," and threatened by pimps if they dared to lodge reports of intimidation. Victims' statements also exposed the mix of seduction, force, and violence used in order for them to acquiesce to their pimps' bidding. Others were told that their freedom could only be gained if they paid a sum varying from €30,000–240,000 to their pimps. The passports of foreign-born women were confiscated, and some women feared being murdered if they escaped.[55]

Since the 2000 law legalized pimping, the pervasiveness of pimping is significant. So-called third-party business managers have turned out to be just regular abusive pimps. Given the fact that pimps commonly exploit women in both the legal and non-legal sex industry, it appears not to matter much whether women are in either quarter, since both are pimp-controlled.

*Legalization of Prostitution Would Reduce Trafficking*

Before passage of the proposed legalization law in 1998, members of the Police Policy and Advice Group on Trafficking in Human Beings had expressed concern that the law would attract traffickers.[56] That concern has been substantiated.

At a 2004 criminology conference, one of the Netherlands' top organized-crime specialists, Cyrille Fijnaut, stated in the opening address that the legalization of prostitution in the Netherlands had "greatly increased trafficking."[57] Criminology expert Louise Shelley, who attended the conference, reported that Russian and Ukrainian attendees who went on one of the famous tours of the red-light district "complained that, all they saw there were women from their own countries."[58]

The Daalder report seems to refute this pervasiveness of trafficked women in speculating, "It is likely trafficking in human beings has become more difficult" owing to increased enforcement efforts. However, this opinion has not been supported by the large-scale closures of prostitution tolerance zones in major Dutch cities and the window brothels in Amsterdam during which increased numbers of women were found trafficked from other countries. The Daalder report did state that 60 percent of the 354 women interviewed in the legal sex industry were foreign-born, and that foreign-born women constitute the majority in the non-legal venues.[59] However, Daalder does not stipulate most foreign-born women found in the licensed windows had been trafficked or forced, as does the National Police Service report.

The National Police Service report specifies that the percentage of women "working against their will" in the window brothels of all three cities investigated is 50–90 percent. "Based on the most conservative estimate of 50 percent, this amounts to 4,000 victims of human trafficking per year in Amsterdam alone."[60] La Strada, the pro–sex work organization, which collects data on victims of trafficking who seek assistance and shelter, reported that the number of registered victims in 2011 was 23 percent more than in 2010 (from 993 to 1,222).[61]

In brothel investigations, officials look for women without legal entry or residence papers. Legal papers, however, do not mean that those who possess them have not been trafficked. Because a number of foreign-born women in prostitution have legal entry documents or come from Eastern European countries within the European Economic Area (EEA), authorities often assume these women are not trafficked and exploited. With legal papers, pimps and traffickers can easily move women into the country. Searching for evidence of trafficking mainly based on women without legal documents is an outdated strategy in a Europe that is increasingly without national borders.

Most women from other countries who are prostituted in the brothels of the Netherlands do not have the financial wherewithal to subsidize their own travel, documents, and "job placement." In other words, it is highly likely they do not get there on their own resources, nor that their "migration" is simply "facilitated" by decent travel agents.

The abusive situation in which women from other countries are found in the Dutch sex industry is also whitewashed by the propaganda of the sex industry apologists that trafficking is simply "migration for sex work" (see chapter 4). They bear immense responsibility for the confusion this misrepresentation has generated in Dutch prostitution policy and its consequences. "Confusion is rife regarding prostitution policy and related legislation," not only among ordinary citizens, but also among those charged with implementation.[62]

*Legalization of Prostitution Would*
*Remove Organized Crime from the Prostitution Sector*
The findings of the National Police Service report confirmed the earlier statements of former mayor Job Cohen in acknowledging that the sex industry continues to be dominated by organized crime. "We have seen that in the last years that trafficking in women is becoming more, so in this respect the legalizing of prostitution didn't work out."[63] In 2011 Lodewijk Asscher, an Amsterdam city alderman, continued to wage his own campaign against the abuse and exploitation that still exist concealed behind the window brothels.[64]

How can the removal, or even the reduction, of organized crime be achieved when the criminals are baptized as newborn legal entrepreneurs? The Daalder report interviewed forty-nine prostitution venue owners, many of whom had once been illegal operators in the sex industry, i.e., former criminals whose status had been transformed into legitimate businessmen overnight by the lifting of the ban on brothels. The Daalder report mildly confirmed that because "a large part of the current owners has already been working as a business owner in that illegal sector, it seems plausible that owners are less inclined to conform to government authority than most other Dutch people."[65]

Another disturbing trend is the lenient sentences that have been imposed on convicted traffickers in the Netherlands. In her 2008 report, the Dutch National Rapporteur on Trafficking indicated, "In 2006 almost half of the custodial sentences [for those convicted of trafficking in human beings] imposed in first instance were for less than one year. . . . The highest average custodial sentence in 2006 . . . where violence was the most serious offence . . . was just over 27 months."[66] Low sentences occurred even after the Dutch Criminal Code was changed in 2005 to set penalties of six to fifteen years for any form of trafficking.

In 2008, the U.S. Trafficking in Persons report stated, "The College of Attorneys-General is investigating whether judges are systematically giving appropriate sentences in trafficking cases."[67] It appeared that judges are skirting Article 273 of the Dutch Criminal Code, which prescribes much larger penalties for any form of trafficking.

These lenient sentences can hardly be viewed as a deterrent to traffickers or as penalties that fit the crime. The removal of organized crime from the prostitution sector is certainly influenced by the political will of the courts to mandate penalties that reflect the seriousness of the crime.

Several past and present Amsterdam city councilors, in addition to the mayor and deputy mayor, have criticized the hold of organized crime on the prostitution sector. Roel van Duijn, an Amsterdam city councilor from the Green Party, spent several years investigating the trafficking in women in the illegal prostitution areas. In 2006 he stated, "The illegal circuit is rife with sex slavery." His criticisms are not limited to the illegal sector. He also wants to abolish legal prostitution because "prostitution has always been an illegal area" with women in the sex industry who "continue to suffer from traumatic experiences."[68]

In 2007 Frank de Wolf, a Labor Party city councilor and an HIV-AIDS researcher, told the *Washington Post*:

> "In the past, we looked at legal prostitution as a women's liberation issue; now it's looked at as exploitation of women and should be stopped" . . . he [de Wolf] said Amsterdam's police force is overwhelmed and ill-equipped to fight the sophisticated foreign organized crime networks operating in the city. Laws designed to regulate prostitution and brothel operators have instead opened the trade to criminal gangs.[69]

In 2008 the National Police Service report agreed. "Current prostitution and human trafficking policy is ill-equipped to detect involuntary prostitution (i.e., human trafficking)."[70] This raises the question of how much more so is the policy "ill-equipped" to detect all forms of prostitution that do not fall under the restricted definition of forced.

*Legalization Will Improve the
Situation of Women in the Sex Industry*
Karina Schaapman, a survivor of prostitution and former Labor Party city councilor in Amsterdam, has spoken publicly about her experience in the Dutch prostitution industry. She also published her autobiography

in which she discusses the harms of prostitution for women and the increase of abuse brought about by the 2000 legalizing legislation. In an interview Schaapman stated, "Legalization did not bring what we expected, the abuses are enormous."[71]

In its investigation, the 2008 National Police Service report listed the ways in which pimps, traffickers, and bodyguards, called the Dürdan Group, exploited the women. The pimps ordered their victims in the windows every day and required them to ask permission to stop being available for sex. Many women were ordered to earn €1,000 per day and were under twenty-four-hour surveillance. The few victims who made statements to the police testified that they were beaten with baseball bats or made to stand in icy water of lakes or parks during winter. Some were branded with tattoos that inscribed the names of pimps on their bodies.[72]

In addition to the pimps and bodyguards, there were other facilitators of women's exploitation. In some cases, the window operators colluded with the women's pimps. A tax consulting firm and small temporary employment agencies provided the women with financial and work papers to establish the appearance of legality of their "sex work." An enlisted abortion clinic performed the procedure, and all women were required to go to the same cosmetic surgery clinic for breast enlargements. "It is likely that nearly all of the above-mentioned facilitators were to some degree aware of the exploitative practices of the Dürdan group. In spite of this knowledge, only one window lessor made a formal report to the police."[73]

All proposals to legalize prostitution and/or decriminalize the sex industry claim with full confidence that normalizing prostitution will radically improve women's health and well-being. Despite its moderate tone, the Daalder report reached damning conclusions about the welfare of women in the Dutch sex industry since legalization went into effect. In addition to his finding that the emotional well-being of women in the sex industry was lower in all respects in 2007 than in 2001, Daalder added, "Prostituted women also suffer high levels of distress." The ability of women in prostitution to exercise autonomy in determining their on-duty schedules has also declined since 2001. In other areas—such as the ability to refuse certain buyers, determine the prices, and decide "the course of action with clients" (i.e., the sexual activities that women must perform)—these remain at the same level measured by studies in 2001.[74] Nothing has improved.

In responding to these failures, however, the recommendations of the Daalder report minimize the exploitation of women in the sex industry by using the language of "labor relations," which tones down abuse. The report recommends that authorities better clarify the "right form of labor relations" within the prostitution sector and enhance the brothel owners' power. "The more instructions are given by the business owner, and the greater his say in all kinds of matters, the sooner the existence of an employer-employee relation will be established."[75]

When a country establishes prostitution as work, it is almost impossible for an officially commissioned report to frame its conclusions and recommendations outside the labor paradigm. This recommendation of the Daalder report to increase the power of brothel owners illustrates the difference it makes in the lives of women when a regime legally institutionalizes their abuse and well-being as a labor issue rather than as violence against women. Thus, the exploitation, the distress, the lack of autonomy, and the low levels of emotional well-being chronicled in the report are summarized as occupational hazards to be remedied by better work conditions.

An aim of the prostitution legislation was to regularize the status of women as workers and to provide them with benefits. The majority of women, however, do not want to be regular-salaried employees for several reasons. Many do not want to pay taxes, arguing that they earn very little. A large number collect social security or employee insurance and fear that these payments may be jeopardized by extra income. Some argue, "This involves my body; I will not pay tax over it."[76] Some want the freedom and flexibility of being independent contractors. More important, the majority wants to retain anonymity because women fear the exposure of providing contact information and registering with relevant authorities.

All paeans to legalized prostitution regimes promote the myth that women can become regular employees with access to social security, disability, and pension benefits. However, when prostituted women in the licensed prostitution sector were asked whether these benefits or others were most important to them, most stated they were not as important as anonymity.[77] They were aware that failing to register would have negative consequences for their future social security entitlements, yet they chose not to institutionalize their "labor status."

Few municipalities have initiated any programs that assist women to leave prostitution despite earlier parliamentary encouragement that urged the cities and towns to launch exit programs. In 2004, the government also sent a brochure to all municipalities offering assistance in developing exit policies and programs. Only 6 percent of municipalities responded.[78]

The 2008 National Police Service report concluded that the lifting of the ban on brothels has done nothing to promote the safety or prevent exploitation of women in prostitution.[79] The signs of victimization were not recognized or acted upon.

---

The National Police Service report of 2008, the Daalder report of 2007, the termination of the major tolerance zones from 2003 through 2009, and the closing of many window brothels in Amsterdam indicate that legalized prostitution legislation has not fulfilled its goals. The situation of women in prostitution has not improved, their emotional well-being is lower than it was in 2001, and most women have not accessed the proclaimed social and economic benefits that were to follow legalization. Pimping is still prevalent in both the legal and illegal sectors, with the added benefit to pimps of being legal entrepreneurs. Trafficking appears to be rampant, as evidenced by the majority of women from other countries, as well as Dutch women who are involuntarily in the legal and non-legal sectors. Former criminals run many of the brothels and sex clubs, and ties with organized crime permeate the legal and non-legal sex industries. As one journalist wrote, "These criminals have terrorized the Red Light District to such an extent that the police officers . . . did not want their real names to appear in [the] . . . article, as they were afraid—they were receiving murder threats."[80]

## THE EXPORTING OF DUTCH PROSTITUTION POLICY

On the eve of the 21st century, under pretext of an analysis that officially equates sexual freedom with prostitution, and arguing, in defiance of all ethics, that the social stigma attached to prostitution will disappear once the profession is legally recognised, the Dutch government is advocating a new human "right," the right to pimp, for which the right to be a prostitute is just a cover.
—*Marie-Victoire Louise*, Le Monde Diplomatique

The exporting of Dutch prostitution policy to other countries began in earnest at a Strasbourg meeting in 1991. In Strasbourg the Dutch advocates promoted a neo-regulatory regime based on a market model of prostitution controlled by better business practices and health and safety standards. It was here that the Dutch also began consistent efforts to use regional and international meetings to proselytize partici-pants and champion legalization of prostitution. In these forums, Dutch government and NGO participants and their allies used an aggressive agenda of censoring opponents who disagreed with pro–sex work policy.

Building on an undemocratic strategy used nationally that had led to the passage of the legalization legislation in 1999, the international exporting of Dutch policy moved forward based on a similar lack of public discussion, debate, and criticism. The Dutch government subsi-dized the advocacy of organizations that promoted the Dutch position and placed Dutch policy advocates in key national and international forums at the same time that it tried to suppress any opposition to the Dutch position.

## European Interventions

*Strasbourg*

As indicated by the title of the Strasbourg Council of Europe meeting called "Traffic in Women and Forced Prostitution," the Dutch policy was already mobile and influential in limiting actionable prostitution only to that which can be proved to be forced. The 1991 Strasbourg meeting, held in association with the Dutch government, attracted gov-ernmental and NGO representatives from most European countries, as well as anti-trafficking NGO representatives from outside Europe.

CATW cofounder Dorchen Leidholdt, one of the international participants in the Strasbourg meeting, characterized the Dutch export policy scheme: "From the start, it was apparent that not only were the Dutch running the meeting—the chair was Dutch and the vast major-ity of the officials espoused what became known as 'the Dutch posi-tion'—but the Dutch had 'packed the house.'"[81] The STV was present "in full force" as part of the official Dutch delegation, and the Dutch representatives had earlier formed alliances with pro–sex work groups from Thailand, Ecuador, and Italy. The Dutch tactics ensured that pro-Dutch policy advocates wrote the recommendations.[82]

Part of the Dutch agenda at this conference was to eliminate the 1949 UN *Convention for the Suppression of the Traffic in Persons and the Exploitation of the Prostitution of Others* from any official regional and UN meetings and documents. This was a prelude to attempts to rescind the convention itself, or at least to bury it in obscurity. Because the 1949 convention makes no distinction between forced and voluntary prostitution, criminalizes pimping and procuring, and works to abolish prostitution and regulationism, the Dutch pro-prostitution advocates wanted to replace it with a convention against forced trafficking. The proposed Dutch convention included no mention of pimping and procuring,[83] thus internationalizing the future Dutch national legislation that would transform pimps into third-party businessmen.

The Strasbourg meeting had its critics. Representatives from several countries—Norway, Sweden, Belgium, and France—objected that the recommendations were all confined to forced prostitution and failed to address pimping and procuring. Tellingly, despite Dutch efforts to pack the house, many of the NGOs present openly opposed the distinction between forced and voluntary prostitution in the recommendations.[84]

"As the meeting progressed . . . the advocates of the Dutch position were incapable of defending it. . . . I don't think they are used to much criticism."[85] So they used other tactics than persuasion to press forward their policies. When NGOs demanded that the recommendations not be published since they did not reflect the views of the majority of participants, "the Chair [Dutch] replied that the meeting was never intended to be democratic."[86]

*Vienna*

The next major European meeting in which the Dutch tried to internationalize their position was the "European Meeting on Trafficking in Women" held in Vienna in June 1996. Anita Gradin in her opening address to the conference as European commissioner stated to all participants, "My hope is that we will be able to avoid a debate on prostitution as such, and concentrate on what measures could be taken for hindering the slave trade."[87]

Vienna added a new strategy to the exporting of Dutch prostitution policy—overcome opposition by driving a wedge between trafficking and prostitution. This enabled the Dutch participants to assert that prostitution per se was not on the agenda of the meeting, which was to be solely concerned with trafficking. Workshop leaders at the Vienna meeting were directed to avoid any discussion of prostitution and limit their remarks to trafficking. Participants were warned at the beginning of the conference that they were only to speak about trafficking, not prostitution.[88] Thus some participants, who wanted to speak about the links between prostitution and trafficking and the ways in which the two could not be separated, were silenced and censored.

The tune changed when sex work advocates who delivered keynote presentations supporting the Dutch position asserted *their* view of prostitution. A Dutch keynoter, Marie van Hemeldonck,[89] argued that the 1949 convention was a weak instrument that did not distinguish between forced and chosen prostitution. In what became a common claim of the sex work apologists about this UN convention, van Hemeldonck falsely asserted that it "endorses a moral or religious point of view towards prostitution as a sin which has to be abolished or eradicated." Finally she called for its replacement with a new convention limited to trafficking in which the definition of trafficking would apply only to those who are transported "without her or their consent."[90]

Helga Konrad, then the Austrian federal minister for women's affairs and later anti-trafficking director at the Organization for Security and Co-operation in Europe (OSCE), in her opening address to the conference said, "We must . . . accept that for many women there is no other possibility than to work in the sex business."[91] Although no recommendations emerged from the conference supporting Konrad's and Hemeldonck's call to recognize prostitution as work, or that attacked the 1949 convention on trafficking and prostitution as obsolete, the exporting of the Dutch legalization policy continued.

*The Netherlands Presidency of the European Union*
When the Netherlands assumed the presidency of the European Union in January 1997, it used this opportunity to aggressively move its prostitution policy forward, engineering a European anti-trafficking campaign that made no mention of prostitution. The campaign's first goal was to promote its ideas at an official EU Ministerial Conference hosted by the Dutch presidency of the European Union. Several months prior to the official Ministerial Conference, the Dutch government subsidized an NGO conference that claimed to lay the "democratic" groundwork to export normalization of prostitution.

## Pro–Sex Work Organizing to
## "Inform" the EU Conference of Ministers
In preparation for the EU Ministerial Conference in April 1997, the Dutch government supported organizations that defined prostitution as sex work—the STV, the de Graaf Foundation, and Tampep. Their mission was to organize an NGO conference on trafficking in women that would "inform" the conference of ministers. Prior to the official ministerial meeting, several NGO meetings took place in the Netherlands for this purpose. As the NGO organizers acknowledged, "The Dutch government has taken the initiative to facilitate networking of NGO's [*sic*] in order to organise their lobby and other activities on the European level." Although the network asserted its independence, it acknowledged, "The Dutch government decided to sponsor a conference of NGOs and asked us to organize it."[92]

The "maximum goals" for the NGO conference, known as NOTRAF, included an "NGO campaign for decriminalization of prostitution" and "full rights for all women in all professions and in all traditionally female designated sectors (prostitution, domestic labour, marriage)."[93] The NOTRAF conference was stacked with participants mainly from pro–sex work groups. A hundred subsidized participants, allegedly representing a spectrum of NGO experience and knowledge, were invited.

The list of participating organizations at the NOTRAF conference represented a Who's Who of sex work advocates, including the Red Thread, Anti-Slavery International, La Strada, the Network of Sex Work Projects, Payoke, Europap, Foundation Esperanza, Amnesty for Women, Ban Ying, the International Committee for Prostitutes' Rights, Pro Sentret, Norway, the GAATW, Pag-Asa, and Bliss Without Risk, along with multiple members of the STV, the de Graaf Foundation, Tampep, and members of the Dutch government. The Dutch organizers planned that the invited NGO attendees would form a European NGO network "to position itself amidst the European debate on trafficking in women."[94]

The NOTRAF conference recommendations reflected a strong pro–sex work position. Organizations that were not in sympathy with the Dutch position were few in number. Others either ignorant or neutral about the Dutch prostitution policy were invited possibly because they took no strong policy positions, were potential supporters of the Dutch position, and/or would create no opposition to the dominant pro-prostitution statements and opinion-leaders.[95]

One conference participant from Tampep, Italy, who had formed no opinion about prostitution policy but failed to find the pro–sex work position of the conference convincing, asked why the conference did not emphasize exit programs for women. The response was that the conference was dedicated to discussion about how to address the situation of women *in* prostitution. When she tried to take the question further, she was not recognized.[96]

Most abolitionists who applied to attend the conference received a letter that a "limited budget" did not enable the organizers to invite them immediately, but that they would be placed "high" on a waiting list.[97] Subsequently, they were not invited. Among the hundred invited participants, I could find only two declared opponents of legalization on the list.

Several organizations that did not participate in the conference issued a press release. They denounced "the anti-democratic process of the Dutch NGOs (at the initiative of the STV) who had convened a future European network of NGOs to the exclusion of all others who reject the professionalization of prostitution as an advancement in the liberation of women."[98] These organizations included the International Federation of Human Rights; End Child Prostitution, Pornography and Trafficking (ECPAT); and the international Coalition Against Trafficking in Women.

### Advanced Placement for
### European Funding of Anti-Trafficking Projects

One of the main benefits to organizers and attendees at the NOTRAF conference was its government sponsorship. In addition to being funded by the Dutch government, the conference was supported by key Dutch politicians. For example, European parliament member Nel van Dijk, who was chair of the European Parliament Women's Rights Committee and a key player in supporting the Dutch prostitution policy in the European region, spoke at the conference. The NOTRAF conference resulted in the formation of a European NGO Network against Trafficking, but in favor of legalizing/decriminalizing prostitution and the sex industry.

The conference gave network members advanced placement for the Daphne grants designated for anti-trafficking projects made available in 1997 by the European Commission. Organizations belonging to this network were favored with anti-trafficking and anti-AIDS funding, a portion of which was spent on promoting the view that legalization and decriminalization of the prostitution industry were intrinsic to combating trafficking and the spread of AIDS.

The Daphne grants were awarded to organizations selected through an application process. These grants funded many of the European pro–sex work groups during critical years of national, regional, and international policymaking on prostitution and trafficking. This funding also helped propel these organizations and their representatives into key governmental positions and media forums within Europe and also within the UN. These groups captured the lion's share of the Daphne funding, giving their members an advantage in the hiring process for consultants on trafficking within the European Union. Marjan Wijers was one of the primary beneficiaries of this government sponsorship, who was later employed as a European consultant on trafficking and prostitution policy.

On the other side, most abolitionist groups who applied for Daphne anti-trafficking funds were rejected. These rejections were so widespread that in the year 2004, Marianne Eriksson, Swedish member of the European Parliament, issued her own report and held an EP hearing in which she maintained that the EU is "allocating funds to NGOs whose policies and sources of revenue are not clear and transparent" (see chapter 1, pp. 6–8).[99]

The government conference following the NOTRAF conference was called "The Hague Ministerial Conference on Trafficking." The Hague Ministerial Declaration was instrumental in encouraging funding for European NGO networks to combat trafficking and urged regular cooperation between these networks and the European Commission. It affirmed the "use of existing budget lines for funding actions by NGOs, to combat trafficking in women."[100] This recommendation was followed by a report from the European Parliament Committee on Women's Rights with Dutch MEP Nel van Dijk at the helm. The report reinforced the Hague Ministerial Declaration by urging more funding for European NGOs working against trafficking and enforced prostitution. It bemoaned the paltry support given to NGOs and turned the funding spotlight on La Strada, a major pro–sex work NGO, calling it the most well-known anti-trafficking organization.[101]

Because the Dutch-subsidized European NGO network was the most well-connected and organized applicant, its member organizations benefited both from the report recommendations of the Hague Ministerial Declaration and the in-tandem report of the EP Committee on Women's Rights to fund more anti-trafficking projects. Both governmental reports helped to effectively accredit the pro-prostitution network's future grant applications to the Daphne Initiative and other European grants.

The globalization of NGO funding has proved to be almost the only way that small countries like the Netherlands become prominent on the international stage. The Netherlands has carved out a global role by funding development projects through NGOs in many countries of the global south—funding not given without self-interest in promoting its own policies. As author David Rieff has pointed out in his critique of humanitarian agencies—a critique that can be aptly applied to the Dutch NGOs as they went about exporting Dutch prostitution policy—"It is first necessary to acknowledge the depth of their commitment to defending their own institutional interests, as well as the degree to which that commitment influences the way they conceive of providing help to people in need."[102] More so, the critique appropriately pertains to the Dutch government, as it became the avatar of pro-prostitution policy within the official UN circuit of conferences.

## Pro-prostitution Advocacy at UN World Conferences and with UN Special Rapporteurs on Women

There were two key UN world conferences during the 1990s—in 1993 and 1995—during which the Dutch position on prostitution was in full bloom, and where Dutch NGOs and their allies aggressively promoted Dutch policy. With the appointment in 1994 of Radhika Coomaraswamy as the first UN Special Rapporteur Against Violence Against Women, Dutch pro–sex work organizations were quick to lobby her for support of their positions. Together the UN conferences and the Special Rapporteur's reports took the debate over legalization/decriminalization of prostitution into the official UN sphere, which puts a high premium on how resolutions, declarations, platforms of action, and conventions, called UN instruments, are worded.

Some may think that debates about language are merely debates about words, but statements that emerge from UN conferences have a moral and political force. NGOs and concerned citizens can use these instruments to advocate with their governments, and hold them to commitments they have signed or ratified. Also with these written tools, NGOs can charge governments with not living up to their international obligations.

Language helps shape legal and political reality. UN instruments institutionalize not only the language that is used in future international and national policy but also the reality of what these words signify. It makes a huge difference if commercial sexual exploitation is worded as prostitution or sex work, and if women in prostitution are recognized as workers in, or victims/survivors of, a brutal sex industry. If only forced prostitution is acknowledged as violence against women, it puts the burden on abused women to prove they have been forced. This is a burden almost insurmountable for women in prostitution who have few resources and little ability to fight this legal battle in the criminal justice system against the far greater resources of the pimps and traffickers.

*UN World Conferences*
International UN conferences during this era typically held both governmental and non-governmental (NGO) forums that informed the governmental meetings. Policy positions that emerged from the NGO forums significantly influenced official governmental documents that resulted from these conferences.

UN world conferences of this period began with draft documents. These initial documents were subsequently amended and finalized throughout the governmental part of the UN conference. At the same time that NGOs met in a separate conference, usually held to overlap with the governmental conference, they also lobbied governmental delegates to include their NGO positions and policies in the final document.

In 1993, Dutch advocates and allies promoted their prostitution policy at the UN World Conference on Human Rights held in Vienna. *The Vienna Declaration and Programme of Action* included sexual slavery and trafficking in women as violence against women but avoided any mention of prostitution.[103] More important was the second pivotal UN event—the 1995 Fourth World Women's Conference—held in Beijing, China, and attended by women's NGOs from all over the world.

The formation of a large NGO caucus was important to influencing positions and use of language for the final report that would result from the governmental Beijing meeting because NGO caucuses are more influential with governmental delegates than single organizations. At the Beijing conference, a large group of NGOs organized as the "Women's Human Rights Caucus." Its leaders included Charlotte Bunch from the Center for Women's Global Leadership and Alice Miller from the International Human Rights Law Group—both allied with the pro–sex work position. The influence of the Dutch position on prostitution was illustrated in the very name of a caucus subgroup on violence against women, entitled "Trafficking and Sex Work." Dominated by activists from the Dutch women's groups and their allies, this subgroup lobbied for several key changes in the draft Platform of Action.

The key change the pro–sex work groups pushed for was to delete the word "prostitution" in favor of the words "forced prostitution" as a form of violence against women. They argued that the terminology of prostitution per se contained in the initial draft would increase "the stigmatization and marginalization of women working in prostitution, rather than create an environment in which women in prostitution are assisted with their own empowerment."[104] NGOs such as the STV, the GAATW, and the International Prostitutes Collective, including the Network of Sex Work Projects, were out in full force lobbying for this goal.

Post-conference, the Network of Sex Work Projects announced a victory in Beijing. They alleged, "Working in tandem with the Human Rights Caucus, a handful of representatives from The Network of Sex Work Projects successfully revised the Platform language to distinguish between forced and voluntary prostitution."[105] Their claim was far from correct, however. These groups were not totally successful in inserting the language of "forced prostitution" throughout the final Platform of Action. Especially in the section on Violence Against Women (Section

D), the language of "forced prostitution" and prostitution per se are equally used.[106]

Members of the caucus also called for deletion of any mention of the 1949 *Convention for the Suppression of the Traffic in Persons and of the Exploitation of the Prostitution of Others*. They lost this battle. Paragraph 122 of the final report explicitly calls for the need to review and strengthen implementation of this abolitionist convention.

*The UN Special Rapporteur on Violence Against Women*

UN Special Rapporteurs are "mandate-holders" who theoretically work independently of governments. They can conduct fact-finding visits to countries to investigate their mandate themes, such as violence against women and trafficking in persons, and they report on these themes. They do not receive any payment for their work but receive the assistance of UN personnel who help with drafting their reports.

UN Special Rapporteurs report to the UN Human Rights Commission in Geneva. Their logistical help comes from the Office of the High Commissioner on Human Rights (OHCHR). OHCHR staff is especially instrumental in helping to draft the reports of UN Special Rapporteurs. For many years, the OHCHR appointed anti-trafficking staff assistants and consultants who were sympathetic to pro–sex work policy. The reports of the first UN Special Rapporteur on Violence Against Women, Radhika Coomaraswamy, and, later the second Special Rapporteur on Trafficking, Joy Ngozi Ezeilo, reflect a pro–sex work predisposition, whether in the language used or the policy positions put forth.

In 1995 the Dutch STV wrote a letter to Special Rapporteur Coomaraswamy, which proposed, "Prostitution per se should NOT be included as an issue of violence against women."[107] In 1996 the STV joined with the GAATW in issuing a preliminary report to Rapporteur Coomaraswamy, recommending "full legal status" for women in prostitution, the recognition of women's rights as workers, and the comprehensive decriminalization of prostitution. The STV report also attacked the abolitionist 1949 convention on trafficking and prostitution as "obsolete and ineffective" and called for a new convention that "should focus on coercion and deception."[108]

Special Rapporteur Coomaraswamy issued three reports during the period of her first appointment. These reports affected the debate about prostitution as violence against women vs. prostitution as work. In her first report issued in 1994, the Special Rapporteur seemed influenced by the language proposed by the sex work advocates. Terms such as commercial sex worker (CSW) made their way into her report, and

Coomaraswamy also stated, "Some women become prostitutes through the exercise of 'rational choice.'" She also appeared to support the legalization of prostitution issue with the claim, "Many groups argue that the only way to control and regulate . . . violence is to legalize prostitution. Legislation allows for the enactment of health and labour regimes which would protect the CSW. However, most societies and cultures do not accept this position."[109]

Before her 1996 report on the issue of trafficking and forced prostitution of women, Special Rapporteur Coomaraswamy participated in an international seminar held in Poland hosted by La Strada and organized by the Dutch STV. After this meeting, Coomaraswamy wrote about "The Role of Non-Governmental Organizations" in her third report on Poland. Every good practice on trafficking and prostitution that she spotlighted were those of La Strada; the Centre for the Advancement of Women in Warsaw; the STV in the Netherlands; PAYOKE in Belgium; Tampep in the Netherlands, Germany, Italy, and Austria; and PHOENIX in Berlin—almost all of which favor normalizing prostitution as work.[110]

Nowhere in her 1996 report did the Special Rapporteur commend any feminist organization working to eliminate prostitution and trafficking. This omission was not owing to lack of familiarity with the positions and work of feminist abolitionist organizations. In 1995 the CATW published its own response to the Special Rapporteur's first preliminary report and sent it to her. The CATW report noted with special concern the Special Rapporteur's seeming approval of renaming women in prostitution as "commercial sex workers" and her implication that a significant number of women in prostitution "become prostitutes through the exercise of 'rational choice.'"[111] CATW followed up this report with a personal interview with the Rapporteur Coomaraswamy during the Fourth World Conference on Women in Beijing in 1995.

Also in her 1996 report, the Special Rapporteur called for an evaluation of existing international mechanisms relating to the question of trafficking and prostitution. She singled out the abolitionist 1949 convention but made some mischaracterizations of its provisions, beginning with the statement that it governed the international framework of trafficking and "forced prostitution." In reality, the 1949 convention governs prostitution per se and does not separate prostitution into forced and voluntary, recognizing that prostitution can occur "even with the consent of the victim" (Art. I). The 1949 convention also is firmly opposed to the regulation, registration, or administrative controls imposed on women in prostitution. Coomaraswamy added, "The Convention is also criticized by many groups for criminalizing prostitution."[112] This is not accurate and needs clarification as to what aspects of prostitution are criminalized. The 1949 convention criminalizes the *system* of prostitution (i.e., procuring, enticing, or leading others into prostitution) as well as brothel keeping. However the convention does not criminalize women in prostitution. It is unfortunate that Special Rapporteur Coomaraswamy did not make this important distinction because some pro–sex work advocates make the claim that the 1949 convention criminalizes prostituted women, and that some abolitionists support their criminalization. For example, Aziza Ahmed in her article "Feminism, Power, And Sex Work in the Context of HIV/AIDS" wrongly implies that I am in the category of abolitionist feminists who support a full criminalization regime that includes "criminal sanctions for 'sex workers.'"[113]

Despite the Special Rapporteur's assertion that she took no position on the "two different schools"—abolitionists and pro–sex work regulationists[114]—all the recommendations in her third report to the government of Poland encourage formulating "a national policy . . . to eliminate the problem of forced prostitution and trafficking,"[115] not prostitution per se. The tendency to normalize so-called voluntary prostitution, in the reports of Special Rapporteur Coomaraswamy, was to change with the appointment of a new Special Rapporteur on Trafficking in 2005, who restored the links between trafficking and prostitution, defined prostitution per se as violence against women, and firmly refuted the ideology of prostitution as sex work (see this chapter's conclusion).

## RETURNING TO THE NATIONAL FRONT: THE DUTCH SEX WORK APOLOGISTS

After years of international advocacy for the normalizing of prostitution as sex work, Dutch NGOs returned to the national front to put the final touches on the legalization legislation. The leading NGOs—partners in the vanguard of the campaign for legalization of prostitution in the Netherlands—were the Mr. A. de Graaf Foundation, the Red Thread, and the STV. All had been active in organizing the pro–sex work European network of NGOs allied with Dutch prostitution policy, discussed earlier in this chapter.

## The Mr. A. de Graaf Foundation

The oldest organization supporting the normalization of prostitution in the Netherlands was the Mr. A. de Graaf Foundation. Described as the Dutch national center for research, documentation, public information, policy development, and advice relating to prostitution issues,[116] the foundation was credited with inspiring the legalization legislation. It also has been described as a semi-governmental organization with at least 70 percent of its funding coming from the state.[117] Originally a major supporter of the 1911 abolitionist legislation in the Netherlands, it changed its colors in the 1970s and began a comprehensive campaign to prepare public opinion "for the juridical recognition of prostitution as merely another 'official occupation.'"[118]

The de Graaf Foundation put forward the controversial claim that "the 'classical type' of brothel-keeper, i.e., someone who buys and who sells women, *no longer exists*."[119] Although a controversial claim, there was no controversy. Within the police, women's magazines, and popular TV shows, the foundation was very successful in engineering its ideological position that women's "protectors" were not the violent pimps and brothel owners of days gone by. They also sold the view that prostitution is not sexual exploitation, and women in prostitution are regular workingwomen who fulfill a needed social function. Sympathetically presented in the Dutch press, this view encountered no major voices who publicly disputed it.[120]

When the age of AIDS began to dawn in the 1980s, the de Graaf Foundation became a foremost beneficiary of prostitution-related AIDS funding. The Dutch Ministry of Health funded its research, which heralded the harm reduction approach.[121] Harm reduction programs, unlike harm elimination programs, assume that there is a "safe" amount of harm that can be tolerated and limited, and those who experience the harm can reduce the risks if, for example, they use condoms or practice safe sex.

However, it is usually those with a stake in a risky business who generally promote harm reduction programs,[122] using, for example, the terminology of safe coal, safe nuclear energy, and safe cigarettes. In the case of prostitution, safe sex programs promote the rights of pimps and brothel owners. Safe sex advocates too often need the approval of pimps and brothel owners to enter the prostitution venues, whose permission might require that these advocates ignore the presence of children in the brothels or not influence the women to leave. Safe sex programs are like gun locks in gun safety programs. They provide minimal harm, but they don't eliminate the source of it. A more integral public health response would be to advocate for the health and safety of women in the sex industry, at the same time that the response makes clear it opposes the sex industry.[123]

The de Graaf Foundation supported a court case brought to the European Court in 2001 that sought to grant prostituted women from non-EEA countries the right to "work" in the Netherlands as long as they are self-employed and possess the legal residence permit. It joined the Red Thread and the brothel owners in "facilitating" the lawsuit of three non-EEA women who were in prostitution in the Netherlands. The Red Thread, allegedly representing the women in prostitution, initially took the Dutch government to court. Jan Visser, who worked with both the de Graaf Foundation and the Red Thread, explained the strategy. "Brothel owners were keen on letting these women [non-EEA women] work in the windows. So *they stimulated and facilitated the women to challenge the Dutch government* by taking it to court and the brothel owners provided them with a professional organisation, business plans and bookkeepers."[124] Together, the de Graaf Foundation and the Red Thread fronted for the Dutch brothel owners who won the right to regularize the legal status of women from other countries in the brothels.

Visser, de Graaf, the Red Thread, and the brothel owners hid behind the prostituted women put forward allegedly to defend the rights of foreign-born women to work in the brothels but in truth defending the rights of the owners. This decision set the stage for the discourse of "migration for sex work" and "facilitated migration" that came to replace human trafficking in many forums.

The Mr. A. de Graaf foundation closed its doors in 2004 when its funding was reduced by the Dutch government and considered the prostitution policy issue resolved.

## The Red Thread and the Prostitution Information Center

The Red Thread defines itself as an organization of independent, self-determining women in prostitution, i.e., "sex workers." Founded in 1985, the Red Thread became a media attraction, especially earning much publicity after two international "whores' congresses" held in the Netherlands. It became the authority on prostitution and claimed to speak from experience about the alleged need to legalize prostitution in order to protect the interests of "sex workers." The Red Thread dismissed the view that women in prostitution were victims, romanticized them as agents of their own destiny, and defended the employment rights of women in prostitution, arguing that they should have the same rights as persons in other occupations. It reminded the public and governmental committees to pay attention to these rights by including "sex workers" within the labor market and improving their "conditions of employment."

The Red Thread was 100 percent government-subsidized for many years,[125] until the government reduced its funding. To further its goal of professionalization of "sex workers," the Red Thread founded the Red School, a place where newcomers to the "profession" could receive training from an experienced woman in prostitution, hone their prostitution proficiencies, and develop pursuits such as erotic introduction of condoms into the act of sex. This school was later taken over by the closely allied Prostitution Information Center. For many years, the center conducted courses including "how to" instructions for becoming "sex workers" and/or strippers. Along with techniques on how to satisfy a customer, the course discussed personal and financial issues, such as leading double lives and filing tax returns.[126]

Beginning in 2006 the Prostitution Information Center sponsored an "open house day" in the red-light area of Amsterdam to counteract the city's concerns about the increasing crime, corruption, and exploitation in the window brothels. Tourists got a free look at the sex clubs, windows, and peep shows, with hundreds of eager visitors entering the premises and talking with the women. One erotic dancer gushed, "It is especially interesting for women [sic]. If they learn what we do here they will realize it is not a big deal if their husbands or boyfriends want to come here."[127]

After the closing of the tolerance zones, the Red Thread continued to defend the zones as sanctuaries for "sex workers." Critics viewed them as sacrifice zones where women could be exploited under the watchful eyes of police and social workers. In 2003, before the Amsterdam City Council closed its prostitution tolerance zone, both the Red Thread and the de Graaf Foundation protested. Marieke van Doornick of the de Graaf Foundation claimed that the closures would not solve the zone's problems. The Red Thread maintained, "The street zone was safe because clients were not allowed to take women away from the patrolled area."[128] Both organizations seemed unconcerned about the presence in the zones of prostituted children, drug-addicted women, and victims of trafficking, who could be "safely abused" there. Nor did they seem bothered by the dominance of criminals who, most of all, enjoyed safe haven.

When the Amsterdam City Council closed the window brothels in the prostitution district, the Red Thread supported Charles Geerts, the main brothel operator allegedly allied with organized crime in the area, who owned most of the windows that were shuttered. The message of the Red Thread proclaimed, "You have pimps and businessmen, and Geerts is a businessman. . . . We never had a problem with him."[129] The major "sex worker" organization in the Netherlands defended a man quite clearly linked with organized crime, drugs, and pimping. The Red Thread went even further: "The more brothels there are, the less exploitation there is."[130] It claimed more brothels give women more choices and help them avoid the more dangerous venues.

The Red Thread and the Prostitution Information Center joined the suspected criminals in charging that the closures were a "crusade against prostitution." The Prostitution Information Center also attributed the anxiety about the red-light area to a Dutch "fear of migrants."[131]

In the aftermath of the brothel closures, former mayor Cohen announced that a ban on pimping was necessary; it was the next step in preventing exploitation and human trafficking in the red-light district. Ignoring the fact that many of the "legal pimps" sanctioned by law as legitimate third-party agents continue to use force, deception, exploitation, and violence, the Red Thread saw no need for a pimping ban, arguing that pimping is already illegal.

Ironically, in 2006 at the same time it was protesting the brothel closures, the Red Thread released a report about the Dutch brothels, essentially stating that the situation in the brothels was appalling. Its conclusion: the brothel operators dominate women in all areas; many women in the brothels are independent entrepreneurs only on paper; still too many women live where they perform sexual activities so they are completely dependent on the operators; there are brothels where grave abuses prevail; and slavery-like conditions permeate many prostitution businesses.[132]

Although the Red Thread specified the situation was worse before legalization, its incriminatory report of the brothels put side by side with its protest against the brothel closures in Amsterdam seems schizophrenic. Reading the report's conclusions, it is difficult to understand why the Red Thread and other Dutch organizations insist that the remedy is better labor rights and "workplace" improvements—not the re-criminalization of both legal and illegal pimping and of brothels and brothel keeping. Additionally, the website of the Red Thread is very explicit about a system of legalization that is more abstract than real. "On paper it looks good. But unfortunately the Dutch authorities just changed the law and never thought of the practical consequences of this law. Most sexworkers don't even know where [*sic*] the new law is about.[133]

## The Foundation Against Trafficking (STV)

The STV's legislative agenda is clear from its mission statement: "Officially set up in 1987, STV's first campaigns were aimed at developing and refining national legislation and litigation for addressing trafficking in women."[134] For many years, Marjan Wijers worked with the STV writing policy, coordinating with the governmental women's policy group and speaking in public forums. Subsequently she assumed the role of senior stateswoman as chair of the European Commission's Expert Group on Trafficking in Human Beings. Perhaps no pro-prostitution advocate has benefited more from leading Dutch prostitution policy initiatives than Wijers, who today holds an influential policy consultant position within the EU sector.[135]

Wijers has criticized the recent trend in the Netherlands that views the legalization legislation as a mistake. She looks upon this trend as harmful and as fulfilling "ancient stereotypes." "In the present political climate prostitutes are often pictured as poor victims or ill women. As women who need to be saved."[136] She disregards the well-documented harmful conditions in the window brothels. Nor does she acknowledge that women are the victims of unscrupulous and violent pimps and traffickers who continue to be dignified as legal entrepreneurs. She describes the closure of the Amsterdam window brothels as a "missed opportunity" for the city to "make a statement" supporting the women in prostitution. Wijers maintained that instead of giving the space to artists and painters, the city should have allocated the space to women who "really work independently."[137] Given the paucity of women who actually do "work" independently and the prevalence of pimp control eight years after the legalization legislation took effect, this seems an irresponsible or naive response.

Marjan Wijers and the STV—along with the Red Thread and the Prostitution Information Center—bear major responsibility for helping to preserve the Netherlands as a prostitution nation. A major mission of the STV was to *democratize* prostitution and the sex industry throughout Europe and the world and embed legalized prostitution within communities as normal work. During this critical period, it transformed the dehumanization of women into voluntary labor and minimized the real abuse of women from other countries who were likely trafficked by defining them as migrants for sex work, whose travel had been facilitated by helpful agents.

## EXPLOITATION OF CHILDREN IN PROSTITUTION IN THE NETHERLANDS

A major goal of the prostitution legislation was to reduce child sexual exploitation, thus separating the women from the children, disregarding the fact that many women in prostitution begin as children. On the day these girls turn eighteen, prostitution does not suddenly become a choice. Supporters of legalization claimed that by focusing on forced prostitution and legalizing voluntary prostitution, the police would be freer to crack down on the sexual exploitation of young girls and boys.

In the year 2000 almost 20 percent of prostituted women interviewed by researchers from the Netherlands Institute for Social Sexological Research said they began in prostitution as minors.[138] Many had been pimped into prostitution by so-called lover boys. Originally lured by these boys into a romantic and sexual relationship and often lavished with attention and gifts, the girls found themselves induced into having sex with the boys' friends and then forced into prostitution.

In 2002 the police reported that 25 percent of all human trafficking investigations involved underage victims.[139] It was noted that these figures may well have been higher because distinguishing underage status when victims have false identity papers is difficult.[140] In 2006 the Dutch National Rapporteur reported, "There was a striking increase in the number of registered under-age victims, particularly in the age group from 15 to 17 years."[141]

Police think that child trafficking occurs mostly for child sexual exploitation. A UNICEF Netherlands 2004 report maintained, "The largest group of vulnerable children are found in the reception and help centres for asylum seekers."[142] Many child traffickers target unaccompanied child asylum seekers who sometimes disappear to unknown destinations. Another category of victims is "supervised solitary asylum-seeking minors." These children often end up inadequately supervised and thus vulnerable to exploitation in the sex industry. Many are found on the illegal circuit or street, rendering them more at risk of being trafficked.[143]

So-called lover boys are very active in recruiting girls, seasoning them for prostitution *before* they turn eighteen. The Daalder report acknowledged, "The process of humiliation and sexual abuse had often already taken place before the girl involved turned eighteen."[144] This "underage" and "private" sexual abuse enables the lover boys to turn the girls out immediately for public prostitution abuse when they reach the legal age of eighteen. The report also stated, "There are indications that girls are forced to start working as prostitutes the moment they turn eighteen."[145]

Using techniques of seduction, these young pimps, many who come from the girls' own countries such as Morocco, Turkey, or Surinam, look for vulnerable young women and then pretend to be their lovers. The lover boys keep constant watch over their victims, their homes, and especially the window brothels where the young women are placed, which are ready-made locations for observation.

Whether there is a direct link between the legalization legislation and the prevalence of child prostitution is difficult to prove. One thing is clear, however. The Netherlands, like other countries, has a culture of commercial child sexual abuse. The difference in the Netherlands is an influential lobby of pedophile networks that fosters the Dutch culture of prostitution.[146] These pedophile networks spread the message that children can consent to sexual activity with adults—actually a convenient excuse for the fantasies and behavior of the child sexual abusers.

The Netherlands may be the only country in the world with a political party dedicated to promoting pedophilia. In 2006 a Hague court ruled that the Party for Brotherly Love, Freedom and Diversity (PVNVD), which had launched a campaign for abolishing the minimum age of sexual consent and for lifting the ban on child pornography, had the right to exist. Founder of the PVNVD Norbert de Jonge said that other goals of the party were to gain at least one seat in the Parliament and the passage of a law that makes it legal for children to have sex with adults.[147] In a media interview, de Jonge was asked what should be the legal age of consent. He promised that the PVNVD would work for an age of twelve, but that this was only the first step. "A minimum age of consent does not make sense at all. . . . Others may wish to experiment (sexually) at the age of 10."[148]

In the press, the pedophile lobby promotes the right of children to sexual self-determination, acting as if it's a lobby for child rights. "Children must have the freedom to make sexual contact with adults,"[149]—a transparent reversal of its ideology that adults must have the freedom and the legal impunity to make sexual contact with children. A planned demonstration against the pedophile party yielded few demonstrators.

In 2001 a Child Rights Information Network (CRIN) *Report on the Sexual Exploitation of Children* cited Interpol and Dutch police statements that the Netherlands played a leading role in creating and sustaining pedophile networks in Europe. "The fact that many foreign paedophiles choose the Netherlands as a residence, because of its tolerance towards 'different-natured' makes it quite possible that 10,000 paedophiles are sexually active in the Netherlands."[150]

Internationally there has been Dutch pedophile involvement in private pedophile hotels and resorts in the Philippines, Sri Lanka, and Brazil, where child sexual abusers either own the venues or are traditionally welcomed. After the breakup of Soviet-bloc countries, Dutch pedophiles also started their own sex resorts in Romania and Poland.[151] These networks make pornography of child sexual abuse and are often involved in the child sex trade, with the Netherlands also being a transit country for children trafficked to Europe from Eastern Europe and other countries.

The Netherlands government has protected child pornographers in Brazil where Dutch pedophile networks have been operative at least since the 1990s. In 2004 the Dutch consulate in Rio de Janeiro facilitated the speedy exit of two convicted child pornographers by supplying them with emergency passports to leave the country. The case was discovered by a TV program conducting an investigation into Dutch sex tourists who used cheap flights to Brazil, where they engaged in the sexual abuse of children. The Netherlands Foreign Ministry was forced to acknowledge that these men should never have been given passports to leave Brazil, and the consulate should never have enabled them.[152]

The information on children in prostitution, child trafficking, and child sexual abuse in pornography and the increasing influence of a pedophile lobby powerfully repudiate the Dutch claim that legalization of prostitution helps protect children from sexual abuse. The 2004 UNICEF Netherlands report addresses this conclusion when it states, "It is not clear whether the lifting of the general ban on brothels really has led to a better protection of minors than was previously the case."[153]

## CONCLUSION

The Dutch prostitution legislation creates the illusion of fighting sexual exploitation by branding the "good" part of prostitution as voluntary and the "bad" part of it as forced. Its deceptive policy is to fight trafficking while making "voluntary" prostitution normal. The Netherlands subsidizes anti-trafficking initiatives worldwide, offering financial support to many NGOs in developing countries at the same time that it legally supports a growing prostitution industry that mainly exploits women from some of these same poorer countries. It acts as if its legal prostitution industry has no effect on the rampant sex trafficking found in both its legal and illegal prostitution venues.

Sigma Huda, the UN Special Rapporteur on Trafficking in Persons from 2005 to 2008 has written, "State parties with legalized prostitution regimes have a heavy responsibility to ensure that the conditions which actually pertain to the practice of prostitution within their borders are free from the illicit means . . . so as to ensure that their legalized prostitution regimes are not simply perpetuating widespread and systematic trafficking." The former special rapporteur maintains that legalized prostitution states "are far from satisfying this obligation."[154]

This chapter has provided evidence of the Netherlands' failure to satisfy its obligation that prostitution as practiced in the country does not promote trafficking and other forms of sexual exploitation, even by the country's own limited standard of forced prostitution. The lifting of the ban on brothels and pimping has facilitated the presence of organized crime even in the legal sex industry to the extent that the major tolerance zones and a large part of the window brothels in Amsterdam have been closed down. Who would have predicted within a period of eight years that the legalized situation would so deteriorate that the Netherlands is now considering a partial ban on purchasing sexual activities?

For years, abolitionists have recorded findings relating to the exploitation of women in the prostitution venues, the prevalence of trafficking and child prostitution, and the pervasiveness of organized crime in the Dutch prostitution sector. Various journalists have written articles describing the failings of the Dutch legislation since its onset in 2000. These "unofficial" findings were followed by official reports documenting the terrible conditions for women that exist in the Dutch legal brothels in the grip of criminals.

In the aftermath of these dismal failures, the Dutch government in 2008 proposed a series of amendments to the prostitution legislation: all women in prostitution venues must be registered, licensed, and twenty-one years of age; buyers would be penalized for use of unregistered and unlicensed women (it's not clear if buyers would also be penalized for use of unregistered and unlicensed venues); municipalities would be allowed to forbid prostitution altogether within their city limits; more exit opportunities would be provided to women who want them; and implementation and enforcement efforts and personnel would be increased.[155] As of March 2013, Parliament had not passed the Prostitution Framework Act containing these amendments.

These amendments simply tweak the legislation and are part of a dispiriting effort to rehabilitate the Dutch legalized prostitution system. The proposed new regulations are of the same old order. Despite evidence to the contrary, the government adheres to its self-generated myth that its prostitution policy is pragmatic and tolerant; that enough women are in the brothels voluntarily; and that pimps and prostitution users are or can be responsible "partners" of the government as it works to assess and refine its prostitution policy. Credible and official reports highlight the difficulty in distinguishing between forced and voluntary prostitution. Yet this distinction continues to be the foundation of the Dutch prostitution legislation. How can a foundation that is not stable hold up the regulatory edifice of the prostitution regime?

Instead of drawing a line between forced and voluntary prostitution, the Netherlands could be a nation that erases this line, a line that continues to normalize violence against women by relying on this dubious boundary. It reminds this American author of the policy line drawn by the Bush administration governing torture of suspected terrorists that separated "mere infliction of pain and suffering" from "severe pain and suffering." The Dutch standard of forced prostitution seems premised on "severe pain and suffering"—not the "mere infliction of pain and suffering." Yet, in the legal brothels, many authorities fail to recognize even the "severe pain and suffering" inflicted on women.

If the forced/free line is difficult to detect and enforce in the brothels of the Netherlands, as evidenced in the Amsterdam brothel closures, the Daalder report, and the National Police Service report, why continue to build further regulations on it? The perennial problem for the Dutch prostitution regime is this porous and indefensible line.

# 4

---

# Economic Development or Economic Opportunism? Trafficking, Migration, and the Military-Prostitution Complex

To its buyers and sellers, the sex trade is just another business.
—The Economist, *"Giving the Customer What He Wants"*

Prostitution has become an economic development policy encouraging both rich and poor countries to take advantage of its economic benefits. Chapter 4 examines how the pragmatic version of prostitution as just another business, in which its entrepreneurs vie not only for profits but also for social and political respectability, has stripped prostitution of any understanding other than one of economic exchange.

UN agencies and international NGOs have called for the legalization and decriminalization of prostitution to allegedly protect the women. In fact, the aim of some governments is to profit from the growing revenues of the sex sector by capturing it within the state's taxation net. Because the sex industry flourishes in times and places of both economic booms and busts, demand for the sex of prostitution does not decline during recessions. The hazards that prostituted women are subjected to, however, become greater because prostitution users can demand more risky and violent sex.

The Netherlands and Australia are examples of prostitution economies—states that have built a percentage of their economy on income from prostitution. The Australian and New Zealand Standard Industrial Classification (ANZSIC) rated "sexual services" as the most productive of the "personal service" industries, earning 80 percent of all the personal service revenue in Australia.[1] Korea, in contrast, is an example of what a government can do to challenge membership in the emerging prostitution economies. Even in the face of a 1 percent GDP decline after the Korean government announced a zero-tolerance approach to prostitution in 2004, Korea held fast to its law penalizing the buyers and enacted more stringent penalties for pimps and brothel owners. Most significantly, it increased its budget to provide services for women in prostitution.

One approach used to promote prostitution economies is by endorsing unions for women in prostitution. "Sex worker unions" have primarily taken hold in Europe. This issue has been a clincher for sex work advocates and their allies who argue that "sex workers" are entitled to the same rights as other workers. However, in the Netherlands, Germany, and Australia, where unions have been proposed or enacted, very few women register because they don't want any public record made of their prostitution.

Sex work advocates have maintained that women in prostitution are financially motivated, meaning that they do not turn to prostitution out of financial desperation or lack of other economic options. Instead they are viewed as economically rational beings that allegedly weigh the various costs and benefits of their economic activities and hire agents who will help them. Sex work advocates reject that "sex workers" are more coerced than workers who choose other low-paying jobs.

The economic rationalism model, however, does not take into account the economic exploitation of prostituted women who see their money quickly disappear in a steady stream of diversion of earnings into drugs, alcohol, pimps, drivers, and other so-called protectors. What has been needed in this debate about women's economic status in prostitution is an evidence-based study that documents how women truly fare financially in prostitution. Linda DeRiviere's 2006 survey, discussed later in this chapter, estimates the lifelong costs of young Canadian women leaving prostitution in which she quantifies the specific diversions of a woman's income over her years in prostitution and measures both her direct and indirect losses. These "human capital costs" of prostitution debunk the economic rationalism model propounded by sex industry advocates.

Chapter 4 also looks at the role of prostitution colonialism and how it has contributed to the promotion of modern sex sectors in developing countries. U.S. prostitution colonialism, especially during the Philippine-American War, created the model for the U.S. military–prostitution complex in all parts of the world. This system of prostitution, adopted from European regulationist methods and enforced under Gen. Arthur MacArthur, assured U.S. soldiers certified sexual

access to Filipinas and at the same time became an intrinsic part of colonial practice in Cuba and Puerto Rico.

The integration of military colonialism and prostitution shaped the
twentieth-century military-prostitution complex in post–World War II
Japan, where the U.S. occupation government colluded in a "contemporary comfort women" system to sexually service U.S. troops. With
full knowledge of Japan's appalling conscription of women into military sexual slavery during World War II, General Douglas MacArthur's
military government officially sanctioned a similar system of brothels
in Japan. These brothels were populated with some of the same Asian
women who had been handed down by the Japanese troops to the American military brothels, along with thousands of other Japanese women
who were told they were serving their country. The U.S. military–
prostitution complex continued in the Philippines and was also enacted
in Korea and, later, in Vietnam. In all these countries, it provided the
sex tourism infrastructure that took hold after the military either exited
or the bases were closed down.

Not only has the globalization of the sex industry but also the globalization of sex industry advocacy contributed to sexual exploitation
worldwide. The silence of many human rights advocates about the prostitution debate has given permission to scores of men, including human
rights defenders who visit developing countries as part of their work, to
abuse poor women in prostitution from the global south. The globalization of sex work advocacy affirms that trafficked and prostituted women
are simply economic migrants who are part of the global migration
economy. This explanation, in its extreme form, becomes the "myth of
trafficking" in which its advocates stereotype anti-trafficking laws as restricting women's international freedom of movement and as criminalizing women's migration. In examining the links and disjunctions between
migration and trafficking, chapter 4 argues that the "myth of trafficking" is itself a myth. Globalization of the sex industry and globalization
of sex industry advocacy have helped to create the huge transnational
business of prostitution.

In 1998 the *Economist* laid out a framework for prostitution as simply
another market enterprise, arguing that although the sex industry traditionally has been seen as the sleazy side of the entertainment industry, it
is highly lucrative and thus worthy of professionalization.[2] This chapter
tells that story, rationalized as economic opportunity for women, for sex
entrepreneurs and for nations. The other story—the principled story
about prostitution—hopefully will aid in understanding why what is rationalized as economic opportunity is in fact economic opportunism.

## THE PRAGMATIC STORY OF PROSTITUTION:
## JUST ANOTHER BUSINESS

Framed as pragmatism, as opposed to moralism, the market model of prostitution is presented as "sexual services" or as part of the entertainment industry. In this version globalization has expanded international sex tourism, and the Internet has facilitated various "sexual adventures." It is said that hundreds of thousands of women and children are moving (not "being moved") from country to country, aided by "people-movers," in search of something better than what they can access at home. Increasingly, they enter the sex industry. It is said that women from other countries drive down the prices of prostitution in Western countries. Thus, it becomes a buyer's market, and the customer fulfills his sexual fantasy of purchasing a suitable exotic woman at a cheap price. A booming sex industry is said to deserve market capitalization.

At the same time that women from poorer countries are increasingly being enslaved in the sex industry, thousands of men are traveling to countries as sex tourists. In 2012 during the economic crisis in Spain, it was reported that prostitution was branching out into small towns as well as big cities. The boom was fueled by hordes of young men who arrived in packs for the weekend, traveling on cheap airfares available in Europe. The growing demand for prostitution came largely from younger-aged men who view the brothels as simply another form of the entertainment business.[3]

The free market prostitution exponents might offer a few caveats to their economic rationalism model of prostitution. Sometimes they acknowledge that the sex trade gets brutal, and the sex entrepreneurs (pimps and traffickers) cut costs by abusing women and forcing them into debt bondage. Various mafias and organized crime minions have a particularly bad reputation for violence and cruelty, they admit. These offenses are treated as aberrations, and the proposed solution is to regulate and make legal the sex trade. A businesslike response to "price pressure" and "global competition" is to go "upmarket." "Upscale prostitution is safer: customers may be nicer; hotels offer more protection than a pimp (they have their reputation to protect) and take a smaller cut."[4] The free market exponents add that going upmarket would allow sex entrepreneurs to find niche markets, perhaps fetish pornography or prostitution, or the pornography or prostitution of pregnant women. What really makes money is building a brand.

There is also a self-defined feminist position defending market prostitution. Wendy McElroy, representing what she calls the individualist school of feminism, states, "Prostitution is a combination of sex and the free market. Which one are you against?"⁵ One understands the slippery slope of this viewpoint with a change in wording: "Child labor is a combination of children and the free market. Which one are you against?"

The free market proponents emphasize that prostitution is not merely an exchange of sexual favors; it is an economic exchange. Individualist feminists champion the free market as well as a woman's self-ownership of her body, along with the choice to use it as a commodity. In this feminist free market view of prostitution, men are given the right to consume women and women the right to be consumed. In the name of equality, prostitution is recast as a form of self-ownership and self-empowerment.

## A Campaign for Political and Economic Respectability

One way in which sex industries seek increased legitimacy, credibility, and market share is by contributing money to politicians and good causes. In promoting its economic interests, the sex industry has found its political voice lobbying legislators and becoming a contributor to liberal and progressive causes—for example, to prevent HIV/AIDS, the very problem that the sex industry has helped to create. In all these campaigns, the sex industry touts not its own economic interests but the benefits of "sex work" for women.

From *Playboy* awarding grants to women's reproductive rights' organizations to Craigslist donating to anti-trafficking organizations, the duplicity is overwhelming. Many women's groups have not been fooled by the hypocrisy of this corporate tactic. And dozens of anti-trafficking groups protested the Craigslist ads, arguing that they promoted the sexual exploitation of women and children who were offered for sale on the site.

The Center for Women's Development in San Francisco gave one of the most courageous rebuffs to Craigslist. As the site was coming under criticism for its barely disguised online prostitution and trafficking ads, the San Francisco center received an unsolicited check of $100,000 from Craigslist. The letter that accompanied the donation stated the money could not be used to influence any sort of legislation or propaganda against Craigslist. In a ceremony saying it would not profit "from a place of exploitation of girls," the Center for Women's Development burned the check. As an organization of women who grew up poor, its members knew that their likelihood of receiving another big grant would be slim. "But it was a chance to stand up for what we believe in and say we won't be easily bought."[6]

Legal brothels in Nevada have sought political legitimacy through voluntary taxation offers. Although legal brothels pay licensing fees, they have never been taxed. In 2005 they expressed their willingness to pay taxes to the state, allegedly to demonstrate their model citizenship but in reality to ease their access into the advertising market. The Nevada Brothel Association of twenty-eight legal brothels licensed in ten of the state's counties agreed that paying taxes will make them good neighbors but, more to the point, ultimately help them to lift the ban on advertising. Thus, they can use billboards, the yellow pages in phone books, and other media to flaunt their services more openly and attract a larger customer base.[7]

Respectability campaigns are not a new tactic used by the sex industry. For many years, sex entrepreneurs have tried to become upstanding citizens by not only contributing to select political campaigns but also by enlisting prominent politicians and celebrities in their cause to normalize prostitution. In 1974 COYOTE staged the First Annual Hookers Ball in San Francisco attended by VIPs such as then state legislator Willie Brown and the San Francisco sheriff. Seeking further respectability, COYOTE garnered support from local and national celebrities including Governor Jerry Brown, psychiatrist Karl Menninger, and Jane Fonda.[8] With this kind of support, COYOTE achieved its goal of early success and growth.

Prostitution entrepreneurs continue to lobby legislators and support their political candidacies in order to remove legal impediments to their sex businesses. There are vast commercial interests in polishing the image of the sex industry, in cleaning up or hiding its exploitation, in gaining respectability, and in entering the economic mainstream. Victoria, Australia, first listed a brothel on a national stock exchange when the Daily Planet started trading publicly on May 3, 2003.[9] In Australia the sex industry has its own political party called the Sex Party, which lobbies for full decriminalization of prostitution in the country free from any government intervention.[10]

From 1998 through 2004, the *Economist* published at least four articles putting prostitution on its global economic agenda. The *Economist* framework in articulating a prostitution economy concludes with this advice: "Wise governments will accept that paid sex is ineradicable, and concentrate on keeping the business clean, safe and inconspicuous."[11]

How a business that wants to advertise its offerings succeeds by being "inconspicuous" is anyone's guess, and in countries that have already legalized or regulated prostitution there is nothing shy or retiring about the sex industry. For example, advertisements line the highways of Victoria offering women as objects for sexual use and teaching new generations of men and boys to treat women as subordinates. Businessmen are encouraged to hold their corporate meetings in strip clubs where owners supply naked women on the club tables at tea breaks and lunchtime.[12]

## THE PRINCIPLED STORY ABOUT PROSTITUTION

Undergirding the rational narrative that sex is simply another emerging market is the very irrational refrain that prostitution is inevitable. Ironically, market pragmatism is founded on an essentialist foundation of prostitution's inevitability. Zurich City councilor Claudia Nielsen, cited in chapter 1, stated, *"It is very pragmatic: what we can't change we have to live with."*[13]

The pragmatic story of prostitution is of one controlled by a benevolent sex industry in which pimps, traffickers, and brothel owners protect their "employees" and are monitored through a regulatory regime. In this narrative, the law regulates pimping and purchasing women, and all that follows is fine. It's a simple fable, promoted by witting and unwitting advocates, including journalists, academics, and NGOs. It preaches salvation through regulation. It's a solution that claims to reduce the risks to women—not eliminate them. Most of the time, it fails even to reduce those risks.

The principled story tells how the sex industry blurs the line between pornography and entertainment, between prostitution and sexual freedom, and how it has become successful in representing its sexual abuse as sexual pleasure. Market forces are determining expansive aspects of human life to the extent that when people speak of something having a value, they often mean an economic value. It has become possible to turn almost every human activity into a market exchange. As Robert Bellah has argued, "All the primary relationships in our society . . . are being stripped of any moral understanding other than market exchange."[14] Supporting prostitution on economic grounds commodifies women by conflating women's rights with market rights.

Trafficking markets ensure not only the future of a sex industry but also "the future of organized crime." In country after country, prostitution networks from Eastern Europe, indentured labor in the Gulf States, and migration gangs out of China constitute what Misha Glenny has called "gangsters without borders," where these criminals are penetrating markets around the globe.[15]

## PROSTITUTION AS ECONOMIC DEVELOPMENT POLICY FOR POOR WOMEN IN POOR COUNTRIES AND IN POOR ECONOMIC TIMES

> As sex is a human need and prostitution is here to stay, we should think about a proactive and realistic approach to deal with the situation. Therefore, I would suggest to pay more attention to sustainable prostitution (SP) in order to transform inevitable prostitution into a more responsible and beneficial industry. . . . Clearly, SP can be a miracle agent for sustained economic growth in the Third World. . . . Under properly planned and managed conditions, SP has the potential to make positive contributions to community development and environmental protection. Most importantly, it can also empower poor and underprivileged women. In its ideal form, SP can create jobs and income, boost foreign exchange, disperse benefits to rural areas, and generate funds for public purposes such as education, health care, preservation of culture and nature.
> —*Anita Pleumarom, "A Sustainable World Through Prostitution,"* The Nation, *Bangkok*

These words were written as a tongue-in-cheek commentary about "sustainable prostitution." Although the author intended them to be a satire on the commodification of sustainable development ideas where "it has become possible to turn virtually every development activity into an environmentally friendly venture," these words in a more tedious style could have been penned by the International Labor Organization (ILO).

Economic policies promoted since the 1980s by international lending organizations such as the World Bank and the International Monetary Fund have mandated "structural adjustments," more recently called austerity programs, in many developing regions of the world. Within the last thirty-five years especially, these policies have pushed certain countries to export persons, including large numbers of women, for labor (the Philippines), making them vulnerable to trafficking; or to develop economies based on tourism (Thailand), with a huge dependence on sex tourism. When structural adjustments or austerity programs are imposed on countries by international monetary agencies, countries are forced to continually reduce or withdraw state support for public services like health, education, and social welfare. The burden of providing these services shifts mainly to women who must supply these services, work harder, or migrate overseas for family survival under worsening economic conditions. Traffickers move into this gap.

Since the economic development policies of many countries are locked into repaying foreign debt, certain countries encourage their citizens to leave the country for work so that the payments, which workers send back to families, can stimulate and stabilize the economy with hard currency. In 1995, 15.3 percent of the Philippine labor force (or an estimated 4.2 million women and men) migrated for labor, making the Philippines the largest Asian exporter of labor. During the 1990s, two thousand overseas contract workers left the Philippines each day, with women constituting 60 percent of these legal migrants.[16] In later years, on several occasions, I witnessed the long lines of mostly women being legally processed one by one as they left Manila, as well as groups of Filipinas returning during holidays from Hong Kong laden with packages for relatives. Traffickers who have set up private employment agencies recruit many of these women into sex industries.

This is the international version of the pragmatic story of prostitution. Developing countries should reap its economic benefits, rather than treat the sex industry like an outcast. International equality of opportunity and nondiscriminatory globalization policies uncritically integrate prostitution into economic development plans. What developed economies consume so should developing economies. Perhaps the most controversial articulation of prostitution as a development strategy for poor countries came from a 1998 report published by the ILO. Entitled "The Sex Sector: The Economic and Social Bases of Prostitution in Southeast Asia," the report called for economic recognition of the sex industry and spotlighted its economic contribution to the gross domestic products of Indonesia, Malaysia, the Philippines, and Thailand.

The ILO report argued that the revenues from a recognized and regulated sex sector could be put to good financial use by the state and allow governments to control the criminal side of the sex industry; it was effectively calling upon governments to cash in on the booming profits of the industry by taxing and regulating prostitution as a legitimate job. The report further argued that because the sex industry contributes directly and indirectly to jobs, national income, and economic growth, developing countries especially cannot ignore this economic infusion and simply consider the welfare of "individual prostitutes."[17] Recognition of the sex sector would include extending labor rights and benefits to "sex workers," improving "working conditions" in the industry, and "extending the taxation net to cover many of the lucrative activities connected with it."[18] Although the ILO report claimed to stop short of advocating legalization of prostitution, the economic recognition of the sex sector that it promotes could not occur without legal acceptance of the industry.

Another UN agency calling for the decriminalization of prostitution in developing countries has been the World Health Organization (WHO). Arguing from both a public health and an economic development framework, WHO Beijing coordinator Zhao Pengfei stated that the profitability of the industry made it almost impossible to control. The WHO West Pacific adviser on sexually transmitted diseases, Gilles Poumerol, called on Asian governments to "move swiftly to decriminalise prostitution" and to "accept the imperfections of society at this stage." He added that decriminalization is a matter of acknowledging that prostitution is a reality that takes place and a short-term strategy to eliminate HIV. Poumerol "insisted that the WHO was not condoning prostitution and supported efforts for its eventual eradication."[19] However, the WHO statements leave unaddressed the tolerated and/or accepted "natural law" of male sexuality—that men's alleged sexual needs must be satisfied and therefore, prostitution is inevitable—if only in the short term.

On the policy level, Joseph Stiglitz has demonstrated that IMF economic policies in many places have set back the development agenda by unnecessarily corroding the very fabric of society.[20] Like IMF policies, the ILO, WHO, and other UN reports calling for legalization or decriminalization of the sex industry are helping to undermine social stability. Where poverty, economic disadvantage, and even crass commercialism dictate that families encourage their daughters into prostitution, women bear the burden of providing not only for family essentials but also for family amenities at great cost to women's health and well-being. Traditional relationships are broken down without a concomitant liberalization of women's roles, women's rights, and women's social, economic, and political power. Instead, prostitution rigidifies women's status as sexual objects and as instruments of sexual pleasure for men when they are bought and sold as commodities.

Media accounts have pointed to prostitution's role in the economic development of India. "There are few more visible signs of India's economic growth than the hive of activity around this transport stop [Sanjay Gandhi Transport Nagar],"[21] which is the largest truck stop in Asia, servicing hundreds of lorry drivers. In addition to showers, bedding, and routine maintenance, men pay for prostituted women and girls, sometimes several times a day, depending on the layover, for as little as thirty rupees (fifty U.S. cents).

Of the truck drivers who stop at this transport hub, 15–18 percent are HIV-positive, according to Dr. Bhanu Pratap who operates a clinic there. Sexual health counselors in the area conclude that the drivers who pass through Sanjay Gandhi Transport Nagar have an average of 150–200 sexual encounters a year with the prostituted women and girls, transmit the infection to many of them, and then take the disease home to their wives and future children. A peripatetic workforce of internally migrating men who come from rural to city areas adds to the legions of truck drivers who buy women and girls in prostitution at these lorry stops. Indian health experts name the phenomenon "the three Ms," i.e., "mobile men with money."[22] This money comes not only from those with cash to spare but also from men who, although economically disadvantaged, still have the money needed to pay for sex in this pit stop of the globe.

During the 1990s, the wealth of the new Asian "tiger economies" fueled an expansion of commercial sexual exploitation. New wealth created huge profits for sex industries and increased demand, with women from indigent rural areas recruited into the sex trade. Even poorer Asian countries such as Vietnam and Cambodia became destinations for sex tourists. Cambodia emerged as a leading country for child sex tourists seeking cheap sex with children; and Vietnam, flush with foreign investor cash, restored its sex industry to wartime highs.[23]

## The Sex Industry in Economic Downturns

The sex industry flourishes in times and places of both economic boom or bust. At the beginning of the recent world economic crisis in 2007, many reports alleged that economic downturns fuel economic upturns in the sex industry. *IBIS World*, which publishes Australian business information, reported that in a 2007 slowing economy in Australia, Australians nonetheless spent A$1.13 billion in prostitution and strip club venues. Although prices continued to rise in 2008, the legal sex industry garnered A$1.22 billion, an increase of 8 percent. "In economic terms, the sex industry does enjoy so-called 'sticky consumption' in that, like tobacco and alcohol, consumption levels remain relatively strong compared with other products during economic downturns."[24] In the United States, Houston-based Rick's Cabaret, which owns sexual entertainment clubs in various states, reported US$60 million in revenue in 2008 versus US$28 million in 2007.

Demand for the sex of prostitution does not decline during recessions. Rather, the prices paid for women decline because prostitution
users can demand lower rates while at the same time forcing women to
take higher risks for the money. During tough economic times, prostitution users enjoy slashed prices and slashing behavior. Ruhama, the
Irish organization giving assistance to women in prostitution, reported
that in 2009 requests from women for its services increased by 20 percent. "The reporting of rape and sexual assault was almost universal.
Women reported having been punched in the face, the stomach, being
kicked down stairs, beaten for refusing to have sex with men, being
locked in and refused food, being burned, being bitten."[25]

In the same period of global economic decline, women entered the
sex industry in larger numbers, and men continued to spend on sexual
entertainment, so much so that the international media became fasci-
nated with the question of how prostitution and pornography were far-
ing in the recession. Featured headlines included "More Women Going
from Jobless to Topless," "Melbourne Adult Venues Beat the Blues,"
and "Does Sex Still Sell?" However, reports of sex industry upturns
in downturn economies do not account for who actually benefits—the
women or the industry. Surely not the women who must resort to taking vacancies in the sex industry because they can find nothing else.

The *Providence Journal* reported that 150 applicants showed up for
thirty-five positions at the strip club Foxy Lady after the club starting
hiring again when lost business returned in the wake of a price cut.
"Employers across the adult entertainment industry say they're seeing
an influx of applications from women who . . . have college degrees and
held white-collar jobs until the economy soured."[26] By and large, it is
the sex clubs, brothels, and other venues that gross profits during economic slumps.

## Counting Prostitution in
## the System of National Accounts

When job production is measured on a national level, the influx of
women into the prostitution sector makes it more normative and thus
easier for countries to count prostitution as work in the system of national accounts and to include it in the employment figures for women.
For example, the Statistical Institute of Jamaica (STATIN), a government agency responsible for measuring the country's GDP, has already
undertaken efforts to capture the prostitution economy. Launched as
a way of including underground and informal labor sectors estimated

to be 40 percent of the formal economy in Jamaica, these efforts to account for the unofficial economy aim to use the data for tax reform and to bring these informal sectors into the formal economy.[27] If struggling countries incorporate the prostitution economy in their systems of national accounts, the employment picture for women looks much better than it is.

The push for women's informal sector work to be counted in the system of national accounts has been the subject of all past UN conferences on women. This laudable effort is belittled by the fact that these discussions are now being used to institutionalize prostitution as work. Then follow proposals to legalize or decriminalize the sex industry. Normalizing prostitution as work helps expand the sex industry and the number of women in it, while allowing governments to affirm that they are complying with women's rights agendas that promote women's employment, and that count women's "unrecognized" work. Including prostitution in the system of national accounts goes far in validating prostitution as recognized work and in authorizing it as a legal sector of the economy.

Prostitution has been an economic mainstay in various countries, not only in those that have legally institutionalized prostitution as work but also in countries that effectively exercise legal tolerance of the system of prostitution and the sex industry. Not only the GDP of the legalizing Netherlands but also the GDP of tolerating Thailand benefit from the prostitution sector. In the Netherlands, the prostitution industry accounts for 5 percent of the GDP,[28] and in Thailand, prostitution represents 10–14 percent of the GDP.[29] Although few countries admit the economic incentive to legalize, regulate, or tolerate prostitution, projected income has been at the heart of a country's enthusiasm for a laissez-faire system, whether legally institutionalized or not. The unspoken fact is that legalization or tolerance policies promote prostitution as an economic option for *poorer* women.

A 2005 University of Philippines study found that prostitution in the Philippines has become the fourth-largest source of gross national product (GNP) in the country.[30] Developing countries like the Philippines have become major centers for the global sex tourism industry. I witnessed this firsthand in 1998 on visits to Olongapo and Angeles City, where it was evident that former U.S. military bases, which had promoted a culture of prostitution in the local area, provided the infrastructure for a later sex tourism industry to thrive. Speaking with the women in prostitution who had been survivors of military sexual exploitation and were now subjected to the current influx of Western sex tourists, I was reminded of the way in which military-based prostitution establishes the groundwork for global sex tourism in many parts of the world. This easy transformation also happened in Bangkok, which had been a rest and recreation (R&R) center for the U.S. military during the Vietnam War.

The broader problem of a prostitution economy and the reasons why a large segment of the world's women end up in prostitution should be at the top of the economic development agenda of UN and national agencies. The question these agencies should be asking on a deeper level is why certain governments are dependent on institution-alizing a prostitution economy to help "solve" the problems of a coun-try's economic development. Does the state really want to become a government pimp and brothel-keeper? Should it?

The touted benefits of legalizing or decriminalizing prostitution sectors sound much like the promised payoffs of trickle-down econom-ics. Proponents of normalizing prostitution confidently assert that in-creased legal recognition of the sex industry will result in less violence, less trafficking, better health, and fairer earnings. In examining the leg-acy of the legal sex industry in the Netherlands, Germany, or Australia, however, studies show these alleged benefits cannot be defended.

The sorry and sordid heritage of normalizing prostitution and the sex industry in these countries repudiates these claims as fanciful and shows that regressive romanticizing of sexual exploitation as voluntary prostitution can be disguised as progressive policy. Not only are these alleged benefits lacking, but also legalization proponents fail to address the larger issue of why women must turn to prostitution when all else fails.

## THE PROSTITUTION ECONOMY

European Parliament policy favors promoting economic growth and the creation of jobs by ensuring the free movement of services within the European Union. For example, in 2006 the European Commission and the European Parliament unanimously adopted a directive encour-aging member states to offer services and products produced or mar-keted in one country to any other member country. Paragraph 1 of the directive states, "The elimination of barriers to the development of ser-vice activities between Member States is essential in order to strengthen the integration of the peoples of Europe and to promote balanced and sustainable economic and social progress."[31] The directive supports the removal of legal barriers to the free movement of services between member states that is essential to establishing a viable internal market.

Several countries in Europe have already legalized or decriminalized prostitution and recognize it as a sexual service. Prostitution policy in these countries, along with the 2001 decision of the European Court that defined prostitution as an economic activity and gave women from countries outside the European Economic Area (EEA) the right to work in the Netherlands, could set precedents for regulating prostitution on the whole continent. In the interests of integrated economic development, such precedents could serve as encouragement for prostitution to be made legal within the EU. As the directive forecasts, member states would need to submit to the same regulatory standards, and these standards would need to be harmonized.

In recent years, there have been attempts to integrate prostitution policy within the EU, but so far these efforts have failed because of opposing legal regimes of prostitution in European countries. Yet if member states of the EU continue to integrate their economic decisions based on a single market vision, economic integration policy combined with political pressure may become a driving instrument for a EU prostitution policy that defines prostitution as a market activity and a sexual service. This directive could be used to encourage an EU-wide market of legalized prostitution "services" to be offered in all EU countries and to discard any domestic policy relating to prostitution that allegedly inhibits integrated economic growth.

## The Netherlands

The more that prostitution is viewed through the lens of economic markets and policy—as a sexual service; as part of the entertainment, tourist, and leisure industries; and as contributing to the GDP and thus the economic development of countries and regions—the more normal and accepted systems of prostitution will become. In the Netherlands, for example, prostitution enjoys not only a large local demand but also attracts and sustains high rates of tourism that increase the local economy. Those who argued against the Amsterdam City Council's decision to close down a large number of the window brothels in the old city maintained that the windows have been immense tourist attractions and generate a large amount of state and private revenue.

Globalization has also influenced Dutch prostitution policy. Looking to the future, the Netherlands is targeting poor women for the international sex trade to remedy the inadequacies of the Dutch free market of "sexual services." *The First Report of the Dutch National Rapporteur on Trafficking* notes there has been a "shortage of workers in prostitution signaled by operators and the general work ban for prostitutes from outside the EEA."[32] Faced with this dwindling number and expanding demand, some Dutch government authorities called for "people from outside the EU/EEA countries to be permitted to work in the prostitution sector," i.e., for more female bodies and more exotic women to service the market. In 2002, the Dutch minister of social affairs and employment and the minister of justice suggested that in the future, the lack of domestic supply could be remedied by exempting the prostitution sector from the Aliens Employment Act.[33] In addition, the Dutch National Rapporteur on Trafficking *seemed* in her 2002 report to support the solution put forward from "the field," that voluntarily prostituted women from non-EU/EEA countries could be given "(measured) legal and controlled access to the Dutch market."[34]

Prostitution is thus normalized as an "option for the poor" and disguised as voluntary migration for sex work. As scientist Vandana Shiva writes,

> Women are selling their bodies to survive. And this growth in prostitution is not a choice that women are making. It's the ultimate destitution into which they are being pushed by the forces of globalization. . . . There's two kinds of survival—there's survival with dignity, simplicity, and autonomy and then there's the kind of survival that globalization is pushing people into—survival with violence, indignity, and total destitution.[35]

## Germany

Germany decriminalized aspects of its prostitution system in 2002. Referred to as the Prostitution Act, the new law permitted procuring for the purposes of prostitution, made it easier to operate brothels and comparable establishments, and lifted the prohibition against promoting prostitution. Theoretically, the new law entitles persons in prostitution to employment contracts and benefits, but very few women have registered for these benefits. Another provision in the law seeks to improve "working" conditions of those in prostitution.

In Germany the sex industry has developed into a legitimate, modern, and constantly growing business. An influential argument for decriminalizing prostitution was that a regulated system would control the expansion of the sex industry. However, as with any legal market, the prostitution industry keeps expanding, not contracting. Germany is one of the most lucrative prostitution economies in Europe. In 2004 revenues from prostitution were reported to be €6.4 billion.[36] In May 2006 annual revenues from prostitution were reported to be €14.5 billion.[37]

In a 1996 report prepared for the Council of Europe, French legal expert Michèle Hirsch estimated that "the total number of prostitutes in Germany was between 60,000 and 200,000." She also noted that half of the women then in the German sex trade were foreign women.[38] In 2004, two years after the new prostitution law was passed, government statistics estimated that 400,000 persons in prostitution are bought by a million prostitution users daily.[39] Ninety percent of those in the German sex trade in 2004 came from foreign countries.[40]

SOLWODI (Solidarity with women in distress, Solidarität mit Frauen in Not), an organization in Germany providing services for prostituted and trafficked women, wrote in its September 2007 newsletter that in the late 1990s it had good relationships with the police and local authorities who in past times referred more than 80 percent of the women the organization assisted. Today, the police refer only 10 percent of victims to this service organization. Why? "Because of the new legal situation, the police now hardly have the opportunity to gain access to victims of human trafficking and to free them. . . . [SOLWODI] fears that the victims of trafficking in women 'will now become altogether invisible.'" Under the Prostitution Act, police have fewer ways of justifying brothel incursions.[41]

In 2012 SOLWODI participated in a panel discussing the situation in Germany ten years after the prostitution law had passed. "It's obvious that the 'market' is 60 times bigger than in Sweden. . . . Pimps become employers. . . . The work of the police became more difficult." SOLWODI also reported that of the 1,772 women from 108 countries who asked the organization for help in 2011, 75 percent were under twenty-one.[42]

A 2007 report of the German Federal Ministry for Family Affairs, Senior Citizens, Women and Youth concluded its five-year evaluation of the 2002 Prostitution Act with these findings:

- "The Prostitution Act has thus up until now not been able to make actual, measurable improvements to prostitutes' social protection."
- As for "working conditions," there is "hardly any measurable, positive impact has been observed in practice. . . . No short-term improvements that could benefit the prostitutes themselves are to be expected."

- "The Prostitution Act has not recognisably improved the prostitutes' means for leaving prostitution."
- "There are as yet no indications that the Prostitution Act has reduced crime. The Prostitution Act has as yet contributed only very little in terms of improving transparency in the world of prostitution."
- Finally, "Prostitution should not be considered to be a reasonable means for securing one's living."[43]

Given these damaging conclusions, the federal government of Germany is drafting a criminal provision to punish the clients of persons forced into prostitution or who are victims of trafficking.[44] As with the Dutch, the Germans may resort to penalizing the buyers of "forced prostitution."

## Australia

Much of Australia is an example of a prostitution economy. Initially, the state of Victoria led the way in legalizing prostitution in 1984 under a Labor government. Subsequent governments expanded legalization culminating in the Prostitution Control Act of 1994. Three other states and territories followed in legalizing prostitution: the Australian Capital Territory (ACT) in 1992; the State of New South Wales in 1995; and the State of Queensland in 1999. Western Australia and Tasmania have so far rejected legalization.

The sex industry in Australia is not simply a legally accepted industry but has had a substantial impact on large sectors of the economy. "Sex-based industries in Australia are the financial equals of the 50 top-ranking publicly traded companies with the industry growing at 5.2 per cent annually between 1999/2000 and 2004/2005, and as high as 7.4 per cent between 2003/2004 and 2004/2005. This is significantly higher than the Gross Domestic Product." The May 2006 *Sexual Services in Australia* review ranked "sexual services" the highest of all personal service industries, constituting 80 percent of all personal service revenue. "Sexual services" also drives the overall growth of all personal service industries.[45]

Australia's tax system allows deductions for brothel and strip club visits paid for as bonuses or gifts from employers to employees. Some businesses dispense such favors around Christmas time, even paying for strip shows at job sites.[46] The prostitution culture in Australia has become so matter of course that brothels such as Scarlet Harem report that especially during the holiday season, fathers drop off families at the shopping centers before betaking themselves to the brothels.[47]

After full legalization of prostitution in the Australian State of Victoria in 1994, the actual growth in the prostitution industry was in the illegal sector, with vendors of the legal brothels also owning the illegal brothels. In only one year, 1998–1999, unlicensed brothels in Victoria tripled in number.[48]

One of the arguments leading up to full legalization of prostitution in Australia was it would promote self-employment for women by removing intermediaries, formerly known as pimps, from the sex industry and allow women to develop cottage-type industries. Proponents believed that women in prostitution would control these residential sites and didn't question its dangers.

Other "sex worker" groups have admitted the downside of cottage-industry prostitution venues. Reports from Hong Kong "sex workers," selling sex out of their apartments, testify to the naiveté of the self-employment argument and, more important, to the dangers posed by women who are indoor solo operatives. In 2008 four women prostituting out of their apartments were killed in different areas of Hong Kong. In writing about these murders, *Action for REACH OUT*, a "sex workers'" newsletter, stated, "They can never be sure if the visitor is a customer or if he is a thief."[49] The newsletter was compelled to publish safety tips for women in "sex work" that included taking self-defense classes, working closely with other women next door, installing safety alarms, and reporting to the police.

Other arguments leading up to full legalization in various states of Australia optimistically forecasted that more profits would be directed to women through "sex worker–owned brothels." In the state of Victoria, however, a prostitution trade representative named Victoria Roberts admitted, "'It's not the nature of women in this industry to build up a large capital base. . . . Most women who come to the industry are in immediate financial difficulty.' She estimated that women owned only 7 percent of Victoria's licensed brothels."[50] Yet, her solution was to advocate for more independent women to enter prostitution and minimize those who are in prostitution as a means of survival, failing to understand that the majority of women in prostitution state they are in the prostitution industry trying to eke out a living.

The "sex worker as independent entrepreneur" argument has been promoted by many advocates who uncritically maintain that legal prostitution will free women from predatory and violent pimps. Alan Young, the lawyer for the applicants in the Canadian legal challenge to the prostitution laws, holds this simplistic view. "The pimp is . . . a creation of the criminal law. If we remove the blunt instrument of criminal law, and take a proper regulatory approach, hookers could oust their pimps in exchange for a safe working environment. The pimp of today may become the union steward of tomorrow."[51] The pimp of today is already the businessman of regulated prostitution, but in regulated regimes such as the Netherlands and Australia, he is still behaving like the pimp of yesterday.

The goal of any industry is to increase its market share. The sex industry is never satisfied with a modicum of legalization but constantly pushes the envelope to pressure governments to accommodate its expansionism through decriminalizing and regulating other prostitution venues and related activities that may not be part of the original plan. Who would have thought, after the decision of the Canadian appeals court that struck down laws against pimping and brothels, that the sex industry would recruit strippers at Vancouver high schools? True to economic form, executive director of the Adult Entertainment Association of Canada (AEAC) Tim Lambrinos has gone public with the prospect of recruiting eighteen-year-old girls, "a market that has been untouched." He proposed that students who want to become future "professionals," and who are "comfortable with . . . taking all . . . clothes off," could earn the funds to pay their tuition. This proposal followed the government announcement that it would curtail recruitment of foreign women at risk for sexual exploitation. Blaming the government for the AEAC decision to recruit at local schools, Lambrinos maintained that the government was telling the industry indirectly that it needed to be "more aggressive and proactive at recruiting locally."[52]

Although Vancouver school officials stated they would not permit any recruiting efforts near Vancouver schools, Lambrinos said that industry representatives will stand on the streets and hand out flyers. With the new Canadian laws effectively decriminalizing the sex industry, it is conceivable someone will challenge the decision of the Vancouver school authorities on grounds of interfering with the right of businesses to hire workers.[53]

## South Korea

Korea passed its groundbreaking anti-prostitution law in 2004. The Korean law stands as an example of what governments can do when they have the political will to punish the perpetrators, combat the sex industry, and provide alternatives for women. With this law, the Korean government announced a zero-tolerance approach to prostitution, which has rewritten a fifty-year-old history of its country's prostitution industry initially generated by U.S. military presence in the country and increasingly servicing Korean men.

The Korean Institute of Criminology found that prostitution activities through the end of 2004 contributed 4 percent to the country's GDP, about the same as agriculture.[54] As in Australia, the sex industry drives other parts of the service economy. But in contrast to Australia where the legal expansion of the prostitution industry drove the overall growth of the related service sector, Korea's legislation helped to drive down the sales of service industries linked with prostitution in some way. By 2005 a report from the Korean National Statistics Office was already finding that many businesses impacted by the sex industry's decline were suffering economic losses. After the enforcement of the new prostitution law in August 2004, the hotel industry fell by 9.1 percent in September 2004, 10.2 percent in October 2004, and 9.8 percent in November 2004 compared with the year before. Sales from drinks and food at bars and pubs dropped for two consecutive months after the prostitution law was implemented. Credit card companies said that workers at entertainment establishments reduced their spending.[55] Experts who follow service industry trends in Korea alleged that these declines derived from the then recently enacted law opposing prostitution that took effect in September 2004.

Enforcement was strong after the law came into effect. Prostitution users faced jail time of up to one year or fines of 100 million won (in February 2013, that was worth almost US$92,000).[56] In 2006, the Ministry of Gender Equality released a survey on the law's second anniversary that found of the 49 percent of men interviewed who had previously used women in prostitution, 85 percent had stopped after the law's enactment.[57]

The 2004 law in Korea also stipulates tougher punishment than preexisting law did for other perpetrators. For example, brothel owners could face up to ten years in jail instead of five. The law includes provisions requiring state confiscation of all profits or assets from brothels and other sex venues accumulated through criminal acts stipulated in the new law. It also widens the interpretation of illegal sexual activities, eliminating a legal loophole for sex venues such as strip clubs that allege their sexual acts don't meet the definition of prostitution.

In September 2004, according to statistics compiled by the National Police Agency, there were 1,679 sex districts around the country containing 5,500 women in prostitution. Twenty months later, the number of sex districts had dwindled to 1,097 with roughly 2,660 prostituted women still in these areas.[58] Red-light areas have thus decreased by 38 percent with almost a 50 percent reduction of women in prostitution.

The dwindling numbers of women used in prostitution were owing to the increased enforcement of the law following its coming into force. The decrease was also because of legal provisions that provided protection and services for thousands of victims. Legal protections include victim counseling, job retraining, medical treatment, a monthly stipend, and legal support. To qualify, women have to demonstrate that they have been harmed, suffer from addictions or other disabilities, or are underage. Bae Suk-ill, director of the Incheon Women's Hotline at the local center for prostituted women, stated, "It's a miracle for them to have an opportunity to find shelter here."[59]

Thousands of women have taken advantage of the protection and assistance provisions. In 2007 the government almost tripled its 2004 budget of 6.8 million to 17.4 billion won used to provide services to women in prostitution.[60] Even critics of the law and of the police crackdown on sex establishments admit the law has also improved the overall lives of women still in prostitution.[61]

Survivors of prostitution "say it is like a miracle that they can escape prostitution through the protective system of law. The experience that they who always believed they live outside the law, are subject to the protection of the law and that the brokers who seemed to live above the law can be punished truly empowers the women."[62]

## Unions

When feminists began to criticize the U.S. sex industry and the system of prostitution in the 1970s, the industry responded by supporting women to promote prostitution as "sex work" and to advocate its decriminalization. The sex industry was learning that organizations like COYOTE could be useful in promoting legislative change that would benefit them. For example, COYOTE received initial funding from the Playboy Foundation. Other funding was given for COYOTE to organize the first prostitutes' "union."[63] COYOTE's primary goal was to promote decriminalization of prostitution, not to assist women in prostitution through badly needed services. "The year of COYOTE's inception, St. James announced that 'changing the law is, of course, the most important job.' Since then, COYOTE's overarching goal has been the decriminalization of prostitution."[64] In the beginning, "sex worker" unions were promoted as a handy tool for promoting "sex worker" rights that in reality promoted sex industry rights. By the late 1980s, however, the sex industry in the United States was no longer promoting "sex worker unions," having realized that it was less costly to hire women as independent contractors.

### Unions Supportive of "Sex Work"

"Sex worker" unions primarily took hold in Europe as the progressive response to the exploitation of the prostitution industry. In 2005 Jose Maria Fidalgo, one of Spain's major union leaders, defended the growing nature of the sex sector there and said, "In a civilised country, we cannot tolerate a non-regulated sector where hundreds of thousands of people, particularly women and immigrants, are being exploited."[65] Unionism became a litmus test for supporters of "sex worker" rights.

In Britain where prostitution is not legalized, some associations of "sex workers" have joined the General Municipal Boilermakers (GMB), the country's fourth-largest union. The London-based International Union of Sex Workers has helped the GMB to form an adult entertainment branch and to recruit persons in prostitution, strip clubs, and pornography.[66] The GMB has also called for the decriminalization of pimping and brothel keeping. Its international union of "sex workers" believes that pimps may be necessary to protect women in prostitution since, it says, most police fail to do so. Julie Bindel, columnist for the *Guardian*, responded to this argument.

> The 150 or so sex workers currently affiliated to the GMB tend not to be the ones who lead chaotic, drug-abusing lifestyles, controlled by pimps. Rather, they are those who speak most vocally about their experiences in the industry being a "positive choice." Women who have left prostitution regularly talk about the horrors they faced on a daily basis when they were in it. So who is really qualified to represent those in the industry?[67]

The Red Thread in the Netherlands is perhaps the oldest union in Europe purporting to represent a substantial number of women in the legal sex industry. Yet in 2004, after twenty years in the country, the Red Thread had collected only a hundred members.[68] In the Netherlands, women in prostitution have stated that legalization or decriminalization of the sex industry does not erase the stigma of prostitution. Because prostituted women must register and lose their anonymity, they feel more vulnerable and pursued by the identity of prostitute. Thus, the majority of women in prostitution still operate underground.

Also in Germany, another legalized prostitution country, women in prostitution have rejected the contract of the ver.di service industry union because they want no public record made of what they do. As of 2004, only about a hundred of Germany's 400,000 prostituted women had joined the ver.di union, and most of them rejected the union contract not wanting to admit what they do for a living.[69] Ver.di is searching for new recruits out of sheer necessity because union membership is at an all-time low in Germany.[70]

Likewise, in Australia unionization has not worked. As of 2002, the Miscellaneous Workers Union had signed up fewer than forty prostituted women who did not envision themselves as long-term "sex workers." "The prostituted women did not see themselves as proud workers who wanted to be identified with their industry but as temporary workers and passing through."[71]

*Unions Opposed to Sex Work*
The push to unionize "sex workers" has been turned back by union policies in other countries. These policies are very clear that prostitution is sexual exploitation, not "sex work." Although Denmark regulates certain aspects of prostitution, Denmark's Confederation of Trade Unions has sent a strong message to its employees and elected officials that they are not permitted to engage in prostitution while traveling abroad on business. This is because they do not want to contribute to the oppression of human beings in other countries, "and we consider prostitution to be an oppression of women."[72]

Likewise, the labor unions in Norway were pivotal in passing a law against the demand in 2008. From 1995 onward many women active in the trade unions worked to encourage their unions to take a stand against prostitution and trafficking in the face of an international lobby for the legalization of the sex industry in Norway. These women also worked to promote policy and legislation that addressed the role of the buyer and his responsibility for the promotion of sexual exploitation.

Success came when the Norwegian Confederation of Trade Unions voted in favor of a new law making the purchase of a sexual act criminal in Norway. Following this vote the youth branches of the Socialist Left Party and the Labor Party at their congresses in 2006 and 2007 "convinced the older generation to see the connection between the demand, trafficking and prostitution . . . [and] both congresses said yes to legislation."[73] In 2008 the Norwegian Parliament voted to pass legislation criminalizing the purchase of a sexual act, and the law came into force in January 2009.

Norwegian unions had also campaigned earlier against pornographic pay-per-view movies in hotels. The Norwegian Hotel and Restaurant Workers Union, representing more than ten thousand workers in the industry, took up this campaign initially on behalf of its female members working in hotel rooms where they were consistently harassed by male hotel guests turned on by the pornography they watched on their TV sets. Male guests, under the guise of calling for fresh towels or other housekeeping amenities, had requested housekeeping staff to come to their rooms, where they were often met by naked men at the door. Complaints ranged from men's sleazy comments to physical assault. Many of these room service and housekeeping personnel are not only female but also immigrants.[74]

In a more recent scenario, which received wide publicity in the United States and elsewhere, Dominique Strauss-Kahn (DSK) allegedly raped and assaulted a Guinean hotel maid in a New York five-star hotel. The Manhattan district attorney declined to prosecute DSK on criminal charges,[75] but the hotel worker brought a civil case against him, which resulted in a legal settlement.

### The Meaning of Unionizing Women in Prostitution

There is no evidence that most women in prostitution want legal unions and legalization of prostitution. In 2003 seventy-five women in prostitution organized the first national conference of Filipino victims/survivors of prostitution in Manila. Alma Bulawan, president of BUKLOD, a survivors' group in Olongapo City, stated, "We want our rights as citizens, but we reject legalization of prostitution which will only maintain women's low status in society."[76]

Promoting unions for women in prostitution is a compelling argument because often people believe that women should be recognized as "sex workers" and awarded the labor protections of unions. However, as Julie Bindel asks, "If prostitutes are the workers, who are the bosses? Pimps and brothel keepers? Is it really acceptable to legitimise these people and call them managers?"[77] One survivor of fifteen years in prostitution has argued that unionizing the sex industry is "saying it's OK for women to be abused. The union is like a pimp because it is encouraging and facilitating. It seems to be there to help the women get in and stay in, not to help them get out."[78]

As part of their mission, unions periodically help launch sexual harassment cases on behalf of their members. The "workplace behavior" that women in prostitution routinely endure is the classic textbook description of sexual harassment from employers and others—actions that are unwanted and unwelcome sexual attention and abuse, as well as conduct that is offensive, threatening, and often violent. Whereas sexual harassment is not a routine part of the job for most union members, it is part of the very "job" for those in prostitution. Unions are in a contradictory situation here. On the one hand, they cannot claim to support the sexual harassment claims of other union members and then, on the other, endorse the routine sexual harassment of their prostituted members as acceptable work.

The majority of women in prostitution come from marginalized groups with a history of sexual abuse, drug and alcohol dependence, poverty or financial hardship, lack of education, and histories of other vulnerabilities. These are not women whose lives will change for the better if prostitution is decriminalized, normalized as work, and unionized. These are women who need exit programs, not programs to help keep them in prostitution.

## PROSTITUTION AS ECONOMIC DEVELOPMENT
## FOR POOR AND DISADVANTAGED WOMEN

How do the women in it see their economic activity in prostitution? Again it depends on whom you ask—those who identify themselves as "sex workers" or "survivors." Sex workers do not consider themselves to be victims. They believe that prostitution is a job like any other; survivors experience prostitution as violence against women. Sex workers state that prostitution is a human right; survivors maintain that prostitution is a violation of human rights. Sex workers want us to believe that international women who end up in local prostitution industries have "migrated for sex work"; survivors tell us that these women are victims of trafficking. From these differing philosophies of prostitution emerge differing views about prostitution as an economically viable job.

### Economic Rationalism

Historically, economists viewed prostitution as an irrational economic activity. A *Research for Sex Work* publication devoted to the topic of "Sex Work and Money" claims that this assessment is changing as economists use their analytical methods to study "illicit networks" and reevaluate the irrationality of markets and the actors in them. In this assessment not only are "sex workers" engaged in sound economic decision making, but also the sex industry rationally responds to incentives and disincentives as in any licit market.[79]

The view that women in prostitution are mainly rational agents applies to trafficked women as well. Writer Melissa Petro states that one should not conclude "migrant workers' participation in sex work is conclusively more a result of coercion than women working in their home country." Although "migrant women experience the sex industry differently as migrant women and ethnic/racial minorities," this does not mean that they don't rationally choose to enter prostitution. Petro concludes that rather than "crusading" to eliminate "sex work" as an option, advocates on behalf of women in prostitution "would do better to address labour and immigration policies."[80]

The economic rationalism model of "sex work" also challenges the dominant health policy that blames the spread of HIV/AIDs on lack of education or access to condoms. Instead it is said "sex workers" rationalize that they will earn more money for forgoing condoms, and they respond to this "economic incentive."[81] No matter that they may end up deprived of long-term economic benefit if and when they become seriously ill or die. Invisible in this rationalist analysis is the buyer's pressure on the woman not to use a condom, his threat of violence if she does not comply, his warning that he will take his business elsewhere, and/or his offer to pay more for this service knowing that she will be put at significant risk of disease. This model offers cold comfort to women in prostitution who are given the explanation they have rationally responded to a "financial experience."

## Financial Motivation: Not Financial Desperation

Self-identified stripper Jo Weldon bemoans that every interviewer asks her whether she was sexually abused as a child, but no one has ever inquired about her "financial mindset or even the financial motivation involved in my decision to work in the sex industry."[82] Sex Worker Education and Advocacy Taskforce (SWEAT) states that the most common reason for women entering prostitution is "unemployment or a desire to improve their income."[83] Weldon decries the notion that women who turn to prostitution do so out of financial desperation rather than financial motivation. "The possibility that the simple exchange every other labourer is assumed to make, that of doing something relatively undesirable for compensation, is treated as deviant, when in fact that element is the most normal thing about the decision to enter the industry."[84]

Valorizing the ability to acquire a job entirely without a resume, Weldon argues, "The sex worker can apply for a job in one day, work that night, and make enough to pay a bill the next day." She continues, "You make money. . . . You watch your income come in physically bill by bill. . . . This is the most immediate way of making money." Sex work fulfills "a unique economic need."[85]

The economic rationalism paradigm is based on the notion that "sex workers" weigh the costs and benefits of their situation and become pragmatic actors in the system of economic exchange. Writer Alys Willman-Navarro argues that like everyone else, women in prostitution are "economically rational beings who choose among the available options the things that make them better off, especially in material terms, and avoid options that do not."[86] Advocates of this view call for the recognition of "a sex worker's agency and ability to make choices in the global arena."[87]

## ECONOMIC EXPLOITATION OF PROSTITUTED WOMEN

The financial motivation and economic rationalism models supported by sex work advocates fail to not only take serious account of the sexual exploitation but also the *economic exploitation* of prostituted women. Much of the economic exploitation of prostituted women comes from the *economic diversion* of any money they might earn. Sex industry advocates often claim that the money women make in prostitution is better than they could earn in other low-income situations. However, they neglect to mention the economic exploitation to which women are subjected due to the steady stream of economic diversion of their earnings into drugs, alcohol, pimps, drivers, so-called protectors, and other intermediaries of women's "financial experience."

The layers of intermediaries that women in prostitution must pay, or for which they are "taxed," are many. Street women in prostitution often have pimps; escort women in prostitution pay drivers and booking agencies who feature as administrative pimps; brothel or sex club women pay managerial pimps, bouncers, and staff who may clean the rooms or perform other chores. Women in countries or states that legalize or regulate prostitution are required to pay personal income taxes to the state or county in which they are located and rental fees in venues, as well as payment to "third-party business managers."

Writing about the legal brothels in Nevada, psychologist Melissa Farley reports, "At least 50% of the women in the brothels are under the control of illegal pimps outside the brothels, and 57% are giving all or part of their earnings to someone other than the legal brothel's pimp." She also notes that, historically, legal pimps (now known as managers) required women to have pimps outside the brothels.[88] Most women "working" in these brothels are controlled by outside agents who initially pimped them into the legal brothels and still control their behavior and take a percentage of their earnings. Women's illegal pimps are often boyfriends, husbands, or other friends.

When they tell the truth about women's lives in prostitution, even pro–sex work articles acknowledge the draining of women's earnings in prostitution. Writer Juhu Thukral concedes that many women responding to a study conducted with fifty-two indoor "sex workers" in New York City report that their initial financial goals of saving, buying a house, and getting an education have not come true. "The money made through sex work is often quickly made and quickly spent."[89]

Prostitution is not sustainable, never mind lucrative, for the majority of women in the system. It is important to assess just how deceptive this economic rationalism model becomes when one understands what has been called the "human capital" costs of prostitution.

## The "Human Capital Costs" of Prostitution

One researcher has developed a methodology for estimating the lifelong costs of young women leaving prostitution. Linda DeRiviere's 2006 study used interviews, case studies, and the tools of economic cost-benefit analysis, surveying sixty-two former "sex trade workers" in Manitoba, Canada, the majority of whom were first-nation or aboriginal women. A subset of eight respondents was interviewed from which more detailed information was collected, including specific economic calculations.[90]

A primary goal of the study was to conduct economic analysis of the lifelong personal costs of prostitution and quantify the economic expenses for the women interviewed. Another goal was to examine the economic rationalism model proposed by advocates who argue that prostitution can be a financially beneficial response compared to work in other low-paying positions in which it is claimed that women earn much less. The human capital approach also calculates the indirect costs of involvement in prostitution in terms of lost productivity and the value of lost time in the labor market.

The average income of respondents was Can$27,071. However, this amount decreased substantially through payment to pimps and escort agency owners (deduct Can$10,068 annually or 37.2 percent of annual income); and the use of drugs and alcohol (deduct Can$12,617 annually or 46.6 percent of annual income). Prostituted women retained only a small portion (Can$2,305 annually or 8.5 percent) of their total annual gross earnings after subsidizing intermediaries and substance use.[91]

The study also broke down costs into direct and indirect, both when women were involved in the sex industry and after leaving prostitution. Average direct costs while in prostitution included earnings handed over to pimps, partners, agencies, or drivers; personal payments for drugs and alcohol; judicial system expenses for fines and lawyers; and direct medical outlays for injuries from abusive clients (Can$23,651 per respondent). Indirect costs while involved in the sex industry included lost earnings resulting from arrest, incarceration, and court appearances; loss of experience, training, and tenure in the job market; and lost income when participating in substance abuse programs (Can$14,799 per respondent).[92]

The intangible costs of "immeasurable value" are psychological harm; physical pain and suffering from past prostitution violence; loss of time with children, friends, and family from incarcerations, substance abuse treatment, programs, and hospitalization; and productivity loss from low self-esteem.[93] Following a transition into mainstream society, the women also bore many of these same consequences of lost opportunities in the mainstream labor market because of foregone labor market experience and tenure, on-the-job training, and missed work from chronic health conditions.

Over two-thirds of the sixty-two respondents reported that they did not use drugs or alcohol before entry into prostitution, or they had been casual and not habitual users. Of the one-third who reported repeated use of drugs and alcohol before their involvement in prostitution, the majority stated that once in the sex industry, they began using more harmful and expensive substances, including crack, crystal methamphetamine, and injected heroin and solvents.[94]

Any small earnings dividend that women in prostitution may have gained at entry into prostitution was short-term relative to the individual's post-prostitution working years and the human capital costs of their prostitution experience and its aftermath. Both during and after being in prostitution, women shouldered consequences of increased substance abuse, lower lifetime productivity, and physical and mental health burdens. Women lost significant opportunities for job training, income-generating experience, and earnings compared to women with similar prospects and backgrounds. "Thus, prostitutes are the most vulnerable to lifelong poverty and other forms of marginalization due to the lack of marketable skills that improve their chances of gaining employment."[95]

The human capital costs of prostitution findings debunk the rational economic perspective of the pro–sex work financial models, especially for ethnic and socioeconomically disadvantaged groups of women who constitute the main populations in systems of prostitution. DeRiviere concludes that there are "multiple reasons for policy-makers to direct their attention to counteracting the conditions of vulnerability that bring young women and men to this lifestyle and perpetuate the social and economic marginalization of people in the sex trade."[96]

Not only do the women bear the economic burden of prostitution but so too does the health system, especially from women's frequent use of emergency rooms and other health venues. In testimony before the Governor's Council on Domestic Violence in Portland, Oregon, the Baldwin Foundation reported that in San Francisco, prostituted persons constituted about 12 percent of the two hundred heaviest users of the city's emergency rooms and health clinics. In the late 1990s, the cost to the city was estimated to be 5 million dollars per year.[97]

## PROSTITUTION COLONIALISM AND THE MILITARY-PROSTITUTION COMPLEX[98]

In many developing countries, the system of prostitution has a history of colonialist underpinning. This is not to say that historically local prostitution was irrelevant. Rather it is to point out the intensification effect that an earlier colonialism contributes to the modern sex sector in these countries.

In 1999 I was part of a group of advocates who went into a major prostitution area in Dhaka, Bangladesh, called Kandupatti. During the late nineteenth and early twentieth centuries when Bangladesh was part of India and the British Raj, Kandupatti served as an R&R area for the British military. After Bangladeshi independence from Pakistan, Kandupatti became a local prostitution area. Walking through the warren of streets past the cinder block hovels serving as home and brothel for the prostituted women, we met women who had never lived anyplace else or seldom ventured out of this compound of sexual exploitation.

Our group had been asked by some of the prostituted women who had participated in a CATW Asia-Pacific conference held in Dhaka to visit the Kandupatti area; they believed it would be a show of solidarity with the women living there whose livelihood had been stolen by the local strongman who had appropriated their money and possessions, allegedly for safekeeping. When the women demanded return of their assets, he evicted them from their fragile shelters. This meant the women were living on the streets and in public areas with their children.

Our walk was short-lived when we were attacked by a group of extremist men. They were irate that a group of mostly women was being led into the area by one of the "fallen women" and that we were supporting the women in protesting the theft of their possessions and their expulsion from the area. Almost immediately after we entered the brothel area, throngs of men began to follow us shouting, raising their fists, and eventually attacking our group's bus with bricks. Fortunately, participants escaped, seeking shelter in a nearby market area.

## The Philippines

I had also seen this legacy of prostitution colonialism in the Philippines when I visited the previous U.S. military base cities of Olongapo and Angeles City. I listened to the formerly prostituted women in Olongapo, who were part of a survivor-led service organization called BUKLOD describe the ways in which they were brought onto the base at Subic Bay on weekends for the rest and recreation of the U.S. military. Ordinarily, no Filipinos were allowed on base unless for work. Even when Mount Pinatubo erupted in the area during 1991, "the commanding officer of Subic refused to allow Pinatubo evacuees access to the base at the height of the more deadly eruptions," but instead sent a truckload of apples as a donation. In a dramatic statement of refusal, the mayor of Olongapo City rejected it.[99]

U.S. prostitution colonialism in the Philippines created the model for the U.S. military–prostitution complex in most parts of the world. Beginning in 1898 when the U.S. military took control of Manila from the Spanish forces that had occupied the Philippines since 1565, the United States established a system of prostitution that followed U.S. forces wherever they were based, particularly in Asia. During the Philippine-American War, the U.S. Army conducted compulsory venereal inspections of women used in prostitution and, if found to be diseased, compelled their incarceration in hospitals for treatment until they were certified as "clean." Authorities weekly inspected women, who were forced to pay the examination fees and penalties themselves.

The U.S. military adopted European methods for containing venereal disease. It based its system on the regulationist model employed in Britain during the period of the Contagious Diseases Acts and used in India in the military cantonment system. The U.S. military–prostitution complex was also founded on practices locally carried out in the Philippines first by the Spanish and then for a short period by the revolutionary government that succeeded it under Emilio Aguinaldo. In 1899 the regulationist system became U.S. army policy assuring soldiers' certified sexual access to Filipinas. Regulation of prostitution was now an intrinsic part of colonial practice in the Philippines, Cuba, and Puerto Rico, and later during the U.S. military occupation of Japan after World War II.

The vast majority of women used for prostitution were Filipinas from rural families, many who became trapped in prostitution and who were regarded by the military authorities to be "inherently diseased." Sexual intercourse with Filipinas meant contagion and was thought to be a cause and symptom of the physical and moral "degeneration" said to afflict white American soldiers.

> The system's first principle was the prostitute as the perpetual and exclusive source of contagion. . . . [It] instituted a sexual double standard that both explicitly and implicitly attributed venereal epidemics to women and rationalized the non-examination of men. . . . Subjecting men to venereal inspection was believed to be intrusive, humiliating, dishonorable and "demoralizing"; prostitutes at home or abroad apparently had none of this burdensome honor to lose.[100]

In response to later protests coming from U.S. suffragists, anti-colonialists, and social purity campaigners against the sexual double standard, soldiers were also ordered to submit to regular venereal inspections. In 1900 U.S. Army physicians admitted that troops disembarking from U.S. military bases, such as the Presidio in San Francisco, were heavily infected with venereal disease. In one of the first regiments to arrive in the Philippines in mid-1898, 489 of the 1,300 men had venereal disease before arrival.[101] Male inspections, however, were never formalized, and enforcement of examinations for men was halfhearted as military authorities were able to exert more stringent control of the local women used in prostitution.

The U.S. Army was successful in hiding its regulationist system of prostitution from the American public during its first years of operation. However, in 1900 a journalist from Chicago divulged the details of the country's prostitution regime in the Philippines. Journalist William B. Johnson reported American flags flew over the houses of prostitution in the red-light districts, the military licensed these brothels, and inspections were conducted under the supervision of the military government by what he called the "department of prostitution."[102]

Following these revelations, various groups called for reform. Purity reformers protested "regulated vice." Anti-colonial protesters joined with anti-militarists arguing, "standing armies meant prostitution, and prostitution meant officers' attempts to regulate it." William Lloyd Garrison, a prominent race abolitionist in the United States, was "saddened by this revelation [of U.S. regulation of prostitution in the Philippines].... My mind reverted to the horrors of the British camps in India whereof I had been reading in Mrs. Josephine Butler's pathetic appeal for aid to prevent the re-enactment of the Contagious Diseases Acts."[103]

Although some American feminists did not recognize anti-imperialism as a common cause with feminism, others supported the Philippine Revolution and vehemently objected to military colonialism. Lida Calvert Obenchain, a contributor to the *Women's Journal*, was one of those who made the connection.

> I cannot understand how any suffragist can uphold this Administration in the Matter of the Philippine war. . . . Every argument that is used to defend our injustice to the Filipinos has been worn threadbare in the defence of injustice to women. I am sick of hearing over and over again of "our duty" to the Filipinos and their "incapacity for self-government," and the necessity laid upon us of "protecting" them from foreign aggression and domestic strife. It is the same old story of "chivalry" and "mercy" being proffered where nothing but justice is asked.[104]

In her remarks to the National American Women Suffrage Association (NAWSA) conference in 1900, Catharine Waugh McCulloch also recognized the shared aims of Filipino and American women, especially invoking their common wish for liberty and emancipation."[105] The NAWSA strongly protested against the military regulation of prostitution in the Philippines. "Rather than being protected by U.S. forces, Filipinas were being degraded, turned into sexual objects to gratify male desires."[106] The 1900 conference drafted a resolution that was sent to President William McKinley calling regulation of prostitution an "insult to womanhood" that "breeds a moral and physical degeneration that will avenge itself upon our American society when these soldiers shall have been recalled to their native country."[107]

The NAWSA resolution was followed by a series of U.S. governmental denials and subsequently by a promise that Gen. Arthur Mac-Arthur—newly appointed governor-general of the American-occupied Philippines in 1900 and father of Gen. Douglas MacArthur—would investigate the subject and make a full report. MacArthur penned a terse refutation of the charges that brothels were licensed, protected, and encouraged by the military. However, he did defend regulation as a more benevolent form of colonialism, stating Manila's condition was "remarkable in view of the general lack of moral tone pervading the seaports of the East."[108] In 1901, the U.S. War Department openly admitted and defended inspections as a health measure comparable to those directed against smallpox and bubonic plague.

A turning point in the campaign came when suffragist Margaret Dye Ellis circulated an official registration book issued by U.S. authorities allegedly certifying a child named Maria de La Cruz for prostitution. The book contained inspection records and a photo that matched the appearance of a twelve-year-old child. Ellis left copies of this book with every member of the U.S. Committee on the Philippines and with U.S. congressmen, whose wives, upon seeing the book, were provoked to indignation and sent a flood of letters to the War Department. Theodore Roosevelt, now president, handed down an order directed to the army authorities to cease regulating prostitution. Instead, Roosevelt instructed that soldiers must practice "self-restraint, self-respect, and self-control." He stated, "Venereal disease could be prevented through a sexually restrained and self-disciplined masculinity." And he pointed out that it was "criminal folly" to believe that "sexual indulgence is necessary to health."[109]

The inspection of Filipinas continued but in a less visible way. Publicly, MacArthur claimed that prostitution was not "licensed, protected or encouraged." For example, American flags were removed from brothels, and inspection booklets were done away with. Privately, however, medical officers were encouraged to keep their own confidential records of inspections of women. In this way, there could be no charge that the military government was maintaining the system of licensed prostitution.

The U.S. military policy of making regulation of prostitution invisible migrated quietly to other outposts of the military-prostitution complex and to bases in the United States. In the postwar period, campaigners turned to other criticisms of military colonialism because the campaign against regulation of prostitution had always been marginal to anti-colonialist protest.

The integration of military colonialism and prostitution shaped the twentieth century's U.S military–prostitution complex in many areas of the globe. Regulationism sotto voce became the practiced policy governing prostitution. In applying rules managing troops in other military outposts, Arthur MacArthur published the specifics of the policy in a "confidential circular" to avoid "adverse criticism." This regulationist prostitution policy would continue to operate in Puerto Rico, Hawai'i, post–World War II Japan, South Korea, Vietnam, and the Philippines, even after the U.S. bases were dismantled there. And soon after, a U.S.-Philippine status of forces agreement insulated soldiers from local prosecution who committed crimes. The military-prostitution complex secured protected male sexual access to women in different parts of the globe.

## Post–World War II Japan

The model for U.S. military prostitution behavior in post–World War II Japan was institutionalized by Gen. Douglas MacArthur, the alleged World War II "savior of the Philippines" and son of Gen. Arthur MacArthur. Shortly after the surrender of Japan, MacArthur's occupation administration approved the Japanese government's recruitment of thousands of "comfort women"—many used by the Japanese during the war—to sexually service the U.S. troops in Japan.[110] The occupation system of "comfort women" for the GIs replicated the system that Japan organized during the Second World War for its soldiers.

> The Japanese government, fearful that "sex-starved" American Occupation troops would behave as Japanese forces often had abroad by raping every woman or girl in sight, recruited thousands of "comfort women" to slake the passions of foreign soldiers in official brothels. The prostitutes and war widows pressed into service were told that their mission "was to be a sexual dike to protect the chastity of Japanese women" and prevent pollution of the race.[111]

Despite reports that women were being coerced into the occupation brothels, and with full knowledge of Japan's appalling conscription of women into military sexual slavery during World War II, U.S. soldiers found an officially sanctioned system of brothels in Japan waiting for them ten days after the country surrendered to the Allies. The chief of public relations for the Japanese Recreation and Amusement Association (RAA)—a network of police officials and Tokyo businessmen who established the network of brothels for the U.S. soldiers—reported that American military police could hardly contain the throngs of men who lined up to be sexually serviced. In the first RAA brothel set up in Tokyo, each woman had to serve fifteen to sixty buyers a day.[112]

At its peak 70,000 women—many who had answered ads calling for them to help their country in working for a "New Japan"—ended up serving the 350,000 U.S. servicemen who occupied Japan in the postwar period. "The US occupation leadership provided the Japanese government with penicillin for women servicing occupation troops, established prophylactic stations near the RAA brothels and, initially, condoned the troops' use of them." The number of unofficial private brothels servicing the U.S. military was probably even higher.[113] The U.S. military's collusion with Japanese government inspections of women for venereal disease, the way in which Japanese women were induced and deceived into prostitution, the continued use of many "comfort women" who were prostituted for Japanese soldiers during the war, and the supervision of brothels for U.S. military use during the occupation all testify to this extension of the U.S. military–prostitution complex.

Historian Toshiyuki Tanaka has researched and written about Japan's violation of the "comfort women," estimated to affect over a hundred thousand mostly Asian women from Korea, the Philippines, and China who were victims of organized sexual slavery by the Japanese military during World War II. Japanese crimes against the "comfort women" constitute for Tanaka "a crime against humanity on an unprecedented scale."[114]

In his 2002 work *Japan's Comfort Women: Sexual Slavery and Prostitution During World War II and the US Occupation*, Tanaka concludes that the Japanese crimes against women should have been prosecuted as crimes against humanity at the International Military Tribunal for the Far East (the Tokyo War Crimes Tribunal) after the war. Tanaka maintains that the U.S. military authorities were well aware of these crimes against women and, of course, held key positions and power during the tribunal. The fact that the "comfort women" crimes were not prosecuted, he states, was owing to the "sexual ideology" of the American occupation officials who were complicit in the establishment of a similar "comfort" system for the U.S. military personnel in Japan. This complicity made it inevitable and self-interested that they would not want their own "comfort women" system exposed. Further, that it was mostly Asian women who were violated by both the Japanese and the Americans added to U.S. lack of accountability.[115]

In the spring of 1946 at the instigation of U.S. military chaplains, General MacArthur was pressured to end the military's use of "comfort stations" in Japan, put them permanently off limits, and relocate women "who had been handed down from the Japanese troops to the Americans." All violations of the new policy would be subject to disciplinary action.[116] By that time, Tanaka maintains, many of the prostituted women had venereal disease and were destitute.[117] More than a quarter of all American military occupation forces in Japan also had a sexually transmitted disease.

The MacArthur military-prostitution regime in Japan was then returned to the Philippines, where a previous regulationist system was officially approved in cooperation with the Filipino local authorities after World War II. In Olongapo, for example, the Social Hygiene Clinic was a joint venture of the Olongapo City Health Department and the U.S. Navy. Women had to be registered with the clinic, undergo X-rays, a VD smear, blood tests, and a stool sample before they were certified to work as hospitality women—another euphemism for prostituted women—in the bars, massage parlors, and other entertainment establishments catering to the U.S. military from the Subic naval base. Women had to pay for the tests themselves, and men could ask for the women's cards to make sure they were "clean." Clubs that failed to check these cards were off-limits to U.S. servicemen.[118] The U.S. military–prostitution complex would also be enacted during the war and postwar periods in Korea (see chapter 1) and, later, in Vietnam.

In 2005, patronizing prostitution became a crime for U.S. servicemen. Under Article 138-4 of the U.S. military's criminal law—the Uniform Code of Military Justice—patronizing prostitution by U.S. servicemen is de jure illegal anywhere in the world. Whether patronizing prostitution by servicemen is de facto illegal depends, of course, on its enforcement.

## Globalization of "Sex Work" Advocacy

Not only globalization of the sex industry but also *globalization of sex work advocacy* has facilitated the return and expansion of sexual slavery in many parts of the globe. Both have enabled the extensive ways in which women become "goods and services"—as prostituted women, as trafficked instruments of exchange, as objects of sex tourism, and as indentured domestic workers who are often sexually exploited as well.

The globalization of sex work advocacy takes an unusual turn in an industry that has grown up to study and create the discourse about sex trafficking and prostitution—what I call the "explanation industry." Alex Renton, who admits to a liberal view of the sex industry, exposes the many people who populate the explanation industry and who indirectly benefit. "There is a harvest here, too, for cultural anthropologists and social historians. . . . There are socioeconomists analysing the 'incomplete dialectic between tourist and prostitute'; anthropologists on the Foucaultian relationship between a Thai prostitute and her body, social historians on the growth of the myth of the exotic Orient."[119]

Renton points out that twenty-one UN agencies and non-governmental organizations concerned with trafficking are based in Bangkok, and every few weeks the city plays host to a new conference, seminar, or forum on the issue. Quoting a former UNICEF worker, he says that within UNICEF, anti-trafficking programs are viewed as "a great collecting bucket," i.e., receiving a stream of steady funding.[120]

Arguing that many NGOs are flush with millions "for the cause," Renton fails to point out that most of these NGOs favored with UN and multilateral agency money in Bangkok and elsewhere favor the decriminalization and regulation of the sex industry, insist on the distinction between voluntary and forced prostitution, and separate trafficking from prostitution. NGOs who are feminist and abolitionist are not "flush with millions" and, in fact, find it very difficult to establish a foothold in Thailand; this is because the "normalization" paradigm of prostitution prevails in both governmental and non-governmental sectors, and the funding is given to those organizations who advocate professionalizing prostitution.

Sex work advocate Laura Agustin also contends that trafficking has become a big cash cow for middle-class academics and professionals.[121] However, as Julia O'Connell-Davidson observes, "If 'trafficking' is a gravy train, Agustin is no mere train spotter observing her passengers from afar. Her own fieldwork, travel and conference attendance was, presumably, funded and supported somehow. . . . She too has secured status and a living on the back of 'trafficking.'"[122]

In my reckoning, the trafficking deniers such as Agustin generate an *ideology of neo-colonialism*. This is the neo-colonialism of alleged modern-day human rights defenders who sentimentalize women's inequality, romanticize women's agency, and sidestep questions such as: Why does globalization channel mostly poor and third-world women into the sex industry at great cost to themselves? Why do third-world women increasingly bear the burden of men's prostitution culture? Why has it become permissible and fashionable for male NGO members engaged in the fight against poverty, repression of human rights, and environmental degradation to use women in prostitution when they travel abroad to international conferences and meetings? Because these alleged human rights defenders are given permission to engage in the sexual abuse of women under the cover of women's choice, sexual freedom, and economic development for poorer women from developing countries in the south and for economically disadvantaged women in the north.

It is the globalized sex industry and its advocates that reify not only the image but also the reality of third-world women as voluntary sex workers. And in the international context of sex trafficking, victims of trafficking have been "explained" away as economic migrants and as migrant sex workers.

## ECONOMIC MIGRANTS OR VICTIMS OF TRAFFICKING?

Migration fuels economic development in poorer countries, especially through remittances sent home that not only benefit families but also banks, industry, and the national budget. Sex work advocates argue that women who end up in prostitution from poorer countries are simply part of the larger global migration stream and are in fact migrant sex workers and economic migrants, not victims of trafficking, who contribute to their countries' economies.

Of course, most countries don't reward migrants for helping to develop their national economies. Countries encourage migration, often because of a poor domestic economy with low job prospects. At the same time, they discredit those who migrate, especially if they return without having produced the fruit of their economic activities. Among those who return, women trafficked into prostitution are especially stigmatized.

Laura Agustin denounces feminist abolitionists who in her view "see anyone who comes from a Third World country as . . . victimized."[123] She quotes women trafficked from countries such as Nigeria and the Ukraine who don't present as tragic victims because they say they voluntarily migrated for "sex work." Agustin asserts women's voluntarism without context and without any nuanced discussion of the differences between consent and compliance—in the cases that she cites, compliance to the few options available to such women.

Agustin is a major proponent of the dominant academic view that abolitionists—especially feminist abolitionists—stereotype women in prostitution as victims in need of rescue. Abolitionists, it is claimed, create a desperate picture of prostituted women as infantilized and incapable of making their own choices. Abolitionists are portrayed as messianic crusaders trying to save all women from the dark dens of the sex industry and as encouraging the sensationalized views of women portrayed in the media.

Survivor of prostitution Suki Falconberg retorts that "the raw truth about prostitution" is hardly ever represented.[124] In her view, the story of what *really* happens to women in prostitution must be made more visible. The problem surely isn't that feminist abolitionists, researchers, and journalists have overdone the portrait of abuse heaped on millions of women and girls who have been sexually exploited in prostitution. In country after country, in sex venue after sex venue, on street after street, the evidence of victimization is overwhelming. Our failing may be that we have not made the "raw truth" visible enough. How many academics or journalists have met women and young girls who service five, ten, twenty men per day sexually? How many academics have attempted to describe and quantify the violence that is suffered by women in prostitution?

Historically, advocates of normalizing prostitution and the sex industry have argued that trafficking was the real problem, not prostitution. In their view, trafficking is forced and prostitution is voluntary "sex work." More recently, however, even trafficking has become normalized as "migration for sex work," and traffickers are said to be helpful facilitators and "people-movers."

## Conflating Migration and Trafficking: The Numbers Game

The conflating of trafficking and migration is based on the view that statistics on trafficking victims are highly exaggerated in both NGO and government circles. Sex work advocates maintain that the numbers of victims of trafficking have been vastly inflated. For example, David Feingold, international coordinator of the HIV/AIDS and Trafficking Projects at UNESCO in Bangkok, has questioned most trafficking statistics on record. Nor, he says, are there any data to substantiate that "the majority of trafficking is for sex" since "Statistics on the 'end use' of trafficked people are often unreliable because they tend to over represent the sex trade. For example, men are excluded from the trafficking statistics gathered in Thailand."[125]

The most accepted statistics of those trafficked annually range from the low end of 800,000 persons trafficked per year,[126] to 2.4 million.[127] Many settle for numbers somewhere in between. The truth is that no one knows the exact numbers. The numbers are plucked from the extrapolations of scholars and the testimonies of NGOs, officials, and government authorities. Critics seem to forget that the debate over numbers is relevant not only to trafficking; advocates who assist battered women acknowledge that it is impossible to obtain accurate statistics because many women never divulge they are abused. This is why anonymous surveys of women will document more cases of violence than the figures provided in police reports. Of course, in the case of trafficking, even surveys that could query the incidence of women who have been trafficked for sexual exploitation will often fail to reach this clandestine and controlled population of women.

The latest 2012 UNODC Report on global trafficking confirms, "Women account for 55-60 per cent of all trafficking victims detected globally; women and girls together account for about 75 per cent." From 2007 to 2010, 57–62 percent of all victims are trafficked for sexual exploitation globally.[128] Both the gender and purpose of trafficking figures may well be underestimated because the UNODC Report counted mostly those victims detected and reported officially. Also the Report did not make clear if, in reporting cases of forced labor, it investigated whether women in this situation had been sexually exploited as well. Nor did one-fourth of the countries providing information include victims who had been domestically trafficked.

## The Myth of Trafficking

Some critics go further than attacking the numbers in their assertion that *sex trafficking itself is a myth*. The Danish Sex Workers' Interests Organisation claims, "Very few who work in the sex industry have been trafficked."[129] Researcher Nick Mai asserts that although anti-trafficking legislation has been "rolled out" in the name of protecting migrants, it is actually anti-migration legislation.[130]

Sex work apologist Laura Agustin maintains, "Establishing this term 'trafficking' was a big mistake. It has caused chaos and damage and we should never have gone along with it." She reiterates the pro-prostitution lobby's claim that anti-trafficking laws restrict women's international freedom of movement and criminalize migration.[131] However, it would be more accurate to state that conflating trafficking with migration leaves victims of trafficking without any kind of recourse and perpetrators without any fear of prosecution. Agustin's "myth of trafficking" is itself a myth.

Journalist Nick Davies comes close to saying that most trafficking is a myth, based on a *Guardian* investigation of Britain's most resourced investigation of trafficking called Operation Pentameter Two. He cites the failure of the operation to find even one case of trafficking and make any arrests, and therefore suggests that "the scale and nature of sex trafficking into the UK has been exaggerated by politicians and media."[132] In the tradition of those who would accuse abolitionist researchers of creating a moral panic over trafficking, Davies asserts that the U.K. government has acted on this "distorted information" about trafficking to produce a bill that would criminalize the buyers.

However, as British journalist Catherine Bennett shrewdly quips, "The police are not much good at prosecuting those responsible for forced marriages and genital mutilation either. To say nothing of bankers and MPs responsible for fraud. But perhaps those stories are, themselves, nothing more than mischievous moral panics?"[133]

The 2006 *Report of the UN Special Rapporteur on the Human Rights Aspects of the Victims of Trafficking in Persons, especially Women and Children* came to this trenchant conclusion:

> For the most part, prostitution as actually practised in the world usually does satisfy the elements of trafficking. It is rare that one finds a case in which the path to prostitution and/or a person's experiences within prostitution does involve, at the very least, an abuse of power and/or an abuse of vulnerability. . . . The Protocol casts an extremely wide net in defining trafficking, one that arguably captures every present manifestation of prostitution.[134]

## The Links and Disjunctions between Trafficking and Migration

The disappearing of trafficking into voluntary and victimless "migration for sex work" covers a multitude of misinformation. Although there are linkages between trafficking and migration, this does not mean that trafficking and migration should be conflated. Trafficking is an issue of violence against women, a human rights violation, an economic and development issue, and a crime in which traffickers often take advantage of the migration hopes of women. Migrating women are especially vulnerable to sexual exploitation and the consequences of sexual violence, having moved outside their social and cultural safety nets where they are not usually fluent in the language and are easier to exploit. Many women who migrate for labor are sexually exploited as well.

There are points at which migration and trafficking intersect. It is instructive to understand what countries women are migrating to and examine the way in which migration flows, patterns, and regulations facilitate trafficking and women's entry points into the sex industry. An investigation of migration trends can help expose the problems of

international and domestic trafficking, aid in the prosecution of traffickers, and protect the rights of women migrants caught in the web of
trafficking networks.

For example, the governmental Philippines Overseas Employment
Agency estimated that of the 47,017 Filipinos who migrated to other
countries in Asia as "entertainers," 95 percent ended up in Japan.[135]
Since the category of "entertainers" is a well-known euphemism for
women in the sex industry, it is likely that for most of these Filipina
migrants, their destination was the Japanese sex industry heavily controlled by the Yakuza, or Japanese criminal networks. Viewed from
a human rights perspective, trafficking is a crime against migrants in
which women's desire to migrate is preyed upon. Within the context of
migration, trafficking can be viewed as exploited migration. Even many
legal migrants have been trafficked.

There are other ways, however, in which speaking about migration and trafficking in the same breath is fraught with problems. Some
trafficking victims are not migrants. Some have been domestically
trafficked into prostitution within their countries of origin. Most have
been forced, deceived, abducted, sold, abused, or induced into situations where they are exploited. Their migration, or "movement" as the
dictionary defines it, was not self-initiated. They have "been migrated"
into a country, state, or city. Simply speaking, they did not want to
move or be moved from one place to another, or to leave their region or
country for the purpose of being sexually exploited. This is trafficking.
To call this simply "migration" is lightweight language and misrep-
resents women's agency. It makes the harm to trafficked women invisible. It reinforces the conservative opinion that women "choose their
own fate" if they end up in prostitution.

There are many disadvantages for victims of trafficking in being
brought under the migration umbrella. In some countries, equating
trafficking and migration basically means that victims of trafficking
come under migration legislation. Thus, migrants are sent back to their
home country if they are found to be in the country illegally.[136]

We should be committed to principles and policies that foster regular and unexploited migration. But in advocating for migrants, it is
important not to confuse trafficking with migration, and thus to legitimate the commercial sex industry as the champion of "migration
for sex work." Attempts to make prostitution a form of legitimate and
legal "sex work" do not promote regular and humane migration. They
merely valorize trafficking as simply another form of migration, giving

the sex industry one of its best rationales for excusing this crime against mostly women and children as migration for labor.

—————

Women have become the sexual playthings of the post-colonial, migrating, and military global economy. Those from developing countries are major earners of foreign exchange in prostitution. Prostitution is further globalized in the explosion of international sex tourism. It is a buyer's market. *Where are all the anti-globalization advocates* as we face the expansive globalization of the international sex industry?

Although the globalized sex industry may mean more "jobs" for women, abolitionist advocates challenge the nature, quality, and type of "work" available and the differential status of men and women in the prostitution economy. Women become consumer goods in a large part of the economy, which depends on the sexualization and commodification of women's bodies. Men are the habitual consumers of women and children in prostitution. No matter how little money they make, even male migrants whose standard of income is much lower than sex tourists' consume women in prostitution. As activist Francini Mestrum has stated, "Poor women are not the same as poor men."[137] Nothing confirms this more than the globalized sexual exploitation that women are subjected to in all areas of the world.

At the 2006 World Social Forum, Juana Vasquez, a Maya Sacapulteca woman from Guatemala, cautioned against attributing the problem of sexual exploitation only to globalization or other outside influences. She stated that Latin America has to face up to its "endemic abuse of women."[138] So too must other countries. The sex industry and its advocates are transforming the gender inequality of prostitution into legitimate and sustaining work for women, thereby monetizing sexual exploitation. As capital is accumulating in the hands of pimps, traffickers, and related perpetrators, *where are all the anti-capitalists?*

Prostitution is economic opportunism, not economic opportunity. The hundreds of thousands of women who end up in prostitution do not dream of prosperity by prostitution. But the pimps and traffickers definitely do. Institutionalizing prostitution and trafficking as sex work or migration for sex work is the sex industry's dream. *Where are all the feminists?*

# 5

## Good Practices for the Future

Truth and justice make their best way in the world when they appear in bold and simple majesty.

—*Elizabeth Heyrick, British abolitionist of race slavery*

Many good practices have been proposed and implemented for preventing the traffic in persons, but most have not addressed trafficking as global prostitution. Certain UN agencies and programs, such as the ILO, WHO, UNAIDS, and UNDP, have sent a long-standing message in their subsidized reports that trafficking and prostitution are not connected—that prostitution is voluntary, but trafficking is forced. For example, the recent UNAIDS Global Commission on *HIV and the Law* report, in replacing prostitution with the term "sex work," asserts that "sex work and sex trafficking are not the same."[1] Reports dealing with HIV/AIDS especially promote legalization or decriminalization of prostitution in the alleged interests of preventing AIDS.

Chapter 5 focuses on alternative good practices that challenge the normalization of prostitution as work and confront the demand for prostitution that promotes trafficking for sexual exploitation. This book has focused on exposing the myths about prostitution and the global sex trade. This also means exposing the myths about alleged good practices and policies promoted by reputable UN programs and the pro-prostitution lobby, not simply criticizing but also presenting alternatives.

## NOT-SO-GOOD PRACTICES: UN REPORTS ON HIV/AIDS

For many years, sex work advocates have used the HIV/AIDS issue to foster their views on legalization/decriminalization of the sex industry.

Perhaps there is no more flagrant misuse of this subject than the views expressed in the 2012 report of the Global Commission on *HIV and the Law: Risks, Rights and Health*, especially in its section on "sex workers." The commission comprised fifteen members including at least one former head of state, legal scholars, and HIV/AIDS activists, and was "guided" by its technical advisory group, most of whom are historical proponents of decriminalizing the sex industry.

## The 2012 HIV and the Law Report

In addressing HIV/AIDS and prostitution, use of language in the *HIV and the Law* report covers a multitude of misrepresentations. Terms such as "laws that criminalize sex work" are conflated with "laws that criminalize sex workers." In fact, the report's theme is that any laws that criminalize traditional perpetrators of prostitution—pimps, buyers, and brothel keepers—put persons in prostitution at risk.

The report quotes UN secretary-general Ban Ki-moon's 2009 statement on World AIDS Day in a context that represents him as endorsing the commission's conclusion to decriminalize "consensual sex work." In his earlier statement, the UN secretary-general actually said, "In many countries, legal frameworks institutionalise discrimination against groups most at risk. Yet discrimination against *sex workers* . . . only fuels the epidemic and prevents cost-effective interventions."[2] I have never seen any report in which the secretary-general calls for laws that decriminalize "sex work," meaning the sex industry.

Indeed the "invisible man" in this report is the sex industry, although this term is not used. Readers may not realize that the agenda of many groups that aim to decriminalize "sex workers" is to decriminalize "sex work," meaning not only decriminalization of the women but also the entire prostitution trade—pimps, brothel keepers, and prostitution users. The report states that criminal penalties against perpetrators are bad for women in prostitution because most of these laws assume that women are victims in need of protection. The claim is that criminalization "in collusion with social stigma makes sex workers' lives more unstable, less safe and far riskier in terms of sex."[3]

The *HIV and the Law* report is bolder about its pro–sex work agenda than past UN reports. It blatantly criticizes the Swedish model, which penalizes the buyers, and calls the Swedish approach "Victimizing the 'Victim.'" The report claims that Swedish legislation penalizing prostitution users "has worsened the lives of sex workers." It reworks the old fictions that the Swedish law drives the sex trade underground, that resources for women in prostitution are scarce, and that "some Swedish authorities" are demanding an investigation of how the legislation affects the underground prostitution trade (see chapter 2).[4] Rather than "Victimizing the 'Victim,'" this section might be better termed "Pimping for the Pimps."

The *HIV and the Law* report is also more upfront in its recommendation to "repeal laws that prohibit consenting adults to buy or sell sex, as well as laws that otherwise prohibit commercial sex, such as laws against 'immoral earnings,' 'living off the earnings' of prostitution and brothel-keeping."[5] Feminists who support abolition of prostitution would agree that laws criminalizing women put women in jeopardy. However, much evidence cited in this book refutes the report's arguments that favor decriminalization of buyers and points to the fact that in legal regimes where the sex industry is decriminalized, women are more vulnerable to violence and abuse.

The *HIV and the Law* section on "sex workers" is not an investigation that takes into consideration any of the evidence that disputes its conclusions. In contrast to other sections of the report, it is not evidence-based. The report simply ignores the wealth of opposing evidence and fails to make even perfunctory criticisms of evidence that would challenge its recommendations. In examining the report's citations, one finds the usual chorus of advocates who oppose the Swedish law, many from its beginning, and who continue to be apologists for decriminalizing the sex industry. The citations include Ann Jordan, Don Kulick, Petra Östergren, Laura Agustin, and Wendy Chapkis, repetitively citing them as experts from one endnote to another. Many of these sources, such as Kulick's fanciful notion of the Swedish "fear of penetration," and Östergren's work that has not been published, have been discredited by scholars.[6] I could only find two known persons on the advisory committee sympathetic to abolitionism, and one stated she had resigned over a year before the report was published.

Perhaps one of the most disturbing aspects of this report is its "lead author," Judith Levine. A longtime proponent of keeping pornography legal, Levine also supports "consensual" adult-child sexual relationships. In a 2002 book entitled *Harmful to Minors: The Perils of Protecting Children from Sex*, Levine casts concern about child sexual abuse as a panic that pathologizes youthful sexual desire. She argues that alleged child sexual abuse is, in many instances, consensual sex if youth find pleasure in the sexual contact.

When the youngster has had what she considers a relationship of love and consensual sex, it does no good to tell her she has been manipulated and victimized. . . . Teens often seek out sex with older people, and they do so for understandable reasons: an older person makes them feel sexy and grown up, protected and special. . . . For some teens, a romance with an older person can feel more like salvation than victimization.[7]

Such a focus on the youth's consent, as if it stands alone in measuring the legitimacy of an adult's sexual act with a minor, gives abusers a convenient legal alibi.

For Levine, legitimate adult-teen sex hinges on a child's consent, seemingly not on an adult's abuse of power or vulnerability. She offers the Netherlands as a model where youth of 12–16 can legally consent to sex with adults who are not parents or authority figures. The Dutch, she says, protect children but do not infantilize them. Nevertheless, in 2002, after Levine's book was published, even the Dutch enacted age of consent reform and, in a unanimous vote of Parliament, changed their sexual age of consent law to sixteen.

The *HIV and the Law* section on "sex workers" omits any discussion of the multiple reports of the Swedish National Rapporteur; the 2010 report of the Swedish government evaluating ten years of the law's successes; the evidence-based articles of Sven-Axel Månsson, Max Waltman, Gunilla Ekberg; the Swedish feminist groups that work with victims of male violence such as ROKS; and the women in prostitution and survivors who have testified to the law's benefits. It makes no mention of the 2006 report of former UN Special Rapporteur on Trafficking Sigma Huda, who concluded that legal and decriminalized regimes of prostitution do not protect women in prostitution from violence and, in fact, exacerbate the harm (see endnote 116, chapter 2).

The Global Commission signed off on this report, thus providing reputable endorsement to pimps, brothel keepers, and prostitution users. The report puts out a welcome mat for all "consenting adults [who] buy or sell sex," at the same time that it transforms perpetrators of prostitution into respectable partners in the fight against HIV/AIDS.

## UNAIDS' Editors' Notes for Authors

The Global Commission report has a history of earlier UNAIDS writings leading up to its recommendation to "repeal laws that prohibit consenting adults to buy or sell sex, as well as laws that otherwise prohibit commercial sex, such as laws against 'immoral earnings,' 'living off the earnings' of prostitution [pimping] and brothel-keeping."[8] In May 2006 UNAIDS published a guide called *UNAIDS' Editors' Notes for Authors* to be used for manuscript preparation. Building on WHO general principles, it originated as an "aide-memoire of preferred terminology of use by staff members."[9] Over time, however, the editors state that wide demand encouraged their use by other UN agencies, NGOs, journalists, students, and writers.

A revised version of the *Notes* was published in 2011 under a different title, called *UNAIDS Terminology Guidelines*. Reiterating its preferred usage of words to be used in writing about HIV/AIDS, the *Terminology Guidelines* was "developed for use by staff members, colleagues in the Programme's 10 Cosponsoring organisations, and other partners working in the global response to HIV."[10] Since the ten cosponsoring organizations are other UN agencies, including UNICEF, UNESCO, WHO, and the World Bank, these guidelines apparently apply to documents also developed through these agencies.

The revised *UNAIDS Terminology Guidelines* stipulates that "sex worker" should be the designated linguistic driver in UN documents that address HIV/AIDS and related issues. The word "prostitution" is a no-no, listed with the warning, "don't use." For adults, the guidelines stipulate using "terms such as 'sex work', 'sex worker', 'commercial sex', or 'the sale of sexual services'." Only if children are involved is the expression "commercial sexual exploitation of children." As for the prostitution users, they should be called "'men/women/people who buy sex or clients of sex workers."[11] In effect the *UNAIDS Terminology Guidelines* acts as a lockdown for appropriate language for anyone wishing to publish through these agencies and serves to dictate that its restrictive, "Language shapes beliefs and may influence behaviours."[12] For anyone who has ever wondered why so many UN reports use the terms "sex work" and "sex worker" consistently, these prescriptions show that any texts submitted by persons not using these terms would likely be redlined by an in-house editor.

The *UNAIDS Terminology Guidelines* alleges that the term "sex worker" is "intended to be non-judgmental and focuses on the working conditions under which sexual services are sold."[13] However, the conditions of harm to which women in prostitution are subjected are seldom spelled out unless in the context of HIV/AIDS. When mentioned, harm is represented as a consequence of the disease rather than of the prostitution industry and the pimps and prostitution users who perpetrate the violence. Certainly the terms "sex work" and "sex worker" *are* judgmental in that they linguistically bolster the normalization of prostitution and the sex industry. It is difficult to characterize the *UNAIDS Terminology Guidelines* as other than an astonishing version of UN agency censorship.

## The 2011 UNAIDS Advisory Group on HIV and Sex Work

The endorsement of prostitution as sex work, and the sex industry as simply another business, was forecast in the 2011 report of the UNAIDS Advisory Group on *HIV and Sex Work*, which promotes several main myths exposed in this book. The recommendations developed in this 2011 report—a predecessor to the *HIV and the Law* report—are more a reinforcement of pro-prostitution tenets and practices than a discussion of good practices to reduce and eliminate HIV/AIDS.

> *Decriminalize Prostitution and the Sex Industry.* The advisory group's *HIV and Sex Work* report describes countries that have decriminalized "sex work" as examples of good practice.[14]
> *Don't Demonize Prostitution Users.* The *HIV and Sex Work* report endorses a shift from "an unrealistic approach that demonises clients and depicts them as criminals or exploiters" to a "more pragmatic approach" that shifts the focus "from reduction of demand for sex work to reduction of demand for unprotected sex."[15] Changing the meaning of demand is a tactic used to demonstrate that some kind of demand is being addressed, but not men's alleged right to the sex of prostitution. The report maintains that "End Demand" campaigns are punitive not only to buyers but also "they do make sex workers more vulnerable." These campaigns, the report claims, generate approaches "demonising and marginalizing clients" and "create major barriers to effective HIV programming with sex workers."[16]
> *Differentiate Sex Work and Trafficking.* In the advisory group report, trafficking is based on coercion and deceit. "Sex work" is free of both. People "who sell sex are exercising their agency to make a realistic choice from the options available to them."[17]
> *Pimps (known here as managers) and Brothel Keepers are Allies.* The *HIV and Sex Work* report states, "Brothel owners or managers can play a supportive role in ensuring that sex workers and their clients have access to condoms. . . . Alliances should be made with managers and agents of sex workers to encourage and support efforts to implement worker safety initiatives."[18]

The practices that proceed from these myths are more geared to what *not* to do, rather than positive recommendations. First, the report discourages anti-trafficking interventions such as rescuing "sex workers" because sex work advocates claim they result in the increased displacement of "sex workers." Laws on "sex work" should be reviewed to ensure they don't conflate sex work and trafficking. The report also alleges that efforts to abolish the sex industry constitute a "simplistic approach" that forces it underground, "making access to [health and social services] to sex workers in need all the more difficult."[19]

The *HIV and Sex Work* report continues to criticize programs that empower women in prostitution, provide them with alternative incomes, and assist them to exit prostitution, claiming *incorrectly* that they fail because they *require* women to leave prostitution or assume that women want to leave. The advisory group maintains that the aim of assistance programs should be to provide women with services to better function *within* the industry. It is the difficult working conditions that "sex workers" labor under that should be targeted.

Although a disclaimer states that *The Report of the UNAIDS Advisory Group on HIV and Sex Work* does not "necessarily" reflect the views of all members of the advisory group, nor of the position, decisions, or policies of the UNAIDS secretariat or any of its cosponsors, the disclaimer is deceptive. In light of the fact that the preferred language in the *UNAIDS Terminology Guidelines* appears to have been approved by the agency, the disclaimer masks what appears to be agency prostitution policy of recognizing prostitution as work. Likewise, the 2012 *HIV and the Law* report contains a similar disclaimer: "The content, analysis, opinions and policy recommendations contained in this publication do not necessarily reflect the views of the United Nations Development Programme."[20] If not, it certainly reflects the views and opinions of those appointed by the UNDP to serve on the Global Commission and of the technical advisory group that wrote the report. There have been no "equal opportunity" UNAIDS or UNDP commissions dominated by abolitionists who would offer a different viewpoint than the prevailing position of the technical advisory committee and the Global Commission calling for the decriminalization of the sex industry.

Given this book's emphasis on exposing the myths about prostitution, trafficking, and the global sex industry, the final chapter on "Good Practices for the Future" concentrates on strategies and projects that challenge these myths. This chapter showcases models that serve to counter these myths and that provide alternatives to those policies and practices that prop up prostitution as a legal business, transform pimps into benign and helpful business agents, and represent prostitution users as responsible buyers of a service.

I begin with the models and practices implemented by my own organization, the Coalition Against Trafficking in Women (CATW), over a twenty-five-year period of working to eliminate global sexual exploitation of women and children. Many of these good practices themselves expose the myths about prostitution and the global sex trade.

## THE COALITION AGAINST TRAFFICKING IN WOMEN (CATW): AN INTERNATIONAL CAMPAIGN TO CHALLENGE MALE DEMAND FOR PROSTITUTION AND THE LEGALIZATION OF PROSTITUTION[21]

### Penalizing the Demand

In the 1990s, CATW began strategic campaigns to support national legislation penalizing the buyers. Advocates spoke about the need to breach the anonymity of men who were the most invisible link in the chain of trafficking and sexual exploitation of women and children. CATW worked on several fronts—policy, legislation, research, and education—to address demand.

In the United States and the Philippines, CATW addressed the role of U.S. military in buying women and children for prostitution all over the world, whether in contexts of military conflicts or bases. CATW Asia-Pacific (CATW-AP) had long-standing ties with organizations of survivors of prostitution in the Philippines and had documented the abuses of military prostitution users around the former U.S. bases at Subic Bay (Olongapo) and Clark Air Force Base (Angeles City). Representatives of CATW International made several visits to the base regions in the Philippines and, with the help of CATW-AP, interviewed survivors of military prostitution.

In 1998 CATW International received a grant from the U.S. Department of Justice to do a study called *Sex Trafficking of Women in the United States: International and Domestic Trends*. In its investigation, men from military bases in the United States were frequently mentioned as buyers of women in prostitution. The researchers found that clubs, massage parlors, and brothels replicated the sexual R&R areas that proliferate near U.S. military bases to serve U.S. servicemen abroad. Further, prostitution establishments were officially off limits to the military at some bases, but the administrative regulation was never enforced.

The prostitution establishments were filled with military men. In 2001 the report to the National Institute of Justice was submitted with the recommendation, "Enforceable policies are needed within U.S. military contexts that enjoin U.S. military from engaging in commercial sexual exploitation at home or abroad."[22]

In 2005 patronizing prostitution became an offense under Article 138-34 of the Uniform Code of Military Justice and recognized as the foundation of sex trafficking. Earlier the no-patronization policy was left up to the local command and seldom enforced. With this change, the maximum punishment for patronizing a prostituted person is dishonorable discharge, military confinement up to a year, and fines or forfeitures. The Department of Defense was also charged with providing mandatory training on the policy for all troops, which has been enacted with service members all over the world.[23]

The United Nations has also made it a punishable offense for their military, peacekeepers, and related personnel to solicit women for sexual activities in prostitution. The human trafficking policy of the UN Department of Peacekeeping Operations recognizes that men's use of prostituted women in mission areas is exploitation. Even if prostitution is legal in the jurisdiction in which the peacekeepers operate, this UN policy prohibits the purchase of "sexual services" because it identifies prostitution itself as an act of sexual exploitation.[24]

This is not to say that good legislation in both the U.S. military and the United Nations is being well enforced. The record so far shows that few U.S. servicemen and UN peacekeepers and related personnel have been punished for offenses of sexual exploitation. As with any legislation or policy, it serves as a starting point for NGOs to advocate for justice and demand that policies be enforced.

*Promoting the Nordic Model*
Another major part of the CATW campaign has been to promote legislation passed in many of the Nordic countries targeting the male demand for prostitution. Based on principles of gender equality, not on moralism, Sweden passed landmark legislation in 1999 that criminalized the buyer of sexual services. The legislation was built on the public consensus that the system of prostitution promotes violence against women by normalizing sexual exploitation. The law does not penalize the persons in prostitution—mainly women and youth—but instead makes resources available to assist them (see chapter 2).[25] Sweden appears to be the only country in Europe where prostitution and sex trafficking have not increased.

Other Nordic countries such as Norway and Iceland followed Sweden's lead in 2009. CATW International and CATW-AP worked with Norwegian feminists, union leaders, government authorities, and parliamentarians to help pass the law penalizing the buyers. CATW-AP's assistance in helping Norwegian NGOs to promote the law in Norway reversed the usual direction of North-South aid to South-North. Jean Enriquez, the director of CATW in the Asia-Pacific region, gave testimony about CATW's work in establishing demand education programs for young men, which helped influence labor union support for the law.

Also leading up to the passage of the law in Iceland, CATW worked with its NGO partner, Stígamót, to support a law penalizing the buyers that passed in 2009. In 2011, however, Icelandic feminists claimed that police were not enforcing the law against the buyers. Police said they lacked both the funds and the personpower to do so. The movement demanded various actions—first, that the laws are complied with and the police enforce them; and second, that ads for prostitution in the media are stopped.

At the same time, a group emerged called Big Sister Watches Buyers of Prostitution in Iceland. After three weeks of investigation and monitoring of buyers who responded to fake ads, Big Sister turned over a list to the Reykjavik Metropolitan Police containing 56 names, 117 telephone numbers, and 29 e-mails of men who expressed interest in purchasing the services of prostituted women through websites set up by Big Sister as a decoy.[26] Big Sister continues to monitor the law's enforcement.

## Preventing the Demand

As the twenty-first century dawned, CATW in concert with the European Women's Lobby (EWL) conducted campaigns with NGOs in the Baltics, the Balkans, and several countries in Eastern Europe to promote the Swedish model of legislation. Recognizing that legislation was not enough, CATW developed programs to promote, support, and implement prevention programs to discourage the male demand for prostitution. These programs continue to educate young boys and men about the harm of prostitution to women, to themselves, and to their societies. For example, in the Philippines, Mexico and other countries in Latin America, and Italy, CATW has sponsored programs in which the overall objective is to change standards of masculinity, as well as the sexual attitudes and practices of boys and young men that result in trafficking for sexual exploitation. Most important, these programs aim to enlist boys and men as catalysts for change.

Led by Jean Enriquez, CATW-AP created a video entitled "First Time," which critiques how young men go through male rites of passage by using women in prostitution. Materials such as flyers, flipcharts, and handbooks detail the causes of prostitution and trafficking, and popular educational materials such as comic books and videos animate the stories of women who have been in prostitution and include the role of male buyers.

In selected regions of the Philippines, CATW-AP organized camps to educate young boys and men about the harm of prostitution and trafficking, men's role in perpetuating sexual exploitation, and men's potential role in being partners for change. By 2012 thousands of young men had either attended the camp sessions or the "echo programs" created by graduates of the camps who have launched their own projects to spread the messages learned.

Under the leadership of Teresa Ulloa in Mexico, CATW Latin America and the Caribbean (CATW-LAC) developed a model for training school teachers to recognize signs of sexual violence and exploitation of children. The program has reached thousands of teachers, as well as students directly impacted by child sexual abuse, offering ways in which young girls and boys can resist both the cultural messages promoting sexual exploitation as well as the actual recruiters and pimps who stalk school areas to lure young girls into the sex industry. The program entitled "Making Visible the Demand Side and its Role in Promoting Trafficking with Sexual Exploitation Purposes" conducts trainings that provide role-playing, in addition to offering models for boys and girls drawn from teachers and peer educators.

With the support of the Federal Preventive Police, CATW-LAC continued its public campaign against child sexual abuse in Mexico with a poster campaign. Displayed in eleven airports of the country, including the Mexico City airport, the posters presented the message, "Because you buy, child prostitution exists—Their lives and their bodies are not merchandise."

In Estonia, CATW, with local partners organized by the Estonian Women Resource Center, conducted public awareness campaigns and promoted prevention projects that developed creative new strategies to address the male buying of women in prostitution. The campaign targeted taxi drivers who take prostitution users to sex venues and to known hotels where buying women for prostitution is tolerated or encouraged. Estonian project leader Ilvi Joe-Cannon authored a *Primer on the Male*

*Demand for Prostitution* to assist European anti-trafficking projects in the Baltic States in challenging the legalization and decriminalization of prostitution industries combined with explanations of alternative policy to eliminate demand.

In Lithuania the Women's Issues Information Center, with the support of the Ministry of Social Security and Labor, organized an innovative campaign designing six-foot-high posters and placing them in 134 bus kiosks in the seven largest cities of the country. The eye-catching posters depicted men clothed from the head down with partially opened trouser fly fronts and included the message, "It is shameful to buy women."

In Albania, CATW worked with project leader Briseida Mema, the Women's Media Group, and journalists to change the sexually objectifying tone of media articles on prostitution and trafficking and to expose the harmful consequences of male demand for prostitution. CATW gave an award to the president of the Albanian parliament, Jozefina Topalli, who supported and assisted the campaign in Albania to combat proposals legally recognizing prostitution as work. Currently, Albanian partner NGOs conduct an ongoing media campaign whose message is "No to Sex Tourism. Yes to Cultural Tourism." The campaign advertises the country's natural resources as a contrast to the sexually objectifying posters of women meant to draw men to Albanian beaches and resorts for sex tourism.

In Hungary, writer Zsuzsa Forgacs coordinated a project to produce and distribute fourteen hundred posters to raise public awareness about prostitution and trafficking. The most creative and hard-hitting poster was of seven men urinating, placed in men's toilets and other public spaces in Budapest. The poster spotlights a wall of graffiti in front of the urinals with twelve messages, beginning with "Every Seventh Man Buys Vulnerable Women and Children for Sexual Use—They Generate Prostitution with Their Money." Postcards of the scene were also distributed.

With the EWL, CATW worked in conjunction with the Centre for Women War Victims—ROSA; Women's Room—Centre for Sexual Rights; and the Centre for Women's Studies all in Zagreb Croatia. As part of the PETRA anti-trafficking network, the three partner organizations helped sponsor a government/NGO seminar to challenge legalization of prostitution proposals. A conference followed that drew participants from fifteen countries and underscored that many participants came from regions devastated by totalitarian regimes, war, or postwar transition, where women were the primary victims of these conflicts.

A key theme of the conference featured the ways in which the UN, NATO, and other troops, police, and foreign presence in these countries promote prostitution, trafficking, and other forms of sexual exploitation and build the infrastructure for future sex tourism in the Balkans. Knowing that a UN zero-tolerance policy of prostitution was in effect but not well enforced, the conference resolution emphasized, "Governments that contribute to peacekeeping operations should publicize the UN policy of zero tolerance for the use of prostituted women by UN peacekeepers and personnel, train their peacekeeping forces, implement the policy, and take responsibility for punishing abusers."[27]

On its website, CATW International publicized a chart of "global good practices," describing police and community actions taken in cities and countries to deter prostitution users.[28] Many U.S. police departments have creatively used local legislation to arrest, charge, and prosecute the men. Some have seized men's cars. Still others have used techniques of "naming and shaming" in which men's names are published in the newspapers or on the Internet when they are caught in the act of soliciting women in prostitution. Other police forces have aired surveillance videos of male buyers, caught in the act of soliciting women in prostitution, on a special TV show. Many of these initiatives have been developed with the purpose of removing male anonymity.

In 2006 CATW launched an extraordinarily successful international campaign called "Buying Sex is Not a Sport" to protest Germany's promotion and public display of prostitution during the World Cup Games in June and July 2006. The campaign, coordinated by Malka Marcovich from France, developed an online petition, available in five languages, and was ultimately signed by more than 150,000 individuals and organizations from 125 countries. At the onset of the games, the petition was delivered to German embassies in all the major world regions.[29]

In the years 2010 and 2012 under the leadership of Norma Ramos, CATW with the support of over a hundred cosponsors led campaigns to protest online pimping and the sexual exploitation of women and children through ads listed on Craigslist and Backpage.com. Both these online sites feature barely disguised ads that facilitate trafficking and prostitution.

A 2010 high-profile protest was held in front of the corporate headquarters of Craigslist in San Francisco, California. Hearing about the protest, Craigslist tried to paint over its corporate logo but was not quick enough to disguise the building to ward off the protestors.[30] Although Craigslist had called in "anti-protesters," few showed up to support the company. Because of the CATW campaign, as well as other actions, that targeted the company for its online exploitative ads, Craigslist closed down its Adult Services section. However, observers quickly saw that some of these ads were reappearing in other sections of the list. Given the closing of the Adult Services section, Craigslist must have recognized that the protest severely impacted its business and reputation.

In 2012 CATW staged a demonstration in front of Village Voice Media, which owns Backpage.com. Protesters knew that Backpage.com would be the beneficiary when Craigslist dropped its Adult Services section. Like Craigslist, its ads fuel demand for prostitution and provide buyers with anonymity and impunity. The protest demanded that Backpage.com take responsibility for facilitating sexual exploitation and remove these ads from its site. CATW held a press conference to publicize the protest at the same time that attorneys general from forty-eight U.S. states were targeting Backpage.com as a sex trafficking hub and called on the Village Voice Media to stop profiting from human trafficking.[31]

## The Campaign against the Legal Normalizing of Prostitution

CATW put prostitution back on the international policy agenda by re-establishing that trafficking is globalized prostitution. These connections had been attacked to the point of becoming the lodestone of a governmental and non-governmental battle about how the very realities of prostitution and trafficking are defined, and whether trafficking and prostitution should be joined or separated in both policies and programs.

Within the United Nations, CATW was very influential in ensuring that the Palermo Protocol on trafficking and particularly its definition would be based on the 1949 convention on prostitution and trafficking. Over a two-year period, CATW organized a network of 140 NGOs to promote a definition of trafficking that would protect all victims of trafficking, not just those who had been forced. CATW and the Human Rights Network were successful in reminding international lawmakers that prostitution should not be separated from trafficking. They successfully fought against significant opposition from legalizing countries and NGOs wanting a definition of trafficking that did not include prostitution and that was based on a definition of force.[32]

Another major campaign of CATW challenged a trend to legalize and decriminalize prostitution internationally. By the turn of the century, several countries in Europe and in Australia and New Zealand, had passed such legislation. CATW documented how these regimes were public policy disasters and worked to reverse a trend of legally normalizing prostitution by testifying before the European Parliament, the U.S. Congress, and legislative committees in various countries that were considering legalization or decriminalization of the prostitution industry. The failed results of legalization of prostitution in Europe and Australia helped many countries reassess the movement to regulate and decriminalize prostitution and put abolitionist principles back on the policy agenda.

In its publications CATW emphasized evidence from the legalizing countries that showed how these regimes had failed. For example, it spotlighted a 2008 Dutch National Police report that denounced the country's legalized prostitution system and stated, "The idea that a clean, normal business sector has emerged is an illusion" (see chapter 3). Likewise, in Germany a federal government report found that the German Prostitution Act had not improved conditions for women in the prostitution industry nor helped them to leave (see chapter 4).

Under the leadership of Esohe Aghatise, Association IROKO in Italy brought together mayors and representatives of the regional Piedmont municipalities, provincial presidents, labor unionists, representatives of the Catholic Church, NGOs that work with prostituted and trafficked women in the region, members of the Italian Parliament, and representatives of various governmental ministries to create a program that addressed the issue of legalization of prostitution in Italy. In 2004 the public program helped to turn back legalization proposals in Italy. One important result of this organizing was that the trade unions announced publicly at the conference that they would not support legalization or decriminalization of the sex industry in Italy.

In Hungary, CATW partnered with the Way Out With You Association in Budapest to establish a drop-in center for women in prostitution that provides an alternative to one that promotes legalization of prostitution. The center offers a hotline, sanitary facilities, food, support groups for women, counseling, employment advice and assistance, a program for endangered youth on the street, schoolwork assistance to children of women in prostitution, and multiple media and education programs about the activities of the drop-in center. These media activities have been key in featuring the experiences of women in prostitution, combined with program and policy discussions to challenge legalization and regulation of prostitution initiatives proposed in Hungary.

In Kosovo, CATW's partner organization was Radio Plus, which created a public awareness campaign about prostitution and trafficking using multiple media—five different forty-second radio spots with succinct messages about prostitution and trafficking, broadcast four times daily for a period of four consecutive months; a web-based campaign that published the radio messages; production and distribution of anti-trafficking brochures; the organizing of several public forums in which human rights experts, international police officers, NGOs, and students were invited to discuss the links between trafficking and prostitution; and CD distribution of the radio spots that were sent to partner stations in Kosovo to rebroadcast.

With local Czech organizations and the European Women's Lobby, CATW helped persuade Czech parliamentarians to reject regulation of prostitution twice in 2005. Pro-prostitution advocates had convinced the government to withdraw the Czech Republic's ratification of the 1949 convention prohibiting the country from regulating prostitution. Had the deratification been successful, regulation of prostitution could have been fast-tracked in the Czech Republic.

In October 2007 Bulgaria reversed its legislative course and declared it would not legalize prostitution and the sex industry.[33] Here CATW worked with the Institute for Democracy, Stability and Security in Southeast Europe (IDSSEE) and the Bulgarian Gender Research Foundation (BGRF) to confront pressures to legalize the sex industry. Bulgaria faces an enormous problem of trafficking in women and children controlled by organized crime and enhanced by political corruption. Owing to the unstinting efforts of MP and former minister of foreign affairs Nadezhda Mihaylova, governmental officials—including the president, the minister of justice, the prosecutor general, and the minister of the interior—announced publicly that the government would not legalize prostitution. The minister of the interior who had earlier proposed legalization reversed his support and distanced himself from pro-legalization legislation.[34]

In Romania with CATW's local partner Caritas and a coalition of human rights, feminist, and religious organizations, CATW also helped to turn back the tide of legalization. In 2007 Interior Minister Cristian David told the U.S. ambassador to Romania that he would defer any "discussion of whether his ministry would explore legalization of prostitution under his leadership." A network of Romanian nongovernmental organizations reported that the Romanian prime minister clearly stated his position against legalization of prostitution.[35]

In launching this campaign to reverse the course of legalization of prostitution and the sex industry, CATW changed the dominant representation of prostitution as work to one that included it as a form of violence against women. Partners in the campaign emphasized that normalizing prostitution was not a solution to a country's trafficking problem but was, instead, part of the problem. In contrast to the message that legalized prostitution protects women in prostitution, CATW answered that women cannot be protected by a legislative package that mainly protects pimps, prostitution users, and brothels. The campaign exposed the fiction that *only* by shielding perpetrators of prostitution can prostituted women be protected. And it showed that legalized and decriminalized regimes of prostitution constitute *state-sponsored prostitution* with the state as the primary pimp benefiting from the profits.

## GOOD PRACTICES, PROGRAMS, AND PROJECTS BY AND FOR WOMEN IN PROSTITUTION

Survivors are the authoritative voices of women in prostitution. An important practice to come out of the abolitionist movement is the growth of websites, blogs, press releases, and manifestos that represent survivors' experiences. Women who have gone through prostitution not only speak for themselves, but they have also developed projects and programs in which survivors help build futures for other women emerging from the sex industry.

Survivors have assumed the crucial task of speaking up about public policy relating to prostitution and trafficking. In testifying about policy and legislation, they have challenged the statements of "sex workers" and the sex work lobby whom the media represent as the authoritative voices of women in prostitution. Their policy involvement has shifted attention from "sex workers" to survivors, as well as exposed the myth that only those who identify as "sex workers" who defend the sex industry represent women in prostitution.

### Manifestos

In 2003 the First National Conference of Prostitution Survivors took place in Manila in the Philippines. Seventy-five prostituted women from eight regions of the country denounced issuing business permits to legitimate prostitution, police abuse of women in prostitution, and police corruption, and called for passage of the Anti-Prostitution Act, a law moving its way through the Philippines national legislature. Alma Bulawan, president of BUKLOD in Olongapo, stated, "Legalization of the industry is not necessary for social security benefits to apply to prostituted women."[36]

Basing its manifesto on the Filipinas' statement, survivors from Denmark, the United Kingdom, Belgium, and the United States issued a similar manifesto during a 2005 press conference held at the European Parliament. The manifesto rejected the ideology that prostitution is work and a job choice like any other. In contrast to an international conference of "sex workers" being held in Brussels at this same time, survivors argued that prostitution is not "migration for sex work," nor is it a form of labor or a human right. Instead, prostitution is a violation of human rights and violence against women. At the press conference, survivors and their allies addressed specific questions such as supporting victims, preventing trafficking, challenging legalization of prostitution, eliminating the demand for sexual exploitation, investigating and prosecuting traffickers, and practical steps to combat trafficking and prostitution.[37]

In 2011 an Asia-Pacific meeting of Survivors of Sex Trafficking and Prostitution, which took place in New Delhi, India, held a regional press conference. Survivors and their allies came from twenty-five countries, including India, Nepal, the Philippines, Japan, South Korea, and Australia. Survivors released a statement urging penalties for prostitution users, as well as greater resources to assist women and girls. "Collectively, we agree to reject the legalization of the prostitution industry which serves as the demand side to sex trafficking, and to punish the buyers and the business, instead of the women." The statement continued:

> Laws in the region have long been criminalizing and stigmatizing those exploited in prostitution, when they are the ones whom society and government should protect. . . . We unite with our sisters in the feminist movement and the labor movement who call for real jobs, not prostitution; for economic programs that create local, sustainable employment. . . . Social movements have to carry out prevention and public information campaigns alongside us, and help in shifting the stigma away from the victims and onto the perpetrators—the buyers and the business.[38]

Fatima Nat Dhuniya, a survivor forced into the sex industry as a child and who managed to escape, said that the idea that governments would legalize prostitution is unthinkable. Twenty-year-old Noor was sold to a brothel in West Bengal at age ten. She was later rescued by activists and became an outspoken community organizer. She stated, "Prostitution is a vicious world. . . . Only traffickers and pimps profit from it. Legalizing prostitution will not empower women."[39]

In their writings and activism, survivors expose the truth about prostitution and the global sex trade. They, more than anyone, can unmask the myths about an industry that severely damages women and children. Survivors continue to speak out singularly and jointly, contradicting the messages from the sex industry lobby that prostitution is good for women. They testify not only to the harms of prostitution but also to the ways in which policy and programs should be developed to prevent sexual exploitation, protect victims, and punish the perpetrators.

## Websites, Blogs, and Press Releases

In Canada, Exploited Voices Now Educating (EVE) comprises former women in the sex industry "dedicated to naming prostitution violence against women and seeing its abolition through political action, advocacy, and awareness-raising that focuses on ending the demand for paid sexual access to women and children's bodies."[40] The EVE website contains actions that people can take to support the abolition of prostitution.

Sextrade101 is a Toronto-based survivors' and abolitionists' organization that offers "public awareness and education on all aspects of the sex trade in order to eradicate myths and stereotypes about prostitution by replacing them with facts and true stories from women who've been enslaved by this dark and lucrative industry."[41] Sextrade101 offers public presentations, police sensitivity training, program development, and educational street tours facilitated by survivors.

Survivors Connect is "a private online meeting place for survivors of sex trafficking/prostitution. This is a space where survivors can come together to communicate, share, network and get the resources we need to help ourselves and each other, like the band of sisters we are. . . . When we act together it is much easier for us to speak the truth about the sex industry."[42] As an article on the site makes clear, however, there are consequences to speaking the truth about the sex industry. Stella Marr writes "How the Sex Industry Threatens Survivors Speaking Out While Pimps Pose as Sexworker Activists." She recounts the ways in which survivors' e-mail accounts have been hacked, private information about them appears online, and they receive cyber-bullying messages.

She traces the threads of anonymous and not-so-anonymous e-mails that she has received, many coming from "sexworker activists." And she cites the tweets of major sex work advocates such as Brooke Magnanti to Elena Jeffreys of the Scarlet Alliance in Australia who try to impugn the credibility of Survivors Connect by comparing it to Operation Rescue, a U.S. extremist anti-abortion group.[43]

These tactics will come as no surprise to feminists who, for many years, have challenged the sex industry and its advocates and have found themselves the recipients of such aggressive smear tactics. The difference is when survivors speak out against prostitution, pornography, and the sex industry, they find their past lives exposed in the most insidious ways. For example, when Shelley Lubben spoke out against her abuse in the pornography industry, she found herself in a YouTube video that depicted her in earlier pornographic scenes and rebutted her accusations of sexual exploitation. The movie was made by Michael Whiteacre, a U.S. lawyer and filmmaker connected with the pornography industry, and includes a male porn actor who discusses her sexual performance in the video as aggressive and "calling the shots."[44] Viewers are led to believe she was no exploited victim but controlled the show. Marr writes that the unspoken warning to survivors who speak out is: "Make waves and this could happen to you."

## Survivors' Legal and Political Advocacy

The media historically has featured "sex workers" as the authoritative voices of women in prostitution. Nowhere was this picture clearer than in the Bedford decision in Canada that decriminalized brothels and pimping. The three "sex workers" who brought the legal challenge known as *Bedford v. Canada* were represented in the media as the experiential experts who speak for women in prostitution. In spite of this bias, survivors articulated their powerful opposition to the court decision.

The constitutional challenge to the pimping and brothel laws in Canada was brought by several former "sex workers": Terri-Jean Bedford, a self-described dominatrix who appears in pictures with a riding whip and who was convicted in 1998 for keeping a "bawdy house" (brothel);[45] Valerie Scott, who plans to open a brothel after attending business school for this purpose;[46] and Amy Lebovitch. In 2008 the three women brought suit in order to operate "legitimate businesses, complete with zoning permits, reimbursable expenses and workers' compensation."[47] The case was advanced on the grounds that the criminalization of pimping and brothels infringed upon the women's right to conduct lawful business in a safe environment—in other words, their rights to pimp women and keep them in brothels.

A contingent of survivors publicly spoke out against the 2010 Superior Court of Ontario's decision to overturn these laws. In an interview, Bridget Perrier, now a social worker, said, "When I see Bedford with her riding crop and the glamorization of sex work, it appalls me, because these are the tools that we see being used on girls, by their pimps.[48] In another interview, Perrier stated the ruling "made those most vulnerable be standing targets for more (Robert) Willie Picktons,"[49] the Canadian serial killer of dozens of prostituted women.

Prior to the decision, nine survivors of prostitution filed affidavits with the lower court challenging the group of three "sex workers" who brought the case.[50] They rejected one premise on which the court decision was based—that brothels are protected indoor spaces much safer than outdoor streets. Survivor Katarina MacLeod stated, "Indoors isn't safer. It is complete hell inside and the customer is always right. They can beat you and take your money. . . . The location didn't make us safer, the men who we were with made us unsafe. Even if there is a panic button in the room, how do you get to it?"[51]

Survivors also protested in front of the court. However, the media highlighted the opposing views of survivors by a photo contrived to look like a catfight between "sex worker" Terri-Jean Bedford and survivor Christine Barkhouse with the caption, "Sex worker advocates clash over landmark ruling."[52] The language of "sex work" and "sex workers" has become so media-dominant that the view that prostitution is not work, and survivors who do not identify as sex workers, gets swallowed up in the title of this article where opposing sides are described as *sex worker* advocates.

The Native Women's Association of Canada and the Aboriginal Women's Action Network (AWAN), both organizations with survivor members, spoke out against the court's decision. The association issued a press release targeting the ruling's contention that it would allow "assistants," otherwise known as recruiters, pimps, and traffickers, to protect the women and their business interests. Rather, the association said that this ruling would make women more vulnerable because it would enable human traffickers to pose as "assistants" when they are simply "living off the avails of prostitution [in many jurisdictions, the legal definition of pimping]."[53]

AWAN issued an eloquent statement in April 2011 representing members who have been prostituted, daughters and friends of prostituted women, and women who have never been prostituted but accept the responsibility to speak out for those they know and love who are being harmed.

> As Aboriginal women, we are whole-heartedly invested in the issue of prostitution. . . . When people support the legalization of prostitution, they tell us that we do not matter. . . . The ruling by Justice Himmel in Ontario takes away what little protection women had from johns, pimps and brothel owners and instead allows these men the legal right to abuse women. . . . When defending the legalization of prostitution or total decriminalization of prostitution, we want you to consider: what am I defending? Because you are defending a hateful, violent, capitalist industry that works to devalue all women but particularly native women, and why would you defend that?[54]

The Asian Women Coalition Ending Prostitution, a network that has long been critical of the legalization and decriminalization of the sex industry, stated that the Ontario court decision makes it more difficult for Asian women in prostitution to obtain legal protection. "The decision . . . to strike down laws that criminalize prostitution activity offers human traffickers, pimps and johns greater legitimacy while stripping away a means for police to use the law in order to stem human trafficking into prostitution."[55]

Survivors Connect also issued a statement joined by thirty-four trafficking and prostitution survivors in support of the Canadian NGOs that challenged the Bedford decision decriminalizing pimping and brothels. "It's especially troubling that the Bedford ruling upholds the criminalization of prostitutes selling sex on the street, as these women are almost always traumatized crime victims who need support not arrest. Meanwhile the ruling empowers the people who terrorize and exploit these women."[56]

## Model Programs and Projects Combining Victim Services and Legal and Political Advocacy

When advocacy is combined with victim services, this grounds legislation and policy in the experience of victims. NGOs that provide both functions perform a huge task, because each is a full-time occupation made all the more consuming by the urgency of removing victims from harm. I have had the opportunity to visit and see firsthand the services at most of these programs and the results of their work. It is instructive that pro–sex work groups claiming to represent women in prostitution rarely provide services other than HIV/AIDS and safe sex education. Their main service is risk management, not risk elimination.

In the United States, survivor Vednita Carter founded the organization Breaking Free in 1993 to provide multiple services to women in prostitution, including counseling, healthcare access, and transitional and permanent housing. Emphasizing the plight of African American women who are disproportionately represented in prostitution in the United States, "Breaking Free is committed to diversity and to the empowerment of women. Our staff come from a variety of backgrounds and areas of expertise, and many are themselves survivors."[57]

In 2011, following the establishment of its earlier Offenders Prostitution Program, Breaking Free organized a Demand Change Project. In cooperation with MATTOO, Men Against the Trafficking of Others, Breaking Free designed a creative two-day program to create public awareness about male demand for prostitution and to educate and involve men in solutions. Breaking Free also conducts trainings and presentations on "Legalization of Prostitution: Laws vs. Reality."

The Eaves for Women/Poppy Project in London gives support and accommodation to trafficked and prostituted women, including financial help, access to health services, counseling, criminal and immigration legal assistance, education, and employment opportunities. Eaves also created a Demand Change campaign that urged the U.K. government to adopt the Nordic model criminalizing the buyers and called upon Parliament to "Vote for Women, not Pimps and Punters [buyers]." The result of this campaign was a change in the U.K. Policing and Crime Act (Art. 14) in 2010 that criminalized the purchase of sex from a person who has been exploited—a strict liability measure, meaning that prosecutors do not have to prove that the buyer had knowledge of the victim's condition of exploitation.[58]

Ruhama is a Dublin-based organization founded on the 1949 convention's principle that "prostitution and the accompanying evil of trafficking for prostitution, is incompatible with the dignity and worth of every human being." Established in 1989 as a joint project of the Good Shepherd and Our Lady of Charity Sisters, Ruhama has a long history of providing services to women in prostitution, including street outreach from a mobile van, casework, and "long term aftercare and support" that helps women to reintegrate into society.

Ruhama increasingly uses the media to create public awareness about the growing problem of sex trafficking and the situation of women in prostitution in Ireland. Working to influence public policy in the country, Ruhama advocates with relevant government agencies to change or develop legislation, including the criminalizing of buyers. In contrast to the view that indoor prostitution is safer than outdoor prostitution, Ruhama's experience shows that women in indoor venues "experience more psychological problems and are in some ways more damaged by the process than those who work on the streets. . . .The added danger [is] that Ireland's indoor sex trade has become predominantly organized and controlled by organized criminal gangs."[59]

In Glasgow, Scotland, a municipal government, which clearly views prostitution and sexually exploitative activities as violence against women, has established the Routes Out Partnership under the former leadership of Ann Hamilton. To an outsider, one of the most remarkable aspects of this partnership is the partnership itself, which includes the Scottish Executive, the city council, the police, and the organizations that provide direct services to women in prostitution. This partnership shows what strides a city can make when it recognizes prostitution as violence against women rather than as a normal job, when it grounds its policy in gender equality, and when it has the will to rebut one of the most degrading industries in the world—the sex industry.

One aspect of the Glasgow City Council's policy is to object officially to the licensing applications for lap dancing clubs. The council has been successful in turning back the majority of these applications by consistently challenging the sex clubs. In an age when some states and cities are permitting tolerance zones for prostitution, which are really protection zones for pimps and predators, Glasgow has rejected this solution.

But Glasgow has not engaged in these battles by diverting funds from programs for women in prostitution. It has put serious resources into a coordinated service program for women through the Routes Out Intervention Team, which helps women involved in street prostitution to get their lives together and choose alternatives. At the same time, Routes Out undertakes public awareness campaigns challenging the social acceptance of prostitution and exposing the true nature of prostitution as sexual violence and as a survival strategy, not a sexual choice, for women.

In 2009 the Glasgow partnership conducted a public campaign called "End Prostitution Now." "The aim of the campaign was to raise awareness of the harm caused through prostitution and to put the focus firmly on the buyers of sex, who create the demand, and who in the past have been invisible from public debate."[60] Councilor Jim Coleman, who led the Glasgow City Council's response to the issue of prostitution, is encouraged by the change in Glasgow public opinion over the past decade but believes that legislation must go further and send an un-equivocal message that buying sex will not be tolerated. In 2009 and 2010, Member of the Scottish Parliament (MSP) Trish Godman pro-posed legislative amendments that would penalize the prostitution us-ers. In 2012, MSP Rhoda Grant submitted a similar proposal for a bill to make it an offence to purchase sex. Although the 2009–2010 efforts were not successful, pimps and traffickers know that the city is not an advantageous place for them to set up shop because of Glasgow's anti-sex industry policy. And the 2012 bill is still pending, as of this writing.

The Women's Crisis Center Secretariat in Oslo is led by Tove Smaa-dahl who has worked for many years to establish the shelter movement in most parts of Norway. Within the last decade, the shelter move-ment has included services to victims of trafficking and prostitution, combined with advocacy to pass the 2009 Norwegian law penalizing the purchasers of sexual activities. After the passage of the Norwegian law, its ROSA project was established to provide services to trafficked women.

Vancouver Rape Relief and Women's Shelter was founded in 1973. Under the longtime leadership of Lee Lakeman, it has an international reputation for its commitment to advancing women's equality and end-ing violence against women. The Vancouver NGO challenges social attitudes, laws, and policies that promote male violence against women and children by participating in feminist, anti-racist, and democratic community building.

Vancouver Rape Relief and Women's Shelter holds an abolitionist view of prostitution identifying it as violence against women. The shel-ter co-organized an equality-seeking coalition to appeal the 2010 On-tario Superior Court's decision to decriminalize pimping and brothel keeping. This coalition was an intervener in the court case that, unfor-tunately, resulted in the higher court's affirmation of the lower court's decision. The case will now go to Canada's Supreme Court.[61]

There are other organizations providing good practices that com-bine assistance to victims of prostitution and trafficking with engaging in legal and political advocacy. Some of these, such as Stígamót in Ice-land, Apne Aap in India, IROKO in Italy, and Kvinnefronten in Nor-way, have already been mentioned in other sections of this book.

## CONCLUSION: THE WORLD'S MISSING WOMEN

Women in prostitution are among the world's "missing women." Many prostituted women have been missing for years, their remains discovered in makeshift graves. Others are missing physically, when their bodies have been mutilated, injured, and diseased. A great number are missing psychologically, when their minds and spirits have been irrevocably damaged. Prostituted women are missing economically, when their lost human capital has deprived them and their families of income and income-generating potential. Prostitution is a systematic gendercide of tragic proportion where many of the world's women are missing in multiple ways in plain view.

There are those who would argue that prostitution and trafficking could be made better for women. In effect they promote a prostitution in which women are made better for men's abuse.

There are those who would argue that prostitution should be re-defined and recognized as work. Although prostitution is an *industry*, it should never be legitimated as a job. If we declare prostitution to be a job like other jobs, we do not dignify the women in prostitution; we simply dignify the sex industry.

There are those who would say that the sexual exploitation of chil-dren is the real problem, because children have no choice. It is critical to make connections between women and children because worldwide many women enter prostitution when they are thirteen or fourteen. The day these girls turn eighteen, their abuse does not magically be-come a self-determined choice.

There are those who would ask us to speak only about the violation of trafficking and not about prostitution as violence against women. But sex trafficking is globalized prostitution. Globalization of the world economy also means globalization of sex industries. The links between domestic prostitution industries and international trafficking networks are critical to the expansion of the sex industry.

There is an urgent need for courage and the political will to act against this global exploitation of women and children. First we must recognize all practices of sexual exploitation for what they are: not sex work but sexual exploitation. Not human rights but a human rights vi-olation. Not the product of women's consent but the result of women's compliance with the only options available to many of them.

The challenge of governments today is to recognize that prostitu-tion is a massive and growing *industry* while *not* ratifying prostitution as *a job*. The challenge of governments today is to provide rights and protections for women in conditions of sex trafficking and prostitution while acknowledging that both abrogate women's rights and violate women's human dignity.

The challenge of governments today is to recognize the difference between decriminalizing the women and decriminalizing the perpetrators, especially when the offenders are rebranded as clients, business managers, and protectors of women.

Governments and non-governmental organizations can acknowledge that there are women and girls attempting to survive in conditions of sex trafficking and prostitution without normalizing prostitution as work. Governments and non-governmental organizations have tended to emphasize short-term solutions for women in sex industries that encourage women to stay in the industry, such as negotiating for safe sex, condoms, and HIV/AIDS testing. However, it is important to advocate for such measures within a context that provides women with alternatives to prostitution. Women have the right to humanitarian assistance to help them out of prostitution rather than humanitarian assistance to keep them in prostitution.

Sexual exploitation is not inevitable. Stopping sexual exploitation requires the same resources that are provided to other victims of violence against women. But most of all, it requires effective actions, programs, policies, and legislation on a national, regional, and international level, as well as intergovernmental cooperation to prevent further violations of women and girls.

# NOTES

## PREFACE

1. Janice G. Raymond and Donna M. Hughes with Carol J. Gomez, *Sex Trafficking of Women in the United States: International and Domestic Trends* (North Amherst, MA: Coalition Against Trafficking in Women, 2000), http://www.catwinternational.org/Home/Article/99-sex-trafficking -of-women-in-the-united-states-international-and-domestic-trends.

2. Robert Jay Lifton, *Witness to an Extreme Century: A Memoir* (New York: Free Press, 2011), 91.

3. Siddharth Kara, *Sex Trafficking: Inside the Business of Modern Slavery* (New York: Columbia University Press, 2009), 22. See figure 1.2, entitled "Slavery and Trafficking Revenue and Profits, 2007." Based on complex methods, especially calculating regional figures, the author estimates both global revenues and profits from modern-day slavery. He estimates that global "Trafficked Sex Slaves" generate total revenues of $51.3 billion and profits of $35.7 billion.

4. This is a modification of Paul Kramer's term "The Military-Sexual Complex," which is a modification of the "Military-Industrial Complex." Paul A. Kramer, "The Military-Sexual Complex: Prostitution, Disease and the Boundaries of Empire during the Philippine-American War," *Asia-Pacific Journal* 9:30, no. 2 (July 25, 2011), http://www.japanfocus.org/-Paul_A _-Kramer/3574.

## INTRODUCTION

1. Amy Goodman, "Barred by U.S. Restrictions, Sex Workers Hold Alternative AIDS Summit in Kolkata, India," *Democracy Now*, transcript and video, July 25, 2012, http://www.democracynow.org/2012/7/25/barred _by_us_restrictions_sex_workers.

2. Lin Lean Lim, ed., *The Sex Sector: The Economic and Social Bases of Prostitution in Southeast Asia* (Geneva: International Labour Organization, 1998). See also my critique of the ILO report in Janice G. Raymond, *Legitimating Prostitution as Sex Work: UN Labour Organization (ILO) Calls for Recognition of the Sex Industry* (North Amherst, MA: Coalition Against Trafficking in Women, 1999), http://www.catwinternational.org/Home /Article/61-legitimating-prostitution-as-sex-work-un-labour-organization -ilo-calls-for-recognition-of-the-sex-industry.

3. Adam Hochschild, *Bury the Chains: Prophets and Rebels in the Fight to Free an Empire's Slaves* (Boston, MA: Houghton Mifflin, 2005), 140.

4. Hugh Thomas, *The Slave Trade: The Story of the Atlantic Slave Trade, 1440–1870* (New York: Simon & Schuster, 1997).

5. Quoted in ibid., 454.

6. Slavery at Jefferson's Monticello: Paradox of Liberty. Smithsonian National Institute of African American History and Culture. Exhibition, January 27–October 14, 2012. http://www.monticello.org/slavery-at-monticello /enslaved-families-monticello/hemings-family. Accessed January 31, 2013.

7. "Sally Hemings," Wikipedia, the Free Encyclopedia. Most Recent Revision, December 24, 2012, http://en.wikipedia.org/wiki/Sally_Hemings (accessed January 13, 2013).

8. UNAIDS Advisory Group on HIV and Sex Work, *HIV and Sex Work* (Geneva: UNAIDS, 2011), annexed to the *UNAIDs Guidance Note on HIV and Sex Work*, updated April 2012, UNAIDS/09.09E / JC1696E,15, http://www.unaids.org/en/media/unaids/contentassets/documents/unaids publication/2009/JC2306_UNAIDS-guidance-note-HIV-sex-work_en .pdf.

9. Jay Tolson, "The Complex Story of Slavery," *U.S. News & World Report*, February 6, 2005, http://www.usnews.com/usnews/culture/articles /050214/14slavery.htm.

10. Hochschild, *Bury the Chains*, 161.

11. Ibid., 160.

12. Henry Bean, "Nye County Lets Brothel Owner Stay in Business, Despite Bribery Confession," *Las Vegas Review-Journal*, October 19, 2011, http:// www.lvrj.com/news/nye-county-lets-brothel-owner-stay-in-business -despite-bribery-confession-105309798.html (accessed October 29, 2011).

Candice Trummel is the former chairwoman of the Nye County, Nevada, Licensing and Liquor Commission. Maynard "Joe" Richards, a legal brothel owner in the county, attempted to bribe her in exchange for a favorable change in the zoning of his brothel. Trummel cooperated with the FBI by wearing a wire that resulted in Richards's confession to bribery. Several years after his conviction, the Nye County commissioners voted to let him keep his brothel license, despite the fact that he was a convicted felon. Even another brothel owner commented, "They should have taken his license. . . . If they're not on the take, they're sure making everyone think they are. . . . I always heard Nye County was crooked. I guess it's true. . . . It's as crooked as hell."

13. Quoted in Hochschild, *Bury the Chains*, 160.

14. Ibid., 87.

15. Sheila Jeffreys, *The Idea of Prostitution* (North Melbournes: Spinifex Press, 1997), 3.

16. Anne Summers, "Which Women? What Europe? Josephine Butler and the International Abolitionist Federation," *History Workshop Journal* 62, no. 1 (2006): 215–32.

17. Margaret Jackson, *The Real Facts of Life: Feminism and the Politics of Sexuality, c1850–1940* (London: Taylor & Francis, 1994), 25.

18. Quoted in ibid., 25–26.

19. Jane Jordan, *Josephine Butler* (London: John Murray, 2001), 243.

20. Ibid., 244.

21. Quoted in Kathleen Barry, *Female Sexual Slavery* (Englewood Cliffs, NJ: Prentice-Hall, 1979), 31.

22. Christabel Pankhurst quoted in ibid., 31.

23. Malka Marcovich, *Guide to the UN Convention of 2 December 1949 for the Suppression of the Traffic in Persons and of the Exploitation of the Prostitution of Others* (North Amherst, MA: Coalition Against Trafficking in Women, 2001), 9, http://www.catwinternational.org/Home/Article/119 -guide-to-the-un-convention-of-2-december-1949-for-the-suppression -of-the-traffic-in-persons.

24. See Janice Raymond, "Ten Reasons for *Not* Legalizing Prostitution and a Legal Response to the Demand for Prostitution," in *Prostitution, Trafficking and Traumatic Stress*, ed. Melissa Farley (Binghampton, NY: Haworth Maltreatment & Trauma Press, 2003), 315–32.

25. Some women who claim the title of sex worker do so because they think it professionalizes and destigmatizes them and what they do. I am not including these women in the group of "sex workers" who actively work to promote prostitution.

## 1. MYTHS AND MYTHMAKERS OF PROSTITUTION

1. Alan Young, "Hookers Deserve Safe Working Environment," *Toronto Star*, October 28, 2003, http://www.google.com/search?client=safari&rls =en&q=Alan+Young,+Hookers+deserve&ie=UTF-8&oe=UTF-8.

2. Charlotte McDonald-Gibson, "Drive-in Sex Plan to Curb Prostitutes in Europe's Playground,"*Independent*, August 2, 2011, http://www.independent .co.uk/news/world/europe/drivein-sex-plan-to-curb-prostitutes-in -europes-playground-2330219.html (accessed September 21, 2011).

3. Carla Del Ponte with Chuck Sudetic, *Madame Prosecutor: Confrontations with Humanity's Worst Criminals and the Culture of Impunity* (New York: Other Press, 2009), 36. Quoting Baron d'Estournelles de Constant, chair

of the International Commission to Inquire into the Causes and Conduct of the Balkans Wars, 1914.

4. Julie Bindel, "Streets Apart," *Guardian*, May 14, 2004, http://www.guardian.co.uk/weekend/story/0,3605,1215900,00.html (accessed May 15, 2004).
5. Rosie Campbell, "Safety at Work: Foreign Sex Workers Need Rights, Not Sensationalism," *Guardian*, October 5, 2004, http://www.guardian.co.uk/world/2004/oct/06/gender.socialcare (accessed October 26, 2011).
6. Eliza Strickland, "Too Sexy for Their Social Services," *SF Weekly*, April 5, 2004, http://www.sfweekly.com/2006-04-05/news/too-sexy-for-their-social-services/ (accessed October 26, 2011).
7. "Trafficking, Rights and Rescue: Sex Worker Perspectives at Arts Festival," *PRWEB*, May 20, 2011, http://www.prweb.com/releases/2011/5/prweb8453485.htm (accessed November 1, 2011).
8. As one example of this literature, see Melissa Farley, "'Bad for the Body, Bad for the Heart': Prostitution Harms Women Even if Legalized or Decriminalized," *Violence Against Women* 10, no. 10 (October 2004): 1087–1125, http://action.web.ca/home/catw/attach/Farley.pdf. Melissa Farley has conducted numerous studies in multiple countries documenting the harm of prostitution to various populations of women.
9. Nick Davies, "Prostitution—the Anatomy of a Moral Panic," *Guardian*, October 19, 2009, http://www.guardian.co.uk/uk/2009/oct/20/trafficking-numbers-women-exaggerated (accessed October 19, 2011).
10. I testified at this hearing.
11. Marianne Eriksson, *The Consequences of the Sex Industry in the European Union*, European Parliament (2003/2107(INI)), January 9, 2004. Incorporated into the report of the European Parliament, Committee on Women's Rights and Equal Opportunities, "Explanatory Statement" section, April 15, 2004, http://www.europarl.europa.eu/sides/getDoc.do?pubRef=-//EP//TEXT+REPORT+A5-2004-0274+0+DOC+XML+V0//EN#title2 (accessed January 7, 2005).
12. Ibid. See also Office of Marianne Eriksson, MEP, "Parliament Refuses to Debate the Influence of the Sex Industry," March 15, 2004. The European Parliament prevented the report from reaching the plenary where it would have been open for discussion and a vote.
13. Leonard Doyle, "Croats Charge Briton with 'Baby-Smuggling,'" *Independent*, March 8, 1995, http://www.questia.com/library/1P2-4703281/croats-charge-briton-with-baby-smuggling. The U.S. adoption organization called the Adams Children's Foundation, whose published aim is "to save babies from abortion," was actually a U.S. organization run by the Solomon Corporation, an offshore enterprise registered in the British Virgin Islands. Leonard Doyle, "Briton Trades in Ethnic Cleansing Victims' Babies," *Independent*, March 13, 1995, http://www.questia.com/library/1P2-4704333/briton-trades-in-ethnic-cleansing-victims-babies.

14. Stephen Grey, "Briton in Prostitute Aid Scandal," *Sunday Times*, January 31, 1999. On file with author.
15. Chris Stephen, "Is He a Placement Specialist or a Baby Trader? Women Cross Borders, Then Abandon Tots," *Washington Times*, May 16, 1995, http://poundpuplegacy.org/node/27317.
16. Bruce Wallace, "Under Suspicion: John Davies Is a Hero to Some Adoptive Parents, a Baby-Selling Profiteer to Many Governments," *Maclean's*, August 21, 1995, pp. 40–43, http://business.highbeam.com/4341/article-1G1-17210123/under-suspicion-john-davies-hero-some-adoptive-parents.
17. Grey, "Briton in Prostitute."
18. Ibid.
19. Dutch Foundation Against Trafficking in Women and La Strada, "STV Withdraws From Cooperation with John Davies," Stop Traffic Listserve posting, February 9, 1999. On file with author.
20. John Davies, "Re: STV Withdraws From Cooperation with John Davies," Stop Traffic Listserve posting, February 10, 1999. On file with author.
21. John Davies, "Independent Audit Clears Hungarian Project," Stop Traffic Listserve posting, May 7, 2000. On file with author.
22. Personal communication by e-mail with Bangladeshi Authority, March 29, 2010.
23. Quoted in Zoltan Dujisin, "More to Trafficking Than Prostitution," *IPS News*, May 26, 2009, http://www.ipsnews.net/news.asp?idnews=46980 (accessed May 30, 2009).
24. Jonathan Portlock, "Esher Man Accused of Rape Tells Court Description Fits His Brother," *Argus*, August 5, 2009, http://www.theargus.co.uk/news/4528554.print/.
25. Andrew Cockburn, "21st Century Slaves," *National Geographic*, September 2003, http://ngm.nationalgeographic.com/ngm/0309/feature1.
26. Ibid.
27. Valerie Jenness, *Making It Work: The Prostitute's Rights Movement in Perspective* (New York: Aldine de Gruyter, 1993), 114.
28. John Hubner, *Bottom Feeders: From Free Love to Hard Core: The Rise and Fall of Counter-culture Heroes Jim and Artie Mitchell* (New York: Doubleday, 1994), 333.
29. Jenness, *Making It Work*, 58–59.
30. In 2004 the Vancouver Network of Sex Work Projects advertised sex industry listings for Vancouver and lower mainland Canada. When I accessed the site at www.nswp.org on January 24, 2004, there were headings for "Commercial Sex Information Services," "Commerce," and "Adult Entertainment Businesses" organized by region on the site. Sex businesses were encouraged to send their listing details to the site where, it was claimed, they would be advertised for free. Since that time, the network has revised the site and is based in Edinburgh, Scotland.

31. See video of the conference, "Not for Sale," http://www.prostitution research.com/how_prostitution_works/000174.html.

32. *Survivors of Prostitution and Trafficking Manifesto*, "Who Represents Women in Prostitution?" (press conference), European Parliament, Brussels, October 17, 2005, http://www.catwinternational.org/Content /Documents/Reports/catw04newsletter1.pdf.

33. Ibid.

34. Shane Holladay, "Working Girls Tell Tales of Torture," *Edmonton Sun*, April 4, 2005, http://www.genderberg.com/phpNuke/modules.php?name =News&file=article&sid=111 (accessed May 2, 2005).

35. Trisha Baptie, "'Sex Worker'? Never Met One!" Sisyphe.org, April 26, 2009, http://sisyphe.org/spip.php?article3290 (accessed June 2, 2009).

36. Bureau NRM, *Trafficking in Human Beings, First Report of the Dutch National Rapporteur* (The Hague, November 2002), 15, www.mvcr.cz/soubor /trafficking-in-human-beings-report-2002.aspx.

37. A. L. Daalder, *Prostitution in the Netherlands Since the Lifting of the Brothel Ban* (Amsterdam: WODC, Ministry of Justice, 2007), 67, www.wodc.nl /images/ob249a_fulltext_tcm44-83466.pdf.

38. Udo Taubitz, "What German Prostitutes Want," *Deutsche Welle*, April 22, 2004, http://www.dw-world.de/dw/article/0,,1176335,00.html (accessed April 26, 2004).

39. Daniel Kurtzman, "Red Cross Knew of Nazi Death Camps, Records Show," JWeekly.com, January 3, 1997. In 2005, a Holocaust-denying group used the Red Cross documents to conclude that there is "no evidence of genocide." Available at www.rense.com/general69/factua.htm.

40. Robert I. Friedman, "India's Shame: Sexual Slavery and Political Corruption Are Leading to an AIDS Catastrophe," *The Nation*, April 8, 1996, 1–11, http://www.scribd.com/doc/29618200/India-s-Shame-The-Nation.

41. UNAIDS Advisory Group, *HIV and Sex Work*.

42. Daalder, *Prostitution in the Netherlands*, 53. Daalder understates his findings: "In view of the fact that a large part of the current owners has already been working as a business owner in that illegal sector, it seems plausible that owners are less inclined to conform to government authority than most other Dutch people."

43. For a discussion of the UN Protocol debate about the definition of trafficking, see Janice G. Raymond, "The New UN Trafficking Protocol," *Women's Studies International Forum* 25, no. 5 (2002): 491–501, http://www .heart-intl.net/HEART/030106/TheNewUNTrafficking.pdf.

44. Mary Lucille Sullivan, *Making Sex Work: A Failed Experiment with Legalised Prostitution in Victoria, Australia* (North Melbourne, Australia: Spinifex Press, 2007), 294.

45. Ibid. See especially chapter 6, "Victoria's 'Safe Sex Agenda': Occupational Health and Safety for the Sex Industry."

46. Ronald Weitzer, "The Social Construction of Sex Trafficking: Ideology and Institutionalization of a Moral Crusade," *Politics & Society* 35 (2007): 463.

47. Gail Dines and Julia Long, "Moral Panic? No. We are Resisting the Pornification of Women," *Guardian*, December 1, 2011, http://www.guardian .co.uk/commentisfree/2011/dec/01/feminists-pornification-of-women (accessed July 2, 2012).

48. Ellen Goodman, "Taking Back 'Values,'" *Boston Globe*, November 7, 2004, http://www.boston.com/news/globe/editorial_opinion/oped/articles /2004/11/07/taking_back_values/.

49. Many commentators have discussed this hypersexualized cultural ethos. See, for example, Madeleine Bunting, "Let's Talk About Sex: Feminism Must Challenge Modern Mores If It's to Consolidate Its Success," *Guardian*, May 24, 2004. For an earlier and fuller acknowledgment of the sexualization of culture and its various defenders, see also Catharine A. MacKinnon, *Feminism Unmodified: Discourses on Life and Law*, especially the afterword (Cambridge, MA: Harvard University Press, 1987).

50. Position of the Netherlands Government, "Human Rights Questions," United Nations Economic and Social Committee (E/1990/33, April 3, 1990).

51. Baptie, "'Sex Worker'?"

52. Maureen Dowd, "Beware a Beautiful Calm," *New York Times*, August 18, 2012, http://www.nytimes.com/2012/08/19/opinion/sunday/dowd-beware -a-beautiful-calm.html.

53. All information relating to the UN Protocol on trafficking, and discussed in the preceding paragraphs of this chapter, is documented in Raymond, "The New UN Trafficking Protocol."

54. "Abe: No Review of Kono Statement Apologizing to 'Comfort Women,'" *Asahi Shimbun*, February 1, 2013. Also, this article cites Abe's seeming change of heart during his second stint as prime minister when he is quoted as saying, "He would shelve his long-held plan to review the 1993 government statement that expressed remorse for the suffering of 'comfort women' before and during World War II," http://ajw.asahi.com /article/asia/korean_peninsula/AJ201302010077.

55. "The Facts," *Washington Post*, June 15, 2007, http://www.occidentalism .org/wp-content/uploads/2007/06/thefact.jpg (accessed November 15, 2011).

56. International Labour Organization, *Human Trafficking for Sexual Exploitation in Japan* (Geneva, 2004), 2, http://www.ilo.org/public/english/region /asro/tokyo/downloads/r-japantrafficking.pdf.

57. Quoted in Brendan O'Neill, "The Myth of Trafficking," review of *Sex at the Margins: Migration, Labour Markets and the Rescue Industry*, by Laura Agustin, *The New Statesman*, March 27, 2008.

58. Katharine H. S. Moon, *Sex Among Allies: Military Prostitution in U.S.-Korea Relations* (New York: Columbia University Press, 1997), 2, 102–3.
59. Moon, *Sex Among Allies*, 1–2, 9–10, 13.
60. Choe Sang-Hun, "Ex-Prostitutes Say South Korea and U.S. Enabled Sex Trade Near Bases," *New York Times*, January 7, 2009, http://www.ny times.com/2009/01/08/world/asia/08korea.html?pagewanted=all.
61. Ibid.
62. Ibid.
63. Coalition Against Trafficking in Women, "Letter to CATW from a Hungarian Activist," *Coalition Report*, 2004, 4, http://www.catwinternational .org/Content/Documents/Reports/catw04newsletter1.pdf.
64. Larry Derfner, "Natasha's 'Choice,'" *Jerusalem Post*, August 18, 2004.
65. Sigma Huda, *Integration of the Human Rights of Women and a Gender Perspective*, Report of the Special Rapporteur on the Trafficking in Person, Especially Women and Children, UN Commission on Human Rights, 62d sess., February 20, 2006 (E/CN.4/2006/62), paras. 42–43, http://daccess -dds-ny.un.org/doc/UNDOC/GEN/G04/169/28/PDF/G0416928.pdf ?OpenElement.
66. U.S. Department of State, Trafficking in Persons Report (Washington, D.C.: Office to Monitor and Combat Trafficking, June 2003), 22.
67. U.S. Department of State, "The Link Between Prostitution and Sex Trafficking," fact sheet, Washington, D.C., Office to Monitor and Combat Trafficking, November 4, 2004.
68. Dorchen Leidholdt, "Successfully Prosecuting Human Traffickers," Testimony before the Committee on the Judiciary, House of Representatives, 110th Cong., November 2007, http://www.catwinternational.org/Home /Article/187-successfully-prosecuting-sex-traffickers-testimony-before -the-committee-on-the-judiciary-house-of-representatives-united-states.
69. Jessica Malmgren, "Sex Worker Measure Splits DOJ, Baptists," *Trans/Missions*, April 7, 2008, http://uscmediareligion.org/printable.php?the Story&sID=836.
70. Ibid.
71. John R. Miller, "The Justice Department, Blind to Slavery," *New York Times*, July 11, 2008.
72. Azriel James Relph, "Potent Weapon to Stem Sex Slavery Left Unused," *NBC News*, July 11, 2011, http://www.msnbc.msn.com/id/43611445/ns /us_news-enslaved_in_america/t/potent-weapon-stem-sex-slavery-often -left-unused/#.TsVDjGBuFH8 (accessed November 17, 2011). Quoting U.S. State Department statistics.
73. Ibid.
74. Daalder, *Prostitution in the Netherlands*, 81.
75. Sex Workers Project, *Behind Closed Doors: An Analysis of Indoor Sex Work in New York City* (New York: Sex Workers Project at the Urban Justice

Center, 2005), 10, http://www.sexworkersproject.org/downloads/Behind
ClosedDoors.pdf.

76. Transcrime Institute (Andrea di Nicola and Others), *National Legislation on
Prostitution and the Trafficking in Women and Children* (Brussels: European
Parliament, 2005), 121, http://transcrime.cs.unitn.it/tc/412.php.

77. Ibid., 114.

78. Jody Raphael and Deborah L. Shapiro, "Violence in Indoor and Outdoor
Prostitution Venues, *Violence Against Women* 10, no. 10 (February 2004):
133, http://vaw.sagepub.com/content/10/2/126.full.pdf+html.

79. Esohe Aghatise, "Trafficking for Prostitution in Italy," *Violence Against
Women*, 10, no. 10 (October 2004): 1150, http://www.catwinternational
.org/Content/Images/Article/25/attachment.pdf.

80. Catharine A. MacKinnon, "Trafficking, Prostitution, and Inequality,"
*Harvard Civil Rights-Civil Liberties Law Review* 46, no. 2 (2011): 271–309,
http://heinonline.org/HOL/LandingPage?collection=journals&handle
=hein.journals/hcrcl46&div=14&id=&page=.

81. Alan Feuer and Ian Urbina, "Affidavit: Client 9 and Room 871," *New York
Times*, March 11, 2008, http://www.nytimes.com/2008/03/11/nyregion/11
night.html.

82. Laura Johnston, "The Latest in Bedford v Canada: What Does It Mean?,"
rabble.com, March 28, 2012, http://rabble.ca/blogs/bloggers/f-word
-collective/2012/03/latest-bedford-v-canada-what-does-it-mean.

83. Rosie DiManno, "Prostitutes Suffer with 'Sinister' Law," *Toronto Star*,
October 7, 2009.

84. Phelim McAleer, "Happy Hookers of Eastern Europe," *Spectator*,
April 5, 2003, http://www.spectator.co.uk/spectator/thisweek/11008/the
-spectator/ (accessed November 17, 2003).

85. Aghatise, "Trafficking for Prostitution in Italy," 1132.

86. Rory Carroll, "Willing Sex Slaves. Human Traffickers are Always Demonised, But Most Help Desperate People," *Guardian*, March 1, 2001,
http://www.guardian.co.uk/comment/story/0,3604,444751,00.html.

87. Roger Matthews, *Prostitution, Politics & Policy* (New York: Routledge,
2008). See also Julie Bindel, "It's Abuse and a Life of Hell," *Guardian*,
February 28, 2008, http://www.guardian.co.uk/lifeandstyle/2008/feb/29
/women.ukcrime.

88. Suki Falconberg, "Tears for Forgotten Women," *The Granville Journal: the Flagship Blog of Cyrano's Journal Online*, May 7, 2008, http://www
.bestcyrano.net/tgi?p=293 (accessed May 22, 2008; no longer available
online).

89. Trisha Baptie, "Why Prostitution, the World's Oldest Oppression, Must
Be Stamped Out," Straight.com, June 12, 2009, http://www.straight.com
/article-232404/trisha-baptie-why-prostitution-worlds-oldest-oppression
-must-be-stamped-out (accessed June 2, 2010).

## 2. PROSTITUTION ON DEMAND: THE PROSTITUTION USERS

1. "Prostitution: Prestigiacomo Levels with Clients," AGI, November 6, 2005, www.agi.it/english/news.pl?doc=200511051757-1171-RTI-CRO -O-NF11&page=0&id=agionline-eng.oggitalia (accessed November 21, 2005). Unfortunately, the same legislation proposed penalizing the women who solicited in public places. It also called for decriminalizing indoor prostitution under certain conditions. The bill was never passed.

2. Department of Peacekeeping Operations (DPKO), "Human Trafficking and United Nations Peacekeeping," *DPKO Human Trafficking Policy Paper*, 2004, paras. 12–13, http://www.un.org/womenwatch/news/documents /DPKOHumanTraffickingPolicy03-2004.pdf.

3. United Nations, *Protocol to Prevent, Suppress and Punish Trafficking in Persons, Especially Women and Children, supplementing the United Nations Convention against Transnational Organized Crime*, 2000, http://www.unhcr .org/refworld/docid/4720706c0.html.

4. Ministry of Industry, Employment and Communications, Government of Sweden, *Fact Sheet on Prostitution and Trafficking in Women*, 2003, http:// naring.regeringen.se/fragor/jamstalldhet/ (accessed, April 30, 2003). For updated information on Swedish the law and the government's policy on trafficking, see Government Offices of Sweden, Against Prostitution and Trafficking, 2009, http://www.sweden.gov.se/content/1/c6/13/36/71/ae 076495.pdf. See also http://www.sweden.gov.se/sb/d/573/a/12566/action /search/type/simple?x=17&y=15&query=prostitution. See also Gunilla Ekberg, "The Swedish Law that Prohibits the Purchase of Sexual Services," *Violence Against Women* 10, no. 10 (October 2004): 1187–1218, http:// www.catwinternational.org/Home/Article/171-the-swedish-law-that -prohibits-the-purchase-of-sexual-services.

5. Gerald N. Hill and Catherine T. Hill, "Domestic Violence," in *The Free Dictionary* (Farlex, 2005), http://legal-dictionary.thefreedictionary.com /Domestic+Violence

6. Louise Brown, *Sex Slaves: the Trafficking of Women in Asia* (London: Virago, 2000), 132–33.

7. Ibid., 133.

8. Max Waltman, "Prohibiting Sex Purchasing and Ending Trafficking: The Swedish Prostitution Law," *Michigan Journal of International Law* 33 (December 1, 2011): 148, http://papers.ssrn.com/sol3/papers.cfm?abstract _id=1966130##.

9. "Stolen Youth: Child Prostitution Plagues German-Czech Border," *Deutsche Welle*, October 29, 2003, www.dw-world.de/English/0,3367,1432 -184677A1016370.00.html (accessed December 2, 2003).

10. Giles Tremlett, "Spanish Men Most Likely to Pay for Sex," *Guardian*, July 29, 2004, http://www.guardian.co.uk/world/2004/jul/29/spain.giles tremlett.

11. Alfred C. Kinsey, Wardell B. Pomeroy, and Clyde E. Martin, *Sexual Behavior in the Human Male* (Philadelphia: W. B. Saunders, 1948).

12. Harry Benjamin and Robert E. L. Masters, *Prostitution and Morality; A Definitive Report on the Prostitute in Contemporary Society and an Analysis of the Causes and Effects of the Suppression of Prostitution* (New York: Julian Press, 1964).

13. Robert T. Michael, Edward Laumann, and Gina Kolata, *Sex in America: A Definitive Study* (Boston: Little, Brown, 1994).

14. Leslie Bennetts, "The John Next Door," *Newsweek*, July 18, 2011, http://www.thedailybeast.com/newsweek/2011/07/17/the-growing -demand-for-prostitution.html. "We had big, big trouble finding nonusers," Farley says. "We finally had to settle on a definition of non-sex-buyers as men who have not been to a strip club more than two times in the past year, have not purchased a lap dance, have not used pornography more than one time in the last month, and have not purchased phone sex or the services of a sex worker, escort, erotic masseuse, or prostitute."

15. Sven-Axel Månsson, as early as 1984, was among the first to write about "The Man in Sexual Commerce." Others who followed include Anderson and O' Connell Davidson (2003); Axel-Månsson (2001 ff.); Bindel and At-kins (2008); Blanchard (1994); Chetwynd and Plumridge (1993); de Graf (1995); Farley et al. (1998, 2011); Farley, Bindel, and Coy (2009); Holtz-man and Pines (1982); Horvath and Kelly (2007); Hughes (1999, 2001, 2004); Lammi-Taskula (1999); Leidholdt (2005); Lowman and Atchinson (2006); Macleod et al. (2008); McKeganey (1994, 1996); Monto (1999, 2000, 2004); Monto and Hotaling (2001); Plumridge et al. (1997); Raymond (2001, 2002, 2004); Vanwesenbeeck et al. (1995).

16. Kristie Blevins and Thomas J. Holt, "Examining the Virtual Subculture of Johns," *Journal of Contemporary Ethnography* 38, no. 5 (2009): 637.

17. Melissa Farley, Julie Bindel, and Jacqueline M. Golding, *Men Who Buy Sex, Who They Buy and What They Know* (London and San Francisco: Eaves-4Women and Prostitution Research & Education, 2009), http://www .eaves4women.co.uk/Documents/Recent_Reports/Men%20Who%20 Buy%20Sex.pdf.

18. *Why Do Men Buy?* trans. Mayu Iwata and Kaoru Kinoshita (Tokyo: Asian Women's Resource Center, 1998), 45.

19. Claire Halliday, "Why Men Go to Prostitutes," *Sun-Herald*, May 21, 2001.

20. Nicole Brady, "Why Men Pay for It," *The Age*, November 13, 1997.

21. Ine Vanwesenbeeck, *Prostitutes' Well-Being and Risk* (Amsterdam: VU Uit-geverij, 1994), 141.

22. Raymond and Hughes with Gomez, *Sex Trafficking of Women in the United States*, 77.

23. Natalie Pona, "The Harm Is Done to Men, Too," *Winnipeg Sun News*, September 24, 2001.

24. Sebastian Horsley, "The Brothel Keeper," *Observer*, September 14, 2004.
25. Finlo Rohrer, "The Men Who Sleep with Prostitutes," *BBC News Magazine*, February 22, 2008, http://news.bbc.co.uk/2/hi/7257623.stm\.
26. Farley, Bindel, and Golding, *Men Who Buy Sex*, 19.
27. Rohrer, "The Men Who Sleep with Prostitutes."
28. Halliday, "Why Men Go to Prostitutes."
29. Victor Malarek, *The Johns: Sex for Sale and the Men Who Buy It* (New York: Arcade Publishing, 2009).
30. Halliday, "Why Men Go to Prostitutes."
31. Rohrer, "The Men Who Sleep with Prostitutes."
32. Bridget Anderson and Julia O'Connell-Davidson, *Is Trafficking in Human Beings Demand Driven? A Multi-Country Pilot Study* (Geneva: International Organization of Migration [IOM], 2003), 24, http://www.compas.ox.ac.uk/fileadmin/files/Publications/Reports/Anderson04.pdf.
33. Martin Nkematabong, "Cameroon: Anti-AIDS: Truck Drivers Deserve More Attention," *Cameroon Tribune*, November 30, 2005.
34. Malarek, *The Johns*, 97.
35. Dennis Duggan, "A Regular John—And Proud of It," *New York Newsday*, August 25, 1994, http://www.loebner.net/Newsday.JPEG.
36. Farley, Bindel, and Golding, *Men Who Buy Sex*, 8.
37. *Why Do Men Buy?*, 44.
38. Anderson and O'Connell-Davidson, *Is Trafficking in Human Beings Demand Driven?*, 24–25.
39. Maddy Coy, Miranda Horvath, and Liz Kelly, *"It's Just Like Going to the Supermarket": Men Buying Sex in East London* (London: Centre for Independent Research, Evaluation, Training, Consultancy and Networking, London Metropolitan University, 2007), 21.
40. Malarek, *The Johns*, 24.
41. "Customers of Prostitutes Say Buying Sex is Hassle-Free," *Helsingen Sanomat, International Edition*, November 17, 2007, http://www.hs.fi/english/article/Customers+of+prostitutes+say+buying+sex+is+hassle-free/1135231427437.
42. Martin A. Monto (quoting Blanchard), *Focusing on the Clients of Street Prostitutes: A Creative Approach to Reducing Violence Against Women* (Final Report for National Institute of Justice Grant #97-IJ-CX-0033, 1999), 34.
43. Sandra Pollock Sturtevant and Brenda Stolzfus, *Let the Good Times Roll: Prostitution and the U.S. Military in Asia* (New York: The New Press, 1992).
44. Malarek, *The Johns*, 95.
45. Pona, "The Harm Is Done to Men, Too."
46. Malarek, *The Johns*, 105.
47. Janice G. Raymond, "Under New Law, France Would No Longer Be Sexual Playground of Men Like Dominique Strauss-Kahn," *Truthout*,

February 10, 2012, http://truth-out.org/index.php?option=com_k2&view =item&id=6604:under-new-law-france-would-no-longer-be-sexual -playground-of-men-like-dominique-strausskahn.

48. Janice G. Raymond, "The Secret Service Prostitution Scandal: It's About More Than National Security," *Guardian*, April 19, 2012, http://www .guardian.co.uk/commentisfree/cifamerica/2012/apr/19/human-trafficking -prostitution.

49. Martin A. Monto and Nick McRee, "A Comparison of Male Customers of Female Street Prostitutes with National Samples of Men," *International Journal of Offender Therapy and Comparative Criminology* 49, no. 5 (October 2005): 525.

50. "Attached Men Have Their Cake and Eat It Too," *IOL Scitech*, April 18, 2005, http://www.iol.co.za/scitech/technology/attached-men-have-their -cake-and-eat-it-too-1.239020#.USz1Q47ENlk.

51. Former Dublin prostitute, "The Harsh Realities of Being Raped for a Living," *Irish Examiner*, February 17, 2012.

52. Kathy Sheridan, "A Prostitute's Life: 'Whether It Hurts the Woman or Not, the Men Don't Care," *Irish Times*, August 8, 2010, http://www.irish times.com/newspaper/features/2010/0830/1224277854132.html.

53. Jean d'Cunha, "Thailand: Trafficking and Prostitution from a Gender and Human Rights Perspective—the Thai Experience," in *A Comparative Study of Women Trafficked in the Migration Process: Patterns, Profiles and Health Consequences of Sexual Exploitation in Five Countries (Indonesia, the Philippines, Thailand, Venezuela and the United States)*, ed. Janice G. Raymond (North Amherst, MA: Coalition Against Trafficking in Women, 2002), 129, http://www.catwinternational.org/Home/Article/96-a-comparative -study-of-women-trafficked-in-the-migration-process.

54. Ibid., 143.

55. Zoraida Ramirez Rodriguez, "Venezuela Interview Findings and Data Analysis: A Survey of Trafficked Women and Women in Prostitution," in Raymond, *A Comparative Study*, 167.

56. Sex Workers Project at the Urban Justice Center, *Behind Closed Doors: An Analysis of Indoor Sex Work in New York City* (New York: Sex Workers Project at the Urban Justice Center, 2005) 11, 51, http://www.sexworkers project.org/downloads/BehindClosedDoors.pdf.

57. Sheridan, "A Prostitute's Life."

58. Gail Dines, *Pornland: How Porn has Hijacked Our Sexuality* (Boston: Beacon Press, 2010), xi.

59. Melissa Farley, *Prostitution & Trafficking in Nevada: Making the Connections* (San Francisco: Prostitution, Research & Education, 2007), 28.

60. Ibid., 29–30.

61. Alexa Albert, *Brothel: Mustang Ranch and Its Women* (New York: Random House, 2001), 259.

62. Houston Chronicle News Service, "Infamous Mustang Ranch Closes/ Brothel's Owners, Manager Convicted of Fraud, Racketeering Charges," *Houston Chronicle*, October 10, 1999, http://www.chron.com/CDA/archives /archive.mpl/1999_3157148/infamous-mustang-ranch-closes-brothel-s -owners-man.html (accessed February 1, 2011).

63. Albert, *Brothel*, 234.

64. Ibid., 235.

65. Gillian Lord, "25pc of Prostitutes Students, Says Sex Industry," *Canberra Times*, June 25, 2005, http://www.canberratimes.com.au/news/local/news /general/25pc-of-prostitutes-students-says-sex-industry/216296.aspx? storypage=2 (accessed June 6, 2006).

66. Girls Educational and Mentoring Services (GEMS), "Fundraising Letter," December 1, 2009. Additional information can be found at http:// www.gems-girls.org.

67. M. Catherine Maternowska, "Truck-Stop Girls," *New York Times*, August 18, 2009, http://www.nytimes.com/2009/08/23/magazine/23lives-t.html ?ref=magazine (accessed February 3, 2011).

68. Meena Sheikh, "Why are Those Who Make Us Suffer Not Punished," *Red Light Dispatch of Apne Aap* 2, no. 3 (December 2, 2008), http://apneaap .org/sites/default/files/Redlight/Red%20Light%20Despatch%20 Issue%203%20%20Vol%202.pdf.

69. Pona, "The Harm Is Done to Men, Too."

70. Albert, *Brothel*, 182.

71. Sarah Catherine Lewis, *Indecent: How I Make It and Take It as a Girl for Hire* (Emeryville, CA: Seal Press, 2006), 52.

72. Ibid.

73. Chris Griffith, "Australia: Brothels Boost to Self-Esteem," *Australian*, January 23, 2007, http://www.theaustralian.com.au/brothels-boost-to-self -esteem/story-e6frfkwr-1111112875218 (accessed June 10, 2008).

74. ANI, "Well, This Is Why Men Visit Brothels," *IBN Live*, September 4, 2008.

75. Action for REACH OUT, "Stories About Their First Respectable Client," *Reaching Out* 16, no. 2 (June 2010).

76. Jeannette Angell, *CALLGIRL: Confessions of an Ivy League Lady of Pleasure* (Sag Harbor, NY: HarperCollins, 2004), 237.

77. Ibid., 238.

78. Noelle Knox, "In Belgium, Brothels are Big Business," *USA Today*, November 5, 2003, http://www.usatoday.com/news/world/2003-11-04-beligan -brothels_x.html (accessed January 2, 2007).

79. Farley, *Prostitution & Trafficking in Nevada*, 22.

80. Ibid., 34.

81. Hubert Dubois and Elsa Brunet, *The Client*, Handbook Accompanying the Film, "The Client" (Paris: Rue Charlot Productions).

82. Sheridan, "A Prostitute's Life."

83. "Sex Service Marketing: Off Streets and Online," *Helsingin Sanomat*, October 30, 2007, http://www.hs.fi/english/article/Sex+service+marketing+off +streets+and+online/1135231327264 (accessed February 1, 2012).
84. Kolbrún Halldórsdóttir, "The Fight to Criminalise the Purchase of Sexual Favours: An Icelandic Fighting Saga," in *The Nordic Approach*, eds. Trine Rogg Korsvis and Ane Stø. (Oslo: Feminist Group Ottar, 2011), 124.
85. "Johns Voice: Providing a Safe Space for Sex Buyers to be Heard," *John's Voice*, http://www.johnsvoice.ca/ (accessed January 3, 2012).
86. John Lowman, "The Hypocrisy of Prostitution Law: A Challenge to the Politicians of Canada," editorial, *The Province*, September 28, 1997, http://www.sfu.ca/sterlingprize/lowmanart.html.
87. Ronald Weitzer, Application Record—Reply Evidence Affidavit of Ronald Weitzer, Bedford et al v. Attorney General of Canada, Ontario, Canada Superior Court, (07-CV-329807PD1), 2–3.
88. For a critique of Lowman, see Ronald-Frans Melchers, Affidavit (examining three empirical studies conducted by John Lowman), *Bedford et al. v. Attorney General of Canada*, Ontario, Canada Superior Court, (07-CV-329807PD1), April 7, 2008, especially 43–44, http://184.70.147.70/low man_prostitution/HTML/Ontario_Charter_Challenge/Joint_Application _Record/Volume_61/Tab_122_Melchers_Affidavit.pdf.
    See also Ronald-Frans Melchers, Supplementary Affidavit, February 4, 2009, http://184.70.147.70/lowman_prostitution/HTML/Ontario _Charter_Challenge/Joint_Application_Record/Volume_61/Tab_123 _Melchers_Supplementary_Affidavit.pdf.
89. Max Waltman, "Sweden's Prohibition of Purchase of Sex: the Law's Reasons, Impact, and Potential," *Women's Studies International Forum* 34 (2011), 462.
    For other critiques of Weitzer's work, see also Factum of Appellant, Court of Appeals for Ontario, Court File No. C52799 and C52814), March 1, 2011. See also Melissa Farley, "Prostitution Harms Women Even if Indoors: Reply to Weitzer," *Violence Against Women* 11, no. 7 (July 2005): 965–70, http://myweb.dal.ca/mgoodyea/Documents/CSWRP/CSWRP CAN/Bedford%20v%20Canada%20OCA.%20Factum%20of%20 apellant%20March%201%202011.%20Part%20III%0.%2070 -110.pdf
90. Sven-Axel Månsson, "Men's Practices in Prostitution: The Case of Sweden," in *A Man's World: Changing Men's Practices in a Globalized World*, eds. Keith Pringle and Bob Pease (London: Zed Books, 2001).
91. Adult and Sex Industry Research Group, *Rethinking Management in the Adult and Sex Industry* (Ottawa: Faculty of Social Sciences, University of Ottawa, 2012), http://www.sciencessociales.uottawa.ca/gis-msi/eng/index .asp (accessed June 20, 2012).
92. Ibid.
93. "Pimp Denied 'Expert' Status at Trial," *Newscore*, November 22, 2011.

94. Brenda Power, "Comment: Stop the Sex Trade by Shaming the Clients," *Sunday Times*, May 13, 2006, www.timesonline.co.uk/article/0,, 2091-2179575,00.html (accessed May 18, 2006).
95. Ruchira Gupta, "Speech at the International Conference on Male Violence Against Women," Reykjavik, Iceland, October 23, 2010. On file with author.
96. Christiane Howe, "Non-Discriminatory Approaches to Address Clients in Prostitution," in *Challenging Trafficking in Persons: Theoretical Debate & Practical Approaches*, ed. The Sector Project Against Trafficking in Women and Commissioned by the German Federal Ministry for Economic Cooperation and Development (Baden-Baden, Germany: Nomos Verlagsgesellschaft, 2005), 99, 101. Italics mine.
97. Ibid., 100. Italics mine.
98. Luke Harding, "Germany: Invasion of the Body Pleasers," Salon.com, November 18, 2005, http://www.salon.com/2005/11/18/world_cup_2/ (accessed November 20, 2005).
99. Andrew Curry, "Soccer's Sex Slaves: Even Before a Ball's Been Kicked, There Is a World Cup Controversy: Are Women Being Smuggled into Germany to Work in the World's Oldest Profession?," *Foreign Policy*, May 2006, http://www.andrewcurry.com/portfolio/FPSoccerSex.html.
100. Howe, *Non-Discriminatory Approaches*, 101.
101. "Forced Labour in Prostitution is a Crime," video, 2006, http://www.rnw.nl/english/article/prostitutes-clients-asked-report-abuses (accessed December 2, 2006).
102. "Netherlands: Ladies of Pleasure or Sex Slaves?," Expatica.com, January 1, 2007, http://www.expatica.com/nl/news/local_news/ladies_of_pleasure_or_sex_slaves.html.
103. United Nations Office on Drugs and Crime (UNODC), "UN Head Welcomes Dutch Campaign Against Sexual Exploitation," press release, January 12, 2006, http://www.unis.unvienna.org/unis/pressrels/2006/uniscp529.html.
104. DSP-Groep, "Customers of Window Prostitution, Summary," November 11, 2009, http://www.dsp-groep.nl/getFile.cfm?dir=rapport&file=11sfijsbee_English_summary.pdf (accessed January 4, 2010).
105. Ibid.
106. "Customers of Prostitutes Say Buying Sex is Hassle-Free."
107. Adam Martin, "What Johns Are Saying about the Long Island Serial Killer," *Atlantic Wire*, April 19, 2011, http://www.theatlanticwire.com/national/2011/04/what-johns-are-saying-about-long-island-serial-killer/36727/ (accessed May 5, 2011).
108. Melissa Farley, Emily Schurman, Jacqueline M. Golding, Kristen Hauser, Laura Jarrett, Peter Qualliotine, and Michele Decker, *Comparing Sex Buyers with Men Who Don't Buy Sex* (San Francisco: Prostitution Research & Education, 2011), 1–62, http://www.prostitutionresearch.com/pdfs/Farleyetal2011ComparingSexBuyers.pdf.

109. "Ministry's 'John' Hotline Fiasco," *Copenhagen Post*, May 7, 2011.
110. Bureau NRM, *Trafficking in Human Beings, First Report*, 116.
111. Daalder, *Prostitution in the Netherlands*, 36–37.
112. Rohrer, "The Men Who Sleep with Prostitutes."
113. Chicago Coalition for the Homeless, *Buying Sex: A Survey of Men in Chicago* (Chicago, May 2004), http://www.enddemandillinois.org/sites/default/files/Buying_Sex.pdf.
114. Malarek, *The Johns*, 102–3.
115. Coy, Horvath, and Kelly, *"It's Just Like Going to the Supermarket,"* 24.
116. Sigma Huda, *Integration of the Human Rights of Women and a Gender Perspective*, Report of the Special Rapporteur on the Trafficking in Person, Especially Women and Children, UN Commission on Human Rights, 62d sess., February 20, 2006 (E/CN.4/2006/62), para. 60, http://daccess-dds-ny.un.org/doc/UNDOC/GEN/G04/169/28/PDF/G0416928.pdf?OpenElement.
117. Antonia Crane, "Paying to Play. Interview with a John," *Rumpus*, June 6, 2012. http://therumpus.net/2012/06/paying-to-play-interview-with-a-john/.
118. Anderson and O'Connell- Davidson, *Is Trafficking in Human Beings Demand Driven?*, 11.
119. Ibid.
120. Ibid., 43.
121. National Criminal Investigation Department, *Trafficking in Women, Situation Report No. 5* (Stockholm: January 1–December 31, 2002).
122. (SOU) Statens Offentliga Utredningar, *Prohibition of the Purchase of a Sexual Service: An Evaluation, 1999–2008*, English Summary (Stockholm, 2010), 29–44, http://www.nj.se/produkt/9789138234198.
123. Anderson and O'Connell-Davidson, *Is Trafficking in Human Beings Demand Driven?*, 10.
124. Evelina Giobbe, "Presentation at the NGO Consultation with UN/NGOs on Trafficking in Persons, Prostitution and the Global Sex Industry," Working Group on Contemporary Forms of Slavery, United Nations, Geneva, June 21–22, 1999.
125. Denis MacShane, "Britain's Sex Trade Needs Tackling," *Guardian*, September 6, 2010, http://www.guardian.co.uk/commentisfree/2010/sep/06/sex-slave-trafficking (accessed January 22, 2012).
126. Karl Ritter, "Once Mocked, Swedish Prostitution Law Attracts World Interest," Associated Press, March 18, 2008, http://agonist.org/20080315/once_mocked_swedens_pioneering_prostitution_law_attracts_world_interest. See also National Criminal Investigation Department, *Trafficking in Women*, 2003. Here the Swedish National Rapporteur on Trafficking states, "Street prostitution has decreased drastically," 35.
127. U.S. Department of State, "Prevention: Fighting Sex Trafficking by Curbing Demand for Prostitution," 2011, http://www.state.gov/documents/organization/167329.pdf (accessed December 22, 2011).

128. Ann Jordan et al., "Letter to Ambassador Luis CdeBaca," Office of Trafficking in Persons, U.S. Department of State, September 22, 2011, http://rightswork.org/wp-content/uploads/2011/10/Ambassador-Cde Baca.9.11.pdf.

129. National Police Board, *Trafficking in Human Beings for Sexual and Other Purposes. Situation Report 11* (Stockholm, 2010), http://www.si .se/uploadHuman%20Trafficking/Läg%2011%20Fin%20ENG.PDF (accessed October 5, 2010).

130. SOU, *Prohibition of the Purchase of a Sexual Service*, 35.

131. Ibid., 36.

132. "Rip Up Prostitution Law, Says Top Oslo Politician," *The Local—Norway's News in English*, June 22, 2012, http://www.thelocal.no/page /view/rip-up-prostitution-law-says-top-oslo-politician.

133. Kvinnefronten, press release, July 2012, http://www.kvinnefronten.no /index.php?option=com_content&view=article&id=211:press-release &catid=41:2009&Itemid=11. Kvinnefronten's press release described the claims of Pro Sentret, the response of the police, and Pro Sentret's subsequent retraction. For Norwegian language press documentation of Pro Sentret's retraction, see Emilie Ekeberg, "Pro Sentret Villeder i ny Rapport om Sexkjøpslaven: Rote rom Sexkjøp," *Klassekampen*, June 23, 2012.

134. Dan Bell, "Can You Outlaw the Oldest Profession?," BBC News, February 28, 2008, http://news.bbc.co.uk/2/hi/uk_news/7258639.stm (accessed March 3, 2008).

135. Meghan Murphy, "Prostitution—Can Canada Learn from the Nordic Model?," *Tyee News*, April 11, 2012.

136. Durba Mahila Samanwaya Committee, "Parliament March 2006, Down Down ITPA," 2006. On file with author.

137. Debolina Dutta and Oisha Sircar, "Sex Work and Pleasure," *Times of India*, April 15, 2007, http://articles.timesofindia.indiatimes.com/2007 -04-10/edit-page/27887214_1_durbar-mahila-samanwaya-committee -bharati-dey-dmsc.

138. Rohrer, "The Men Who Sleep with Prostitutes."

139. Brian Steele, "Franklin County Selectmen Express Concern About Effects on Workers of Possible Vermont Yankee Nuclear Power Plant Shutdown," *Republican*, February 23, 2011.

140. Ibid.

141. Ekberg, "The Swedish Law that Prohibits the Purchase of Sexual Services," 1204.

142. Kim Rahn, "Police to Crack Down on 24 Sex Trade Districts," *Asia-Views*, April 16, 2006, http://www.asiaviews.org/index.php?option=com _content&view=article&id=25980:reportalias7155&catid=2: regional-news-a-special-reports&Itemid=9 (accessed April 28, 2006).

143. Upasana Bhat, "India Sex Workers Stage Protest," *BBC News*, Delhi, December 9, 2005, http://news.bbc.co.uk/2/hi/4513286.stm.

144. Durba Mahila Samanwaya Committee, "Why the Sex Workers of India Marched to Parliament Demanding Repeal of the IT(P)A," 2006. On file with author.

145. Ruchira Gupta, "Remarks to the 63rd Session of the United Nations General Assembly," Interactive Dialogue on Taking Collective Action to End Human Trafficking, United Nations, New York, May 13, 2006, http://www.un.org/ga/president/63/letters/htprogramme060509.pdf.

146. Ibid.

147. Twiss Butler, personal e-mail communication with author, May 5, 2011.

148. For example, the 2011 *UN Development Index* ranks countries according to a gender inequality index and related indices (table 4). Several of the Nordic countries are listed in the top 10 of those ranked for gender equality: Sweden ranks #1; Norway #6; and Iceland #9. http://hdr.undp .org/en/media/HDR_2011_EN_Table4.pdf.

   A more dynamic look at the current closing of the gender gap in countries around the world is the sixth annual World Economic Forum *Global Gender Gap Report 2011*. This report rates countries on success in closing their social and economic gender gaps. The report ranks Iceland, Norway, Finland, and Sweden as the top 4 countries that have closed over 80 percent of their gender gaps. http://www.weforum.org/issues /global-gender-gap.

149. Ministry of Industry, Employment and Communications, Government of Sweden, "Fact Sheet on Prostitution and Trafficking in Women," April 2003, http://naring.regeringen.se/fragor/jamstalldhet/ (accessed May 4, 2003).

150. SOU, *Prohibition of the Purchase of a Sexual Service*, 29–44.

151. Ibid.

152. Kitty Holland, "Call to Criminalise Kerb Crawlers," *IrishTimes*, September 26, 2011, http://www.irishtimes.com/newspaper/breaking/2011 /0926/breaking 43.html (accessed September 26, 2011).

153. Max Waltman, "Prohibiting Sex Purchasing and Ending Trafficking: the Swedish Prostitution Law," *Michigan Journal of International Law* 33 (2011): 135n8, http://papers.ssrn.com/sol3/papers.cfm?abstract_id= 1966130##.

154. Max Waltman, "Sweden's Prohibition of Purchase of Sex: The Law's Reasons, Impact and Potential," *Women's Studies International Forum* 34 (2011): 465.

155. Ekberg, "The Swedish Law that Prohibits the Purchase of Sexual Services," 1200.

156. Jonas Troll, Stockholm Police Surveillance Unit, personal e-mail communication with author, January 7, 2011.

157. Ekberg, "The Swedish Law that Prohibits the Purchase of Sexual Services," 1193, citing the director for the Anti-Trafficking Group at the Police Authority in Gothenburg.

158. Waltman, "Sweden's Prohibition of Purchase of Sex," 458.

159. Ibid., 459.
160. Ministry of Justice and Public Security, "Criminalizing the Purchase of Sexual Activity," Government of Norway, December 12, 2008, http://www.regjeringen.no/en/dep/jd/whats-new/news/2008/criminanlizing-the-purchase-of-sexual-ac.html?id=537854.
161. Asta Håland and Ane Stø, "A Grassroots Story," in *The Nordic Approach*, eds. Trine Rogg Korsvik and Ane Stø (Oslo, Kolofon Forlag, 2011), 51 citing the Norwegian newspaper.
162. Harald Bøhler, leader of Oslo Police STOP Unit Combating Sex Trafficking, personal e-mail communication with author, November 17, 2010.
163. Agnete Strøm, "A Glimpse into 30 Years of Struggle Against Prostitution by the Women's Liberation Movement in Norway," *Reproductive Health Matters* 17, no. 33 (May 1, 2009).
164. Bøhler, personal e-mail communication.
165. Farley et al., *Comparing Sex Buyers*.
166. Julie Bindel, "Iceland: the World's Most Feminist Country," *Guardian*, March 25, 2010. Icelandic parliamentarian Kolbrún Halldórsdóttir stated, "These women work 24 hours, seven days a week with their campaigns and it eventually filters down to all of society."
167. Gudrún Jónsdóttir, director of the Icelandic NGO, Stígamót, personal e-mail communication with author, April 17, 2013.
168. Bindel, "Iceland."
169. For the full text of the resolution in French passed in the National Assembly, see http://www.assemblee-nationale.fr/13/ta/ta0782.asp. For the full text of the law proposal in French, see http://www.assemblee-nationale.fr/13/propositions/pion4057.asp. See also Coalition Against Trafficking in Women and Mediterranean Network Against Trafficking in Women, French Parliamentary Mission on Prostitution Supports Criminalizing the Buyer, press release, 2011, http://www.catwinternational.org/Home/Article/437-french-parliament-mission-on-prostitution-supports-criminalizing-the-buyer.
170. Raymond, "Under New Law." I also testified at these hearings on December 9, 2010.
171. U.S. Department of State, "Prevention: Fighting Sex Trafficking by Curbing Demand for Prostitution," Office to Monitor and Combat Trafficking, June 2011.
172. Trine Rogg Korsvik and Ane Stø, "The Nordic Battle for the Minds of Men," in *The Nordic Approach*, eds. Trine Rogg Korsvik and Ane Stø (Oslo: Kolofon Forlag, 2011), 10.
173. Niskanen Tuomo from Statistics Finland, personal e-mail communication with author, February 23, 2011, with attached numbers and categories translated from Finnish to English.

174. Waltman, "Prohibiting Sex Purchasing and Ending Trafficking," citing the National Criminal Statistics Database, 149.

175. Pia Levin, "Finnish Legislation on the Purchase of Sexual Services: Potential Revisions?," *Nordic Prostitution Policy Reform. A Comparative Study of Prostitution Policy Reform in the Nordic Countries*, July 11, 2011, http://nppr.se/2011/11/07/finnish-legislation-on-the-purchase-of-sexual-services-expected-to-be-revised/.

176. "HS: Minister Wants a Total Ban on Buying Sex," *Yle Uutiset*, July 20, 2012, http://yle.fi/uutiset/hs_minister_wants_a_total_ban_on_buying_sex/6224559.

177. Devon Brewer et al., "A Large Specific Deterrent Effect of Arrest for Patronizing a Prostitute," *PLOS ONE: A Peer-Reviewed Open-Access Journal* 1, no. 1 (December 20, 2006): e60, http://www.ncbi.nlm.nih.gov/pmc/articles/PMC1762352/. This research was funded by the U.S. National Institute of Justice.

178. Ibid.

179. Russ Buettner, "Prosecutors Focus on Pimps and Clients, Instead of Prostitutes," *New York Times*, May 2, 2012.

180. Derek Marsh, "Testimony on Human Trafficking: Recent Trends," Hearing before the U.S. House of Representatives Subcommittee on Border, Maritime and Global Counterterrorism, 111th Cong. (March 19, 2009), 7–14, http://www.hsdl.org/?view&did=10574.

## 3. PROSTITUTION NATION:
## THE STATE OF PROSTITUTION IN THE NETHERLANDS

1. Fiona Campbell and Barry Thorne, "Human Trafficking is One of the Most Lucrative Forms of Organised Crime in the World: A Brutal Industry Worth Billions of Dollars," *Radio Netherlands*, 2007. Quoting the Dutch National Rapporteur on Trafficking at a panel of experts on prostitution and trafficking in front of a live audience in Amsterdam. Although the Dutch Rapporteur distinguishes between trafficking and prostitution and continues to support the Dutch legal system, it is instructive that a proponent of the regime acknowledges its failures.

2. Lotte Van de Pol, Affidavit of Dr. Lotte Constance Van de Pol, *Bedford et al. v. Attorney General of Canada*, Ontario, Canada Superior Court, September 3, 2008 (07-CV-32987PD1), 14.

3. Ibid., 17.

4. Ibid., 19.

5. Joyce Outshoorn, "Legalizing Prostitution as Sexual Service: The Case of the Netherlands" (Copenhagen: ECPR Joint Sessions WS 12, 2002), http://www.google.com/search?q=cache:pwnWQtQTg9UC:www.essex.ac.uk/ecpr/jointsessions/Copenhagen/papers/ws12/outshoorn (accessed

November 17, 2002). I am indebted to Outshoorn for her work on the influence of "state feminism" on the 2000 prostitution legislation in the Netherlands and her history of Dutch prostitution policy and legislation. I am aware that she might not draw similar conclusions as I have drawn from this history.

6. Daalder, *Prostitution in the Netherlands*, 47.
7. Bureau NRM, *Trafficking in Human Beings, First Report*, 19.
8. Paul Ames and Agence France Presse, "Amsterdam Raises Legal Age for Prostitution to 21," *Global Post*, February 26, 2013, http://www.globalpost .com/dispatch/news/afp/130226/amsterdam-raises-legal-age-prostitution -21
9. Outshoorn, "Legalizing Prostitution as Sexual Service," 4.
10. Ibid., 5.
11. Ibid., 8.
12. Ibid., 5.
13. Yumi Wijers-Hasegawa, "Dutch Approach Prostitution with Pragmatism," *Japan Times*, March 16, 2002, http://www.japantimes.co.jp/text /nn20020316b3.html (accessed March 10, 2004).
14. Outshoorn, "Legalizing Prostitution as Sexual Service," 5.
15. Bureau NRM, *Trafficking in Human Beings, First Report*, 105.
16. Outshoorn, "Legalizing Prostitution as Sexual Service," 5–6.
17. Ibid., 5–8.
18. Wijers-Hasegawa, "Dutch Approach Prostitution with Pragmatism."
19. Outshoorn, "Legalizing Prostitution as Sexual Service," 15.
20. Ibid., 12.
21. Robert Crew, "Amsterdam's Dark Side," *The Star*, April 27, 2006, http:// nchro.org/index.php?option=com_content&view=article&id=2934: amsterdams-dark-side&catid=57:press&Itemid=37.
22. Ibid.
23. Gemma Bowes, "Red Light Area Condemned as Sick," *Observer*, November 12, 2005, http://www.guardian.co.uk/travel/2005/nov/13/travelnews .genderissues.observerescapesection (accessed November 26, 2005).
24. The above information was subsequently deleted from its website after a successful campaign to halt the tours by many NGOs, including the international Coalition Against Trafficking in Women.
25. Perro de Jong, "Netherlands to Crackdown on Clients of Illegal Prostitutes," *Radio Netherlands Worldwide*, November 9, 2009, http://www.rnw .nl/english/article/netherlands-crack-down-clients-illegal-prostitutes (accessed November 23, 2009).
26. Ibid.
27. Reuters, "Dutch Rein In Sex and Drug Excesses," *Straitstimes*, September 5, 2003.
28. "Why Dutch Street Walkers Are Getting the Boot," Expatica.com, December 12, 2003, http://www.expatica.com/nl/essentials_moving_to/country _facts/why-street-walkers-are-getting-the-boot-2958_9579.html.

29. Ibid.
30. Esther Wittenberg, "Eindhoven Prostitutes Back to Working the Streets," NRC.nl, October 3, 2009, http://vorige.nrc.nl/international/Features/article2175713.ece/Eindhoven_prostitutes_back_to_illegally_working_the_streets.
31. Van de Pol, Affidavit, 33.
32. Andrew Balcombe, "Human Trafficking in Holland: Experts Talk About Sex Slavery," *Hague/Amsterdam Times*, December 1, 2009.
33. "City Revokes 37 Permits in De Wallen," *Hague/Amsterdam Times*, December 8, 2006.
34. "Netherlands Orders Escort Services to Get Licensed or Close Down," Associated Press/Fox News, February 13, 2008, http://www.foxnews.com/story/0,2933,330588,00.html
35. Van de Pol, Affidavit, 25.
36. Emma Thompson, "Amsterdam to Clean Up 'Red Light' District," *New York Times*, December 17, 2007, http://www.reuters.com/article/2007/12/17/us-dutch-prostitution-idUSEIC76462920071217.
37. National Police Service, Criminal Investigations Department (KLPD), *Beneath the Surface (Schone Schijn): The Identification of Human Trafficking in the Licensed Prostitution Sector*, English summary, trans. Lotte Constance Van de Pol, in Addendum to Lotte Van de Pol, Supplementary Affidavit, *Bedford et al. v. Attorney General of Canada, Ontario*, Canada Superior Court of Justice (07-CV-32987PD1), June 5, 2009, 12. Quoting the Dutch government's *National Action Plan on Trafficking in Human Beings*, 2004.
38. Ibid., 12.
39. Daalder, *Prostitution in the Netherlands*, 15.
40. National Police Service, *Beneath the Surface*, foreword.
41. Van de Pol, Supplementary Affidavit, 6.
42. National Police Service, *Beneath the Surface*, 20.
43. Ibid., 3.
44. Van de Pol, Supplementary Affidavit, 2.
45. Daalder, *Prostitution in the Netherlands*, 13.
46. National Police Service, *Beneath the Surface*, 10. Italics mine.
47. Ibid., 8.
48. Van de Pol, Supplementary Affidavit, 6.
49. National Police Service, *Beneath the Surface*, 9.
50. Ibid., 9–10.
51. Ibid., 11.
52. Daalder, *Prostitution in the Netherlands*, 79.
53. Ibid., 69.
54. Ibid., 13.
55. National Police Service, *Beneath the Surface*, 18.
56. Bureau NRM, *Trafficking in Human Beings, First Report*, 84.
57. Louise Shelley, "The Price of Sex," *St. Petersburg Times*, October 20, 2004, http://www.freerepublic.com/focus/f-news/1250770/posts.

58. Ibid.
59. Daalder, *Prostitution in the Netherlands*, 33, 84.
60. National Police Service, *Beneath the Surface*, 7.
61. Human Rights Without Frontiers, "Figures on Human Trafficking in Netherlands in 2011," March 7, 2012, http://www.hrwf.net/images/news letters/trafficking/2012/2012%20trafficking.pdf. Quoting figures of La Strada International.
62. National Police Service, *Beneath the Surface*, 8.
63. Malarek, *The Johns*, 220. Quoting Job Cohen.
64. Klaas den Tek, "Crusading Against Amsterdam's Red Lights," *Radio Netherlands Worldwide*, October 19, 2011, http://www.rnw.nl/english/article /crusading-against-amsterdams-red-lights.
65. Daalder, *Prostitution in the Netherlands*, 53.
66. Bureau NRM, *Trafficking in Human Beings: Supplementary Figures, Sixth Report of the Dutch National Rapporteur* (The Hague, 2008), 36.
67. U.S. Department of State, "The Netherlands," *Trafficking in Persons Report 2008* (Washington, DC: Office to Monitor and Combat Trafficking, 2009).
68. Margaret Strijbosch, "Legalised Prostitution: A Dying Trade," *Radio Netherlands Worldwide*, October 31, 2006, http://www.rnw.nl/english/article /legalised-prostitution-dying-trade (accessed March 18, 2012).
69. Molly Moore, "Changing Patterns in Social Fabric Test Netherlands' Liberal Identity," *Washington Post*, June 23, 2007, http://www.washington post.com/wp-dyn/content/article/2007/06/22/AR2007062202015_pf .html (accessed March 18, 2012).
70. National Police Service, *Beneath the Surface*, 10.
71. Carolina Lo Galbo, interview with Karina Schaapman, trans. Karin Werkman, *Vrij Nederland*, June 14, 2008.
72. National Police Service, *Beneath the Surface*, 4.
73. Ibid., 5.
74. Daalder, *Prostitution in the Netherlands*, 15, 71.
75. Ibid., 61, 63.
76. Ibid., 66.
77. Ibid., 67.
78. Ibid., 70.
79. Van de Pol, Supplementary Affidavit, 7.
80. Ibid., 29.
81. Dorchen Leidholdt, "Trafficking in Women and Forced Prostitution," notes, Council of Europe Meeting, Strasbourg, October 4, 1991. On file with author.
82. Ibid.
83. Leidholdt, "Trafficking in Women and Forced Prostitution," notes.
84. Dorchen Leidholdt, "Keynote Address: Demand and Debate," in *Demand Dynamics: The Forces of Demand in Global Sex Trafficking*, eds. Morrison

Torrey and Sara Dubin (Chicago, IL: International Human Rights Law Institute, De Paul University, 2003), 8–9.

85. Leidholdt, "Traffic in Women and Forced Prostitution Notes."

86. Ibid.

87. Anita Gradin, "Opening Statement by the European Commissioner," Conference on Trafficking in Women for Sexual Exploitation, Vienna Conference Papers, June 10–11, 1996. On file with author.

88. Donna M. Hughes, "Note on European Conference on Trafficking in Women," June 10–11, 1996, Vienna, Austria. A workshop rapporteur related that "in the briefing session prior to the conference they were given specific instructions to avoid talking about prostitution. This was only a conference on trafficking."

89. Marie van Hemeldonck, "Trafficking of Women to Countries of the European Union: Clarification of Concepts, International Instruments, Present Social and Political Context," Conference on Trafficking in Women for Sexual Exploitation, Vienna Conference Papers, June 10–11, 1996. On file with author.

90. Ibid.

91. Helga Konrad, "Statement of the Austrian Federal Minister for Women's Affairs," Conference on Trafficking in Women for Sexual Exploitation, Vienna Conference Papers, June 10–11, 1996. On file with author.

92. "Information Sheet Included in the Invitation to Participate," European NGO Conference on Trafficking in Women (NOTRAF), Noordwijkerhout, the Netherlands, April 5–7, 1997. On file with author.

93. "Steering Group Meeting," European NGO Conference on Trafficking in Women (NOTRAF), Noordwijkerhout, the Netherlands, February 7–8, 1997. On file with author.

94. "List of Participants," European NGO Conference on Trafficking in Women (NOTRAF), Noordwijkerhout, the Netherlands, April 4, 1997. On file with author.

95. Ibid.

96. Esohe Aghatise, personal communication with author, July 10, 2001.

97. Hansje Verbeek, Letter to Anne Søyland from Kvinnefronten in Norway re her application to attend NOTRAF, March 11, 1997, On file with author.

98. CATW, "Traffic and Sexual Exploitation in Europe: A Dutch Code of Conduct?," press release, Brussels, April 21, 1997. On file with author.

99. Eriksson, *The Consequences of the Sex Industry in the European Union.*

100. Ministerial Conference, *The Hague Ministerial Declaration on European Guidelines for Effective Measures to Prevent and Combat Trafficking in Women for the Purpose of Sexual Exploitation*, April 24–26, 1997, http://legislationline.org/documents/action/popup/id/8747.

101. European Parliament, "Explanatory Statement."

102. David Rieff, *A Bed for the Night: Humanitarianism in Crisis* (New York: Simon & Schuster, 2002), 85, 106.
103. World Conference of Human Rights, *Vienna Declaration and Programme of Action*, UN General Assembly, July 12, 1993 (A/CONF.157/23), http://www.unesco.org/education/information/nfsunesco/pdf/VIENNA.PDF.
104. Center for Women's Global Leadership, *Report of the Women's Human Rights Caucus at the Fourth World Conference on Women Beijing 1995*, Sub-Group on Trafficking and Sex Work, 1995, 16. On file with author.
105. Janice G. Raymond, "Prostitution as Violence Against Women: NGO Stonewalling in Beijing and Elsewhere," *Women's Studies International Forum* 21, no. 1 (1998): 109n2, quoting an October 10, 1995, COYOTE press release.
106. *Report of the Fourth World Conference on Women, September 4–15, 1995*, United Nations, Beijing, 1996 (A/CONF.177/20). See paras. 113, 122, and especially 129, Strategic Action D.3, which states, "Eliminate trafficking in women and assist victims of violence due to prostitution and trafficking."
107. STV, "International Campaign Networking, Advocacy, Policy and Strategies, 1994–1996," *News Bulletin* 2 (March 1996): 2.
108. Marjan Wijers and Lin Lap-Chew for the GAATW and STV, "Trafficking in Women, Forced Labour and Slavery-like Practices in Marriage, Domestic Labour and Prostitution," Summary of Preliminary Report, October 1996, 1–2, 22.
109. Radhika Coomaraswamy, *Preliminary Report on Violence Against Women, Its Causes and Consequences*, Special Rapporteur on Violence Against Women, UN Commission on Human Rights, November 22, 1994 (E/CN.4/1995/42), paras. 205–19. http:/www.unhchr.ch/Huridocda/Huridoca.nsf/0/75ccfd797b0712d08025670b005c9a7d?Opendocument.
110. Radhika Coomaraswamy, *Report on the Mission of the Special Rapporteur to Poland on the Issue of Trafficking and Forced Prostitution of Women* (May 24 to June 1, 1996), UN Commission on Human Rights, December 10, 1996 (E/CN.4/1997/47/Add.1), paras. 121–33, http://www.unhcr.org/refworld/docid/3ae6b0db8.html.
111. Janice G. Raymond, *Report to the Special Rapporteur on Violence Against Women* (North Amherst, MA: Coalition Against Trafficking in Women, May 1995).
112. Coomaraswamy, *Report on the Mission . . . to Poland*, paras. 134, 171, 175.
113. See Aziza Ahmed, "Feminism, Power, and Sex Work in the Context of HIV/AIDS," *Harvard Journal of Law and Gender* 34 (2011): 234, where Ahmed writes that "some abolitionist feminists have also supported full criminalization," with reference to note 56. In turn, note 56 refers the

readers to note 52 where my work is cited in the context of being an abolitionist feminist who supports *partial* criminalization schemes that do not include criminalizing "sex workers [italics mine]." Ahmed's documentation is either sloppy or lacking in due diligence. A lack of accuracy underscores much of the pro-prostitution writings.

114. Ibid., note 29.
115. Ibid., section B, "At the National Level."
116. "Netherlands," *Virtual Library Women's History*, December 7, 2010, http://www.iisg.nl/w3vlwomenshistory/netherlands.html.
117. Wijers-Hasegawa, "Dutch Approach Prostitution with Pragmatism."
118. Sari van der Poel, "Solidarity as Boomerang. The Fiasco of the Prostitutes' Rights Movement in the Netherlands," *Crime, Law and Social Change* 23, no. 1 (1995): 45.
119. Ibid., 45. Italics mine.
120. Ibid., 49.
121. Ibid., 53.
122. H. Patricia Hynes and Janice G. Raymond, "Put in Harm's Way: The Neglected Health Consequences of Sex Trafficking in the United States," in *Policing the National Body: Race, Gender, and Criminalization*, eds. Jael Silliman and Anannya Bhattacharjee (Cambridge, MA: South End Press, 2002), 218.
123. For a fuller discussion of harm reduction and the public health aspects of prostitution, see Hynes and Raymond, "Put in Harm's Way," 197–229.
124. Jan Visser, "Work Permits for East European Prostitutes in the Netherlands?," Stop-Traffic Listserve posting, November 21, 2001. Italics mine. On file with author.
125. Wijers-Hasegawa, "Dutch Approach Prostitution with Pragmatism."
126. Ibid.
127. Alexandra Hudson, "Green Light for Visits to Red-Light District," Reuters, April 1, 2007, http://www.reuters.com/article/2007/04/01/us-dutch-prostitutes-idUSL3172421720070401. Italics mine.
128. "Why Dutch Street Walkers Are Getting Their Marching Orders," Expatica.com, December 9, 2003, http://www.expatica.com/nl/essentials_moving_to/country_facts/why-street-walkers-are-getting-the-boot-2958_9579.html.
129. Rohan Minogue, "World's Oldest Professions Link Hands in Amsterdam," dpa.German Press Agency, January 3, 2007, http://rawstory.com/news/2006/World_s_oldest_professions_to_link__01032007.html.
130. Eric Hesen, "Pimping Ban in Amsterdam?," *Radio Netherlands Worldwide*, September 21, 2007, http://www.radionetherlands.nl/currentaffairs/ams070921mc (accessed May 2, 2008).
131. Geraldine Baum, "Sex, Drugs and Second Thoughts," *Los Angeles Times*, January 4, 2008, http://www.latimes.com/news/nationworld/world/la-fg-dutch4jan04,0,5071903.story.

132. The Red Thread, *A New Red Thread Report*, November 4, 2006, http://fleshtrade.blogspot.com/2006/11/new-red-thread-report.html.

133. "The Situation in 2000," De Rode Draad, http://archief.rodedraad.nl/index.php?id=951 (accessed February 10, 2013).

134. Foundation Against Trafficking (STV), statement, Prostitutes Educational Network, http://www.bayswan.org/FoundTraf.html (accessed December 2, 2003).

135. Wijers was a principal consultant for the 2011 *Prevent, Combat, Protect: Human Trafficking. A Joint UN Commentary on the EU-Directive—A Human Rights Approach*, OHCHR, UHCR, UNICEF, UNODC, UN Women, ILO, http://www.unwomen.org/publications/prevent-combat-protect-human-trafficking/ (accessed April 8, 2012).

136. Dorien Pels, "Let the Prostitutes Speak for Themselves," *Trouw*, February 7, 2008.

137. Ibid.

138. Bureau NRM, *Trafficking in Human Beings, First Report*, 55.

139. UNICEF Netherlands in Cooperation with ECPAT NL/Defence for Children International-Netherlands, *Unseen and Unheard: Child Trafficking in the Netherlands, a Preliminary Survey* (The Hague, 2004), 17.

140. Ibid., 18.

141. Bureau NRM, *Trafficking in Human Beings: Supplementary Figures*, 10.

142. UNICEF Netherlands, *Unseen and Unheard*, 15.

143. Ibid., 19.

144. Daalder, *Prostitution in the Netherlands*, 79.

145. Ibid., 14.

146. I use this term "pedophile" not in the clinical sense but because it is widely used of child sexual abusers. My use of this word is not meant to imply that some men are biologically or psychologically driven to commit sexual acts with children, thereby removing men of responsibility for the abuse.

147. Dave van Ginhoven, "Pro-Paedophile Political Party Aims at Second Chamber Seat," *Amsterdam Times*, June 16, 2006. Reuters version available on rense.com: http://rense.com/general71/legal.htm.

148. Daniel Denisiuk, "NVD Want to Legalize Pedophily," *Metro*, May 31, 2006, trans. Hannelore Schröder.

149. van Ginhoven, "Pro-Paedophile Political Party."

150. Child Rights Information Network, *Report on the Sexual Exploitation of Children* (Amsterdam, Netherlands, January 1, 2001), http://www.crin.org/resources/infodetail.asp?id=1456 (accessed March 8, 2004).

151. Ibid., 5.

152. "Dutch Consulate Helped Child Porn Traders Escape," *Expatica News*, September 2, 2004, http//www.expatica.com/source/site article.asp?subchannel_id=19&story_id=11349 (accessed September 6, 2004).

153. UNICEF Netherlands, *Unseen and Unheard*, 23.

154. Huda, *Integration of the Human Rights*, para. 43.
155. Van de Pol, Supplementary Affidavit, 12.

## 4. ECONOMIC DEVELOPMENT OR
## ECONOMIC OPPORTUNISM? TRAFFICKING, MIGRATION,
## AND THE MILITARY-PROSTITUTION COMPLEX

1. Cited in Sullivan, *Making Sex Work*, 2 and note 3.
2. "Giving the Customer What He Wants," *Economist*, February 14, 1998, 22, http://www.economist.com/node/113208 (accessed January 4, 1999).
3. Suzanne Daley, "In Spain, Women Enslaved by a Boom in Brothel Tourism," *New York Times*, April 6, 2012, http://www.nytimes.com /2012/04/07/world/europe/young-men-flock-to-spain-for-sex-with -trafficked-prostitutes.html?pagewanted=all (accessed April 8, 2012).
4. "Giving the Customer What He Wants."
5. Wendy McElroy, "An Overview of 'Solutions' to Prostitution," ifeminists .com, March 24, 2009, http://www.wendymcelroy.com/articles/prostsol .html (accessed March 28, 2011).
6. Lauren Smiley, "Craigslist's $100K Donation Burned by Women's Group," *SF Weekly Blogs*, September 16, 2010, http:blogs.sfweekly.com /thesnitch/2010/09/san_francisco_non-profit_rejec.php (accessed September 30, 2010).
7. "Nevada Brothels Want To Be Good Neighbor," Associated Press, May 10, 2005, http://www.msnbc.msn.com/id/7805733/ns/business-personal _finance/t/nevada-brothels-want-be-good-neighbor/#.T5geEe1yFlk (accessed May 23, 2011).
8. Jenness, *Making It Work*, 59, 61.
9. Sullivan, *Making Sex Work*, 146.
10. Meagan Tyler, "Political Party or Lobby Group? The Dark Side of the Australian Sex Party," *The Conversation*, July 31, 2012.
11. "The Sex Business," *Economist*, February 14, 1998, 18, http://www .economist.com/node/113208 (accessed January 4, 1999), 18.
12. Mary Sullivan and Sheila Jeffreys, *Legalising Prostitution Is Not the Answer: The Example of Victoria, Australia* (North Amherst, MA: Coalition Against Trafficking in Women, 2001), http://www.catwinternational.org/Content /Images/Article/95/attachment.pdf.
13. McDonald-Gibson, "Drive-in Sex Plan to Curb Prostitutes in Europe's Playground."
14. Robert Bellah, "Class Wars and Culture Wars in the University Today: Why We Can't Defend Ourselves," *CSSR Bulletin* 27, no. 1 (February 1998): 2.
15. Misha Glenny, *McMafia: A Journey Through the Global Criminal Underworld* (New York: Knopf Books, 2008).

16. Aida F. Santos, "The Philippines: Migration and Trafficking in Women," in *A Comparative Study of Women Trafficked in the Migration Process: Patterns, Profiles and Health Consequences of Sexual Exploitation in Five Countries (Indonesia, the Philippines, Thailand, Venezuela and the United States)*, ed. Janice G. Raymond (North Amherst, MA: Coalition Against Trafficking in Women, 2002), 23, http://www.catwinternational.org/Home/Article /96-a-comparative-study-of-women-trafficked-in-the-migration-process. The authors cite original sources of Mitchell P. Duran, "Facing Globalization and Its Challenges," *Philippine Labor Review* 22, no. 2 (July–December 1999): 57–101; and statistics from the Philippines Overseas Employment Administration (POEA), *Information Primer for Deployment of Overseas Performing Artists* (Manila: POEA Manpower Development Division, Employment Branch, 1998).

17. Lim, *The Sex Sector*, 11. See also the extensive critique of this report authored by Raymond, *Legitimating Prostitution as Sex Work*.

18. Lim, *The Sex Sector*, 213.

19. Steve Kir, "Changes in Asia's Sex Industry Threaten HIV Explosion: WHO," *Agence France Presse*, August 13, 2001.

20. Joseph E. Stiglitz, *Globalization and Its Discontents* (New York: W. W. Norton, 2002), 76.

21. Dan McDougall, "Truckers Take India on Fast Lane to Aids," *Observer*, November 26, 2005, http://www.guardian.co.uk/world/2005/nov/27/india .aids.

22. Ibid.

23. Andrew Sherry, Matthew Lee, and Michael Vatikiotis, "For Lust or Money," *Far Eastern Economic Review*, December 14, 1995.

24. Sean Plambeck, "No Bust in Sight During Sex Boom," *Perth Now*, August 31, 2008, http://www.perthnow.com.au/aussies-spend-big-on-strippers /story-fna7dq6e-1111117360860.

25. Steven Carroll, "Prostitutes Forced To Take More Risks, Says Charity," *Irish Times*, August 24, 2010, http://www.highbeam.com/doc/1P2 -25545640.html.

26. "More Women Going from Jobless to Topless," Associated Press, MSNBC.com, March 30, 2009, http://www.nbcnews.com/id/29824663/# .UTOZd47ENlk.

27. "STATIN to Add Prostitutes, Ganja Farmers to Data," *Jamaica Gleaner*, October 15, 2008, http://jamaica-gleaner.com/gleaner/20081015/lead /lead4.html.

28. "Amsterdam Travel: Sex Tourism and Human Trafficking," *Just Means, Business Better*, August 19, 2010, http://www.justmeans.com/Amsterdam -Travel-Sex-Tourism-Human-Trafficking/27438.html.

29. Lim, *The Sex Sector*, 10, quoting a Chulalongkorn University, Thailand Political Economy Centre Report for the Period 1993–95, in which prostitution accounts for two-thirds of the total illegal income. Annual income from prostitution during this period was between 450–550 baht—with the

prior conversion rate amounting to US$22.5 and 27 billion. This is a stunning total considering that today global human trafficking profits are said to total US$35.7 billion.

30. Paul How, "Prostitution Fourth Largest Source of GNP," *Business World* (Philippines), April 6, 2005.
31. Directive 2006/123/EC of the European Parliament and of the Council of the European Union of 12 December 2006 on Services in the Internal Market, *Official Journal L376, 27/12/2006 P. 0036-0068*, para 1, http://eur-lex.europa.eu/LexUriServ/LexUriServ.do?uri=CELEX:32006L0123:EN:HTML.
32. Bureau NRM, *Trafficking in Human Beings, First Report*, 40.
33. Ibid., 137.
34. Ibid., 140. I use the terminology of "seems" because in her third report of 2005, the National Rapporteur on Trafficking criticized me for using this quote in a truncated way.

   Bureau NRM, *Trafficking in Human Beings, Third Report of the Dutch National Rapporteur* (The Hague, 2005). In a text box entitled "Use of Suggestive and Incorrect Information," she singles out several critics of the Dutch legalized system (5–6). She faults me for citing her wrongly in my article on "Ten Reasons for *Not* Legalizing Prostitution" "in a manner that suggests that the (B) NRM is in favour of opening the borders for prostitutes from non-EU/no-EEA countries, whereas this is not the case" (5–6).

   In her first report, the Special Rapporteur quotes an anonymous suggestion from "the field" related to giving women from outside the country, but within the EU/EEA, access to the Dutch prostitution market. In the context of reporting a shortage of Dutch women in the legal sector who may have turned to the illegal sector, she states that "from the field the solution put forward for the problem of the outflow is to offer prostitutes from non EU/EEA countries, who voluntarily choose to work in prostitution, (measured) legal and controlled access to the Dutch market" (140). However the Special Rapporteur mentions the EU/EEA point earlier in her report (137). Here, she states that an increasing demand for people from outside the EU/EEA countries to be permitted to work in the prostitution sector *should be taken into account*. However, it is not easy to determine for these people . . . whether they are opting for this work freely and out of a conscious free choice. Because of the need to watch for risks of THB [trafficking in human beings] the thus approaching scenario does not look reassuring" (137, italics mine). Her caveats aside, and in this fuller context, I stand by my original statement that "the Dutch National Rapporteur has stated that in the future, a solution *may be* to "offer" [to the market] prostitutes from non EU/EEA [European Economic Area]."

35. Vandana Shiva, "Prostitution," *Interview with Teen Talking Circles Project*, on ProCon.org, 2004, http://prostitution.procon.org/view.source.php?sourceID=003625.

36. Jurgen Wohlfarth, "Anclaje Jurídico y Social de la Prostitución en Alemania," *Las Ciudades y la Prostitución* (Madrid: Dirección General de Igualdad de Oportunidades, 2004), 70.
37. Matthew Scofield, "Germans Reconsider Legalized Prostitution," Knight Ridder, May 12, 2006.
38. Michèle Hirsch, "Plan of Action against Traffic in Women and Forced Prostitution (Brussels: Council of Europe, 1996), 9.
39. Scofield, "Germans Reconsider Legalized Prostitution."
40. Wohlfarth, "Anclaje Jurídico."
41. SOLWODI, *Newsletter* 73, September 2007. On file with author.
42. SOLWODI, *Newsletter* 92, June 2012, http://acrath.org.au/wp-content/uploads/2012/07/Solwodi-Newsletter-921.pdf.
43. Federal Ministry for Family Affairs, Senior Citizens, Women and Youth, *Report by the Federal Government on the Impact of the Act Regulating the Legal Situation of Prostitutes (Prostitution Act)*, (Berlin: 2007), 79–80, http://www.bmfsfj.de/RedaktionBMFSFJ/Broschuerenstelle/Pdf-Anlagen/bericht-der-br-zum-prostg-englisch,property=pdf,bereich=bmfsfj,sprache=de,rwb=true.pdf.
44. Ibid., 57–58.
45. Cited in Sullivan, *Making Sex Work*, 2.
46. Mark Alexander, "Family Fury Over Brothel Bonuses," *Sunday Mail*, November 28, 2004, http://www.ar15.com/archive/topic.html?b=1&f=5&t=299531.
47. Ibid.
48. Sullivan and Jeffreys, *Legalising Prostitution*, 4.
49. Action for REACH OUT, "Personal Safety of Sex Workers," *Reaching Out*, May 2008.
50. Quoted in Sullivan, *Making Sex Work*, 153.
51. Young, "Hookers Deserve Safe Working Environment."
52. Jeff Green, "Adult Entertainment Lobby Group Threatens to Recruit Strippers at Vancouver High Schools," *Province*, July 26, 2012.
53. Ibid.
54. Anna Fifield, "South Korea Cracks Down on World's Oldest Trade," Ft.com, October 13, 2004, http://www.ft.com/cms/s/0/662b9d06-1cb5-11d9-8d72-00000e2511c8.html#axzz1titOHZ7t.
55. Jong-se Park, "Anti-Prostitution Law Takes Its Toll on Service Industry: Experts," *Chosun Ilbo*, January 6, 2005, http://english.chosun.com/site/data/html_dir/2005/01/06/2005010661037.html (accessed August 1, 2007).
56. Kim Ton-hyung, "Illegal Sex Trade Dying Hard," *Korea Times*, September 17, 2006, http://times.hankooki.com/1page/nation.200509/kt2006091719493710510 (accessed September 17, 2006).
57. "Anti-Prostitution Law Gets Makeover for Second Birthday," *Chosun Ilbo*, September 20, 2006, http://english.chosun.com/w21data/nthml/nes/200609/200609200028.htm (accessed September 20, 2006).
58. Ton-hyung, "Illegal Sex Trade Dying Hard."

59. Quoted in Paul Meyer, "Hoping to Craft a Fresh Start: S. Korean Laws Offer Prostitutes Job Retraining, Counseling," *Dallas Morning News*, May 7, 2006.
60. "As Brothels Falter Amid Crackdown, S. Korea's Sex Trade Reemerges," *Asia News*, September 22, 2008.
61. Ibid.
62. Center for Women's Human Rights, "Who Will Benefit from the Law? Prostitution Law and the Empowerment of Prostitutes," 2008, www.stop.or.kr/board.html (accessed August 19, 2009).
63. Valerie Jenness, *Making It Work*, 42.
64. Ibid., 47.
65. Julia Hayley, "Spanish Union Launches Push for Prostitute Rights," Reuters, May 18, 2005, http://www.freerepublic.com/focus/f-news/1405961/posts (accessed June 6, 2011).
66. Robin Young, "Oldest Profession Says Yes to Union," *Times*, London, March 5, 2002.
67. Julie Bindel, "Sex Workers are Different," *Guardian*, July 7, 2003, http://www.guardian.co.uk/politics/2003/jul/07/tradeunions.gender (accessed September 4, 2003).
68. Amanda Norejko, "Prostitutes' Union Under Threat," *Australian*, August 13, 2004.
69. "German Prostitutes Reject Employment Contract," Ananova.com, August 25, 2004, http://www.dailytimes.com.pk/default.asp?page=story_26-8-2004_pg9_12 (accessed September 4, 2004).
70. Doreen Carvajal, "The Workplace: Organizing the Oldest Profession," *International Herald Tribune*, April 27, 2004, http://www.nytimes.com/2004/04/28/business/worldbusiness/28iht-workcol28_ed3_.html.
71. Sheila Jeffreys, "UK: Prostitutes To Vote To Join Union," CATW Listserve posting, March 4, 2002.
72. "No More Prostitutes, Danish Union Says," *Agence France Presse*, June 30, 2003, http://www.walnet.org/csis/news/world_2003/afp-030630.html.
73. Agnete Strøm, "A Glimpse into 30 Years of Struggle Against Prostitution by the Women's Liberation Movement in Norway," *Reproductive Health Matters* 17, no. 34 (May 1, 2009), http://pubget.com/paper/19962635/A_glimpse_into_30_years_of_struggle_against_prostitution_by_the_women_s_liberation_movement_in_Norway.
74. "Norway Hotel Staff Want Porn Ban," BBC News, July 27, 2004, http://news.bbc.co.uk/2/hi/europe/3928441.stm.
75. Raymond, "Under New Law, France Would No Longer Be Sexual Playground of Men Like Dominique Strauss-Kahn."
76. Coalition Against Trafficking in Women, "First National Conference of Prostitution Survivors, Manifesto of Filipino Women in Prostitution," *Coalition Report 2003*, 2, http://www.catwinternational.org/Content/Documents/Reports/catw2003report.pdf (accessed February 2, 2013). They state, "Because, the innumerable methods of physical violence, rape and degradation

inflicted by customers and others who gain from prostitution, by the police and by the public, cause deep wounds in our being . . . protection for victim-survivors of prostitution is necessary: respect their rights, hear their demands, stop arrests. . . . Prostitution has to be eliminated, thus, it should not be legalized."

77. Bindel, "Sex Workers are Different."
78. Quoted in ibid.
79. Melissa Ditmore, ed., *Sex Work and Money*, Research for Sex Work 9 (Global Network of Sex Work Projects, 2006), http://www.nswp.org/resource/research-sex-work-9.
80. Melissa Petro, "'I Did It . . . For the Money': Sex Work as a Means to Socio-Economic Opportunity," in *Sex Work and Money*, 27.
81. Alys Willman-Navarro "Money and Sex: What Economics Should Be, Doing for Sex Work Research," in *Sex Work and Money*, 19.
82. Jo Weldon, "Show Me the Money: a Sex Worker Reflects on Research into the Sex Industry," in *Sex Work and Money*, 12.
83. Ibid., 13.
84. Ibid., 14.
85. Ibid.
86. Willman-Navarro, "Money and Sex," 19.
87. Petro, "'I Did It . . . For the Money,'" 25.
88. Farley, *Prostitution & Trafficking in Nevada*, 31.
89. Juhu Thukral, "Sex Workers and Finances: A Case Study of New York City," in *Sex Work and Money*, 19.
90. Linda DeRiviere, "A Human Capital Methodology for Estimating the Lifelong Personal Costs of Young Women Leaving the Sex Trade," *Feminist Economics* 12, no. 3 (July 2006): 367–402.
91. DeRiviere, "A Human Capital Methodology," 377.
92. Ibid., 382.
93. Ibid.
94. Ibid., 383.
95. Ibid., 396.
96. Ibid., 397.
97. Lola Greene Baldwin Foundation, testimony, Public Hearing on Domestic Violence, Governor's Council on Domestic Violence, Portland, Oregon, February 4, 2005.
98. Paul Kramer, "The Military-Sexual Complex: Prostitution, Disease and the Boundaries of Empire during the Philippine-American War," *Asia-Pacific Journal* 9, issue 30, no. 2 (July 25, 2011): 7, http://www.japanfocus.org/-Paul_A_-Kramer/3574.
99. Aida F. Santos, "Gathering the Dust: The Bases Issue in the Philippines," in *Let the Good Times Roll: Prostitution and the U.S. Military in Asia*, eds. Saundra Sturdevant and Brenda Stoltzfus (New York: New Press, 1997), 36.
100. Kramer, "The Military-Sexual Complex," 6–7.
101. Ibid., 11, 10.

102. Ibid., 11.

103. Ibid., 13.

104. Kristin Hoganson, "'As Badly Off as the Filipinos.' U.S. Women's Suffragists and the Imperial Issue at the Turn of the Twentieth Century," *Journal of Women's History* 13, no. 2 (Summer 2001): 6.

105. Ibid.

106. Ibid., 5.

107. Kramer, "The Military-Sexual Complex," 15.

108. Ibid., 17.

109. Ibid., 18.

110. Toshiyuki Tanaka, *Japan's Comfort Women: Sexual Slavery and Prostitution During World War II and the U.S. Occupation* (London: Routledge, 2002). See also "Recreation and Amusement Association," Wikipedia, the Free Encyclopedia, February 7, 2013. "To cover the country [Japan] . . . Allied GHQ (General Headquarters) commandeered these institutions (22 places of prostitution) on September 28, 1945."

111. Michael Schaller, *Altered States: The United States and Japan Since the Occupation* (London: Oxford University Press, 1997). See especially chapter 1.

112. Eric Talmadge, "American Military Ignored Japan's Sex Slave Abuses, New Records Show," Associated Press, April 27, 2007, http://www.msnbc.msn.com/id/18355292/ns/world_news-asia_pacific/t/us-troops-used-japanese-brothels-after-wwii/#.T7FTI-1yFl.

113. Ibid.

114. Tanaka, *Japan's Comfort Women*, 84.

115. Ibid., 87.

116. Hudson "Bill" Phillips, "The Flag of My Father," *Panama News* 14, no. 2 (January 22–February 2, 2008).

117. Talmadge "American Military Ignored Japan's Sex Slave Abuses."

118. Saundra Sturdevant and Brenda Stoltzfus, eds., "Olongapo: the Bar System," in *Let the Good Times Roll*.

119. Alex Renton, "Learning the Thai Sex Trade," *Prospect Magazine*, May 5, 2005.

120. Ibid.

121. Laura Maria Agustin, *Sex at the Margins: Migration, Labour Markets and the Rescue Industry* (London: Zed Books, 2007).

122. Julia O'Connell-Davidson, "Book Review—*Sex at the Margins: Migration, Labour Markets and the Rescue Industry*," *Feminist Review* 96 (2010): e1–e4.

123. Cited in Natalie Rothschild, "Exploding the Myth of Trafficking," *The Spiked Review of Books* 12 (April 25, 2008), http://www.spiked-online.com/index.php?/site/reviewofbooks_article/5027.

124. Suki Falconberg, "Tears for Forgotten Women," *The Granville Journal: The Flagship Blog of Cyrano's Journal Online*, May 7, 2008, http://www.bestcyrano.net/tgi?p=293 (accessed May 22, 2008).

125. David A. Feingold, "Human Trafficking," *Foreign Policy*, August 30, 2005.
126. U.S. Department of State, *Trafficking in Persons Report 2007* (Washington, D.C.: Office to Monitor and Combat Trafficking, 2007), 8, http://www.state.gov/j/tip/rls/tiprpt/2007/82799.htm.
127. UN Office on Drugs and Crime (UNODC), "General Assembly President Calls for Redoubling of Efforts to End Human Trafficking," April 3, 2012, http://www.unodc.org/unodc/en/frontpage/2012/April/un-general-assembly-president-calls-for-re-doubled-efforts-to-end-human-trafficking.html?ref=fs1.
128. United Nations Office on Drugs and Crime, Global Report on Trafficking in Persons, 2012, at 10 and 35, available at http://www.unodc.org/documents/data-and-analysis/glotip/Trafficking_in_Persons_2012_web.pdf. A summary finding at the beginning of the report is confusing, listing 58 percent of victims trafficked for sexual exploitation. When one reads further into the report, the reader sees that the finding of 58 percent was reported only for 2010, but during the entire reporting period from 2007 through 2010, between 57–62 percent of the victims were reported trafficked for sexual exploitation. An average figure for these years would not be 58 but rather 59.5 percent.
129. Cited in Natalie Rothschild, "More Evidence That Trafficking is a Myth," *Spiked*, April 27, 2009.
130. Quoted in ibid.
131. Quoted in ibid.
132. Nick Davies, "Inquiry Fails to Find Single Trafficker Who Forced Anybody into Prostitution," *Guardian*, October 19, 2009, http://www.guardian.co.uk/uk/2009/oct/20/government-trafficking-enquiry-fails.
133. Catherine Bennett, "No Trafficking? Well, There's a Hell of a Lot of Women Suffering," *Observer*, October 25, 2009.
134. Huda, *Integration of the Human Rights*, paras. 42 and 48.
135. Quoted in Aida F. Santos, "The Philippines: Migration and Trafficking in Women," in *A Comparative Study of Women Trafficked in the Migration Process*. See note 16.
136. Anne Winsnes Rødland, "Human Trafficking: Demands for Better Protection," *NIKK Magasin* 1 (2009): 44.
137. Quoted in Natalie Obiko Pearson, "A Call to Aid Poor Women of Latin America," *Boston Globe*, January 27, 2006.
138. Quoted in ibid.

## 5. GOOD PRACTICES FOR THE FUTURE

1. Global Commission, *HIV and the Law: Risks, Rights & Health* (New York: UN Development Programme, HIVAIDS Group, Bureau for Development Policy, July 2012), See especially 36–43, 99, notes 140–200, http://

www.undp.org/content/undp/en/home/librarypage/hiv-aids/hiv-and
-the-law--risks--rights---health/.

2. Neil Marks, "World AIDS Day 2009, Ban Ki-moon Calls for Removal of
   Laws Which Hinder Fight against Disease," *Kaieteur News Online*, July
   30, 2012, http://www.kaieteurnewsonline.com/2009/12/01/world-aids
   -day-2009-ban-ki-moon-calls-for-removal-of-laws-which-hinder-fight
   -against-disease/. Italics mine.
3. Global Commission, *HIV and the Law*, 36–37.
4. Ibid., 38.
5. Ibid., 43.
6. On Östergren, for example, see Max Waltman, "Prohibiting Sex Purchasing and Ending Trafficking: the Swedish Prostitution Law," *Michigan
   Journal of International Law* 34 (December 1, 2011): 148, http://papers.ssrn
   .com/sol3/papers.cfm?abstract_id=1966130##.
7. Judith Levine, *Harmful to Minors: The Perils of Protecting Children from Sex*
   (Minneapolis: University of Minnesota Press, 2002), 85–86.
8. Global Commission, *HIV and the Law*, 43.
9. UNAIDS, *UNAIDS' Editors' Notes for Authors* (Joint United Nations Programme on HIV/AIDS: August 2006), 1.
10. UNAIDS, *UNAIDS Terminology Guidelines*, Revised Version (Geneva,
    Switzerland: UNAIDS, October 2011), 4, http://www.unaids.org/en
    /media/unaids/contentassets/documents/unaidspublication/2011/JC2118
    _terminology-guidelines_en.pdf.
11. Ibid., 1–36.
12. Ibid., 4.
13. Ibid., 26.
14. UNAIDS Advisory Group, *HIV and Sex Work*, 7–8, 13–14, 20, 23–26.
15. Ibid., 15, 4.
16. Ibid., 11, 14.
17. Ibid.
18. Ibid., 12.
19. Ibid., 21.
20. Global Commission, *HIV and the Law*, copyright page.
21. All the CATW campaigns and projects listed in the following sections
    are described in further detail in the *Coalition Reports* from the years 1999
    onward, and various press releases and reports on the CATW website at
    www.catwinternational.org.
22. Raymond and Hughes with Gomez, *Sex Trafficking of Women in the United
    States*.
23. U.S. Department of State, *Fact Sheet*, Office to Monitor and Combat
    Trafficking, 2007.
24. UN Department of Peacekeeping Operations (DPKO), "Human Traf-
    ficking Resource Package," 2004; and "Human Trafficking and United
    Nations Peacekeepin, DPKO Policy Paper," March 2004, 12. "These

scenarios may or may not involve trafficking, but are likely to be highly exploitative nonetheless. It thus becomes very difficult to differentiate between trafficking victims, particularly victims of domestic trafficking, and vulnerable individuals in local populations that have had to resort to prostitution for income. The use of prostitutes by UN personnel in these environments is an exploitative activity . . . the procurement of sexual services from nationals in a vulnerable context by a UN staff member (in a position of disproportionate power) constitutes an act of sexual exploitation, even where prostitution is not a crime." http://www.un.org/womenwatch /news/documents/DPKOHumanTraffickingPolicy03-2004.pdf. Further information at http://www.peacekeepingbestpractices.unlb.org.

25. Ministry of Industry, Employment and Communications, Government of Sweden, "Prostitution and Trafficking in Human Beings," *Fact Sheet*, April 2005, legislationline.org/download/.../ee4eb3cbfa0adeec87ad87067a6f.pdf.

26. "Big Sister Watches Buyers of Prostitution in Iceland," *Iceland Review*, October 19, 2011, http://icelandreview.com/icelandreview/daily_news /Big_Sister_Watches_Buyers_of_Prostitution_in_Iceland_0_383393 .news.aspx.

27. Coalition Against Trafficking in Women, "Balkans Conference on Trafficking in Conflict and Post-Conflict Situations," *Coalition Report 2006*, 4, http://www.catwinternational.org/Content/Documents/Reports /CATW06newsletter.pdf. Full text of conference resolutions on file with author.

28. Coalition Against Trafficking in Women, "Good Practices: Targeting the Demand for Prostitution and Trafficking," 2006, www.catwinternational .org (accessed November 10, 2006). On file with author.

29. Coalition Against Trafficking in Women, Online Petition, "Buying Sex Is Not a Sport," 2006. Petition signatures on file with author and with Coaliton Against Trafficking in Women, Europe.

30. Norma Ramos, Report to the Board of Directors on Craigslist Campaign, 2010. On file with Coalition Against Trafficking in Women, New York.

31. National Association of Attorneys General, "Letter Re Backpage.com's Ongoing Failure to Effectively Limit Prostitution and Sexual Trafficking Activity on Its Website," August 31, 2011, http://illinoisattorneygeneral .gov/pressroom/2011_08/BackpageWGLetterAug2011Final.pdf.

Coalition Against Trafficking in Women and Prostitution Research and Education, Press Release, "Leading Human Rights Groups CATW and PRE to Protest Village Voice Media in NYC on 6/20/12," June 20, 2012, http://www.catwinternational.org/Home/Article/472-leading-human -rights-groups-catw-pre-to-protest-village-voice-media-in-nyc-on-62012.

32. Janice G. Raymond, "The New UN Trafficking Protocol," *Women's Studies International Forum* 25, no. 5 (2002): 491–502.

33. Nicholas Kulish, "Bulgaria Moves Away from Legalizing Prostitution," *New York Times*, October 5, 2007, http://www.nytimes.com/2007/10/05 /world/europe/05iht-bulgaria.4.7773739.html?pagewanted=all.

34. Coalition Against Trafficking in Women, "CATW Challenges Legalization and Regulation of the Sex Industry in Bulgaria and Romania, Bulgaria Reverses Its Course," *Coalition Report 2007*, 7. Online Report header is mistakenly dated 2008.
35. Cable Search, "Ambassador's Meeting with New Interior Minister Cristian David," Embassy Bucharest, April 19, 2007, http://cablesearch.org /?id=07BUCHAREST452&v (accessed February 10, 2013). See also, Coalition Against Trafficking in Women, "CATW Challenges Legalization and Regulation," 7.
36. Coalition Against Trafficking in Women, "First National Conference of Prostitution Survivors, Manifesto of Filipino Women in Prostitution," *Coalition Report 2003*, 2, http://www.catwinternational.org/Content /Documents/Reports/catw2003report.pdf.
37. See video of the conference, "Not for Sale." Available at http://www .prostitutionresearch.com/how_prostitution_works/000174.html.
38. *Statement of Asia-Pacific Meeting of Sex Trafficking and Prostitution Survivors* (New Delhi, India: April 3, 2011), http://www.catw-ap.org/?m=201104.
39. Azera Rahman, "India: Please Don't Legalise Prostitution, Say Victims," Calcutta News.Net, April 7, 2011, http://gulfnews.com/news/world /india/please-don-t-legalise-prostitution-say-victims-1.788921.
40. "About EVE," *Exploited Voices Now Educating*, http://educatingvoices.ca/.
41. "About US," *Sextrade101*, http://sextrade101.com/.
42. Survivors Connect Network, http://survivorsconnect.groupsite.com /main/summary (accessed February 6, 2013).
43. Stella Marr, citing a tweet of Brooke Magnanti, author of the blog on which the British TV series, *Secret Diary of a Call Girl* (Belle de Jour), was based. http://stellasscreenshots.files.wordpress.com/2012/06/scasoperation rescue.png.
44. "The Devil and Shelley Lubben—Episode #2." Uploaded to YouTube .com, October 15, 2011, http://www.youtube.com/watch?v=oxd2Vkkz 19w.
45. Harold Levy, "Madame Guilty in Sado-Sex Trial," *Toronto Star*, October 10, 1998, http://www.walnet.org/csis/news/toronto_98/torstar-981010 .html (accessed January 6, 2002).
46. "Is a Major Shake-up of Canada's Prostitution Laws on the Horizon?," *Women's Views on the News*, October 29, 2010, http://www.womensviews onnews.org/2010/09/is-a-major-shake-up-of-canadas-prostitution-laws -on-the-horizon/ (accessed November 11, 2010).
47. Emanuella Goldberg, "Canadian Judge Strikes Down Prostitution Law," CNN.com, September 29, 2010, http://edition.cnn.com/2010 /CRIME/09/29/Canada-Prostitution/index.html?iref=allsearch.
48. "Prostitution Problem Unfixed," *SunNews Video, Prime Time*, March 26, 2012, http://www.sunnewsnetwork.ca/video/1531340793001.
49. Linda Nguyen, "Prostitution Ruling Makes Sex Workers 'Targets' for Abusive Men: Protester," *Postmedia News*, October 5, 2010, http://www

.canada.com/news/Prostitution+ruling+makes+workers+targets+abusive +Protester/3626589/story.html.

50. At the request of the Ontario Regional Department of Justice Office in Canada, I submitted an affidavit as an expert witness and was cross-examined during a full day in the *Bedford et al.* case.

51. Kevin Connor, "Former Prostitutes Picket Trade," *Cnews*, October 6, 2010, http://cnews.canoe.ca/CNEWS/Canada/2010/10/06/15597891.html.

52. Aaron Vincent Elkaim, "Sex Worker Advocates Clash Over Landmark Ruling," *Star*, April 4, 2012, http://www.thestar.com/news/gta/article /1152078--sex-worker-advocates-clash-over-landmark-ruling.

53. Native Women's Association of Canada, "Concerned over Superior Court Decision Striking Down Legislation on Pimping, Brothels," press release, October 1, 2010, http://sisyphe.org/spip.php?article3669.

54. Aboriginal Women's Action Network, "AWAN Address to the People's Tribunal on Commercial Sexual Exploitation," Mohawk Territories (Montreal, QC), March 18–20, 2011, http://www.apneaap.org/policy -work/our-resources/awan-address-peoples-tribunal-commercial-sexual -exploitation-march-18-20-2.

55. Asian Women Coalition Ending Prostitution, "Ontario Supreme Court Decision," Joint Statement of the Aboriginal Women's Action Network, Asian Women Coalition Ending Prostitution, and the South Asian Women Against Male Violence, September 29, 2010, http://sisyphe.org /spip.php?article3671.

56. Survivors Connect Network, "34 Trafficking/Prostitution Survivors Vote to Stand with Our Canadian Sisters against the Bedford Prostitution Decision," March 28, 2012, http://survivorsconnect.wordpress.com/2012/03/28 /survivors-connect-network-votes-to-stand-with-our-sisters-in-canada -regarding-the-bedford-prostitution-decision/.

57. Breaking Free, "Who We Are," http://www.breakingfree.net/who_we _are.aspx (accessed February 11, 2013).

58. Eaves for Women/the Poppy Project, London, United Kingdom, http:// www.eavesforwomen.org.uk/.

59. "About Us," *Ruhama*, http://www.ruhama.ie/page.php?intPageID=4.

60. "Glasgow Calls for an End to Prostitution Now," *Living in Glasgow Archives*, December 8, 2009, http://www.glasgow.gov.uk/en/News/Archives /2009/December/end+prostitution+now.html.

61. "Prostitution and Trafficking," Vancouver Rape Relief and Women's Shelter, http://www.rapereliefshelter.bc.ca/category/topics/violence-against -women/prostitution-and-trafficking.

# INDEX

austerity programs, 128–29
  links and disjunctions with
    trafficking, 163–65
  as a myth of trafficking, 123, 162
  Netherlands, 81, 93–94
  volunteers or victims, 23–24,
    160–61
Mihaylova, Nadezhda, 182
Milakovic, Milorad, 8–9
military-prostitution complex, xvi
  British Army in India, xxxviii–xxxix
  U.S. in Japan, 156–58
  U.S. in Korea, 24–25
  U.S. in Philippines, 122–23, 133–34,
    152–56, 174
Miller, Alice, 106
Miller, John, 27
Miscellaneous Workers Union, 144
missing women, 191–92
Mitchell Brothers, 10
Mittendorf, Mariet, 88
monetary agencies, 128–29
monkey houses, 25
Monto, Martin, 43
Moon, Katharine, 24
moral panic, 16–17, 163
moralism, 12–13, 17–19
Morava Foundation, 7
Mr. A. de Graaf Foundation, 81–82,
  101, 109–11, 112
Mustang Ranch, 46
myths of prostitution
  abolitionism is moralistic, 12–14
  forced *versus* free prostitution, 21–23
  inevitability, xxxi, 2–4, 127
  off-street is safer than on-street,
    29–32
  overview, 1–2
  prostitutes are not victims, 32–36
  prostitution is a choice, xii, 19–21
  sex worker representation, 9–12

naming and shaming buyers, 74,
  179
National Action Plan on Trafficking in
  Human Beings, Dutch, 89
National American Women Suffrage
  Association (NAWSA), 154

National Conference of Prostitution
  Survivors, 183–84
National Council of German Women's
  Organizations, 56–57
National Network of Sex Workers,
  India, 68
National Police Service Report of
  2008, Dutch
  control and exploitation of pimps and
    traffickers, 92, 96, 98
  forced prostitution, 91, 93, 95
  organized crime, 94
  overview, xv, 79, 90
National Rapporteur, Swedish, 62–63,
  170
National Rapporteur on Trafficking in
  Human Beings, Dutch, 79, 94, 115,
  135–36
Native Women's Association of
  Canada, 187
natural law of male sexuality, xxxvii, 40,
  54, 76, 80–81, 130
neo-colonialism, 159
Netherlands, 79–119
  age of consent, 170
  Amsterdam's red-light district, 12, 79,
    81, 86–89, 93, 112–13
  child exploitation, 115–17
  closing of brothels and tolerance
    zones, 88–89
  control and exploitation of women,
    92, 96–97
  Crimestopper Campaign, 57–58
  dignifying demand, 59
  exporting prostitution policy at
    European meetings, 98–104
  exporting prostitution policy via the
    UN, 105–9
  failure in identifying victims, 90–91
  history of prostitution tolerance,
    80–85
  migration and trafficking, 92–94,
    135–36
  normalization of prostitution, 4, 13,
    14, 85–87, 109–15
  organized crime, 94–95
  overview of legalized prostitution, xv,
    79, 117–19

Romania, 6–7, 117, 182
Roosevelt, Theodore, 155
ROSA (Centre for Women War
Victims), 178–79, 191
Routes Out Partnership, 190
Ruhama, 45, 132, 189–90
*Rumpus*, 61

Safe and Green, 67
Safe Harbor law, 35
safe sex programs, 110–11
Salomon Alapitvany Foundation, 7
SANGRAM, xxxii
Sanjay Gandhi Transport Nagar,
130–31
Scarlet Alliance, 186
Scarlet Harem, 138–39
Schaapman, Karina, 95–96
scholarship and advocacy, x–xiv
Scotland, 190–91
Scott, Valerie, 186
Secret Service, U.S., 43
self-employment, prostitute, 139–40
sensationalism of prostitution, 16–17,
33
sentencing of sex criminals, xxxv, 72,
76–77, 94–95
Seshu, Meena, xxxii
*Sex at the Margins* (Agustin), 24
sex industry
causes of expansion, 61–62
economic downturns, 131–32
globalization, xl, 123, 129, 135–36,
165, 192
human rights advocates, 9, 14, 17, 123
language of, xlii–xliii
lobbying, x, 2, 81–82, 85, 105,
125–26, 183
market tradition of, 85
Sex Party, Australia, 126
sex tourism
Asia, 123, 128, 131, 133–34
Balkans, 178, 179
Germany, 56
globalization of, 124, 158–59, 165
Netherlands, 81, 86–87, 112, 117,
135
sex trafficking. *See* trafficking

*Sex Trafficking of Women in the United
States* study (CATW), 174–75
sex work, term of, xlii, xliii, 171
Sex Worker Education and Advocacy
Task Force (SWEAT), 147
sex workers, term of, xlii–xliii
Sex Workers Project (SWP), 30, 45
Sextrade101, 185
*Sexual Exploitation of Children* (CRIN),
116–17
sexual harassment, 86, 145–46
sexual liberation, xvii, 18
*Sexual Services in Australia* review, 138
sexual slavery comparison to race
slavery, xxxii–xxxviii, xxxix
Shapiro, Deborah, 30
Sheikh, Meena, 47
Shelley, Louise, 93
Sherwood Castle, 9
Shiva, Vandana, 136
slavery, sexual compared to race, xxxii–
xxxviii, xxxix
Smaadahl, Tove, 191
SOLWODI (Solidarity with women in
distress), 137
Sonagachi, 68–69
South Korea. *See* Korea
Spain, 30, 39, 124
Spitzer, Eliot, 31–32, 43
Sri Lanka, 117
St. James, Margo, 10, 142
State Department, U.S., 64
state feminism, Dutch, 79, 82–85
Statistical Institute of Jamaica
(STATIN), 132–33
Stígamót, 74, 176, 191
Stiglitz, Joseph, 130
Strasbourg Council of Europe
meeting, 98–100
Strauss-Kahn, Dominique, 43, 145
street prostitution
Norway and Denmark, 73
*versus* off-street, 29–32, 64–65, 187,
190
penalizing buyers, 65–66
Sweden, 62, 64–65, 72–73
strip clubs, 30, 75, 127, 131–32, 138,
141, 190

student recruitment, 140, 177
STV (Dutch Foundation Against
    Trafficking in Women), 7, 83–85,
    99, 101, 102, 107, 114
substance abuse, 149–50
Suk-ill, Bae, 142
Sullivan, Mary, 15
survival, strategy of, 19–20
survivors
    as advocates against prostitution,
        11–12, 146, 183–88
    penalizing buyers, 69–70
    supporters of, 9–10
    term of, xliii
Survivors Connect, 185–86, 188
Survivors of Sex Trafficking and
    Prostitution meeting, 184
Sussex Centre for Migration Research,
    8
sustainable prostitution (SP), 4, 128
"Sustainable World Through
    Prostitution, A" (Pleumarom), 128
Sweden
    demand for prostitution, 39, 62–63,
        175
    legislation criminalizing buyers, xv,
        xxxv, xli, 38, 61, 63–65, 68, 71–73
    numbers of prostitutes, 73
    sex crime convictions, 77
    UN report criticism, 168–69, 170
Swedish National Police Board, 64
syphilis, 81
systems of national accounts, counting
    prostitution in, 132–33

T-visas, 29
Tampep, 101–2, 108
Tanaka, Toshiyuki, 157–58
tax revenues, xxxiii, 84, 121, 129–30,
    133, 148
teacher training, 177
television, 33, 87–88
*Terminology Guidelines* (UNAIDS),
    171–72, 173
Terre des Femmes, 57
Thailand, 38, 128, 134, 158
Thomas Cook, 86–87
thrill of transgression, 41

Thukral, Juhu, 149
tobacco industry, 3
tolerance of prostitution, pragmatic,
    80–85, 127–28
tolerance zones, xv, 4, 25, 79, 88–89,
    112
Topalli, Jozefina, 178
torture, 15, 22
tourism, sex. *See* sex tourism
"Traffic in Women and Forced
    Prostitution" meeting, 98–100
trafficking
    anti-trafficking legislation, xxxv,
        27–28, 68, 76
    austerity programs, 128–29
    children and babies, xv, xxxv, xli, 7
    consent and, xl, 22–23, 29, 160
    decriminalization, xxxii
    domestic, xxxv, 28, 162, 164
    economy of, 123
    human rights, 22–23, 159–60, 163,
        164
    language, 23
    links and disjunctions with migration,
        123, 161, 162, 163–65
    Netherlands, 81, 84, 92–94
    overview, xxxi
    sex work apologists position, 5–6
    "Trafficking and Sex Work," 106
    *Trafficking in Persons* reports, U.S., 27,
        95
Trafficking Victims Protection Act
    (TVPA), U.S., xxxv, 27–28, 76
*Transcrime* (European Parliament), 30
Trolle, Jonas, 72
TVPA (Trafficking Victims Protection
    Act), U.S., xxxv, 27–28, 76

Ulloa, Teresa, 177
UNAIDS, 167–73
    Advisory Group, xxxiv
    *Editors' Notes for Authors*, 171
    *HIV/AIDS and Sex Work* report, 14,
        172
    *HIV/AIDS and the Law* report, 167–
        70, 172, 173
    position on sex work, xxxiv, 6
    *Terminology Guidelines*, 171–72, 173

# ABOUT THE AUTHOR

Janice G. Raymond, professor emerita of women's studies and medical ethics at the University of Massachusetts at Amherst, has been a leader for many years in the campaign to promote the recognition of prostitution as violence against women. From 1994 to 2007, Raymond served as the co–executive director of the Coalition Against Trafficking in Women, International (CATW), a non-governmental organization in consultative status with the United Nations Economic and Social Council. In 2007, she was given the International Woman Award by the Zero Tolerance Trust in Scotland for her work to eliminate sexual exploitation. She is the author of four books and coeditor of a fifth: *The Transsexual Empire: The Making of the She-Male*; *A Passion for Friends: Toward a Philosophy of Female Affection*; *The Sexual Liberals and the Attack on Feminism*, edited with Dorchen Leidholdt; *RU 486: Misconceptions, Myths and Morals*, with Renate Klein and Lynette J. Dumble; and *Women As Wombs: Reproductive Technologies and the Battle over Women's Freedom*. She has published many articles, which have appeared in the *Guardian, Portside,* and the *Christian Science Monitor*, among other publications. She lives in western Massachusetts.